SAVING AMERICA

SAVING AMERICA

USING DEMOCRATIC CAPITALISM TO RESCUE THE NATION FROM ECONOMIC FOLLY

Thomas Bonsell

Algora Publishing
New York

Library of Congress Cataloging-in-Publication Data —

Bonsell, Thomas.
    Saving America: using democratic capitalism to rescue the nation from economic folly
/ Thomas Bonsell.
        p. cm.
    Includes bibliographical references and index.
    ISBN 978-0-87586-867-7 (soft cover: alk. paper) — ISBN 978-0-87586-868-4 (hard
cover: alk. paper) — ISBN 978-0-87586-869-1 (ebook) 1. United States—Economic
policy—2009- 2. Democracy—United States. 3. Capitalism—United States. 4. Right and
left (Political science)—United States. I. Title.
    HC106.84.B66 2011
    330.973—dc22
                            2011014301

Printed in the United States

TABLE OF CONTENTS

There is no doubt the United States of America—well into its third century of existence—has many problems; some real and serious, others phony and distracting. Many of these problems have been created in the private sector and many solutions came, likewise, from that area. Government created some problems and many solutions were derived from government. Numerous problems were created by one sector and solved by the other. There should be no argument the nation has problems, but there also should be no argument the nation is benefactor to many conditions superior to conditions in most other nations. Angry Americans in the past quarter century have been inflicted with new or lingering problems while problems afflicting past generations have been solved.

It has been all too easy recently for Americans to blame all problems on the federal government while excusing themselves from any of the blame. In this age of victimization in which it seems most everyone is self-perceived to be victimized by outside forces, many Americans claim government has caused all their problems and has solved none while they are ever being victimized by politicians and bureaucrats. But the truth is that Americans—except those too young or otherwise incapacitated to be responsible—have created the nation's problems through their collective will and/or actions. It has become much too tiresome to hear Americans blame government for being out of touch with them while they themselves remain out of touch with government.

Americans put themselves in what they now call "a mess" and it is up to them to face up to the truth and make the necessary decisions to get out of that mess. Politicians, always seeking election, continue to play on the voters' collective fear but seldom address the nation's needs. The foremost example of that has been the one-upmanship played out during campaigning on which politician is "tough on crime" while accusing the opponent of being "soft." Texas is a particularly disgusting place with politicians claiming they will execute more criminals than will their political foes. Nothing is ever said about why these same politicians use the power of government to continue creating new criminals to take the place of the ones they execute. Nor do those politicians ever say what they would do to stop creating criminals. Executing people who have already killed—usually more than once before being caught—does no good for those who were the victims. Logic would dictate it would be far more advantageous for the nation and for all Americans that there be a halt to creation of criminals before thousands of victims have to die in order for a "tough on crime" governor to execute murderers.

Most importantly, Americans must solve the massive federal debt they brought on themselves and which they had a chance to cut short only to ignore the warnings. Republican presidential primary candidate George H. W. Bush told the American public in 1980 that the economic proposals of Ronald Reagan amounted to "Voodoo economics". Walter Mondale told them in the 1984 campaign that the growing debt was a danger that should be addressed with taxes. President Reagan, who campaigned "to stay the course," offered what at best could be termed a fairy tale. Americans voted overwhelmingly for the fantasy while at the same time claiming they were not responsible for the looming problem; career politicians were the culprits. But politicians will always give what it appears the people want, and the people spoke loud and clear for more fiscal recklessness which future generations may have to pay for. It's not known if Mondale could have created a corrective course, and that will never be known.

The author began working on this book midway through the administration of President Bill Clinton in response to the economic conditions left by Reagan and Bush, but was lulled into complacency by the economic growth under Clinton and his budgetary surpluses in the last three years of his administration and the first year of the administration of George W. Bush. There was no way then to foretell the presidency of Bush the Younger and the utter destruction he left, making what the book says more important now than it was when begun.

There is a way to a new-and-improved America that may not be as painful or require as much sacrifice as some mainstream pundits believe but will require much more than many politicians claim or most Americans want. Politicians on the right continue to tell Americans all will be okay and an economic paradise will bloom if taxes—usually their taxes—are lowered and government simply spends less, except for the military and to pay interest to those persons and institutions which spent years loading up on Treasury bills, notes and bonds. That is the most-irresponsible position any person can take, as this book is intended to show. The solution, this book is also intended to show, is to recommit the nation to a path toward Democratic Capitalism and to reject the desire to return to the robber-baron past—fundamentalist capitalism—that existed when the United States wasn't much more than what is now called a Third World nation. That path means rebuking the far right's regression to supply-side (fundamentalist) capitalism. It means strengthening the Democratic Capitalism begun under Franklin D. Roosevelt to combat the Great Depression, but which has been under attack since the days of the Vietnam Conflict.

Clinton ran on a promise of change in the 1992 presidential campaign then offered a relatively painless beginning to slowly reverse previous stupidities. But, it seems, many Americans dare not tread into a wilderness of cautious change, preferring to rely on the fairy tale that promises overnight successes through lower taxes and less spending, which were the driving forces that turned a noticeable debt from the Vietnam Conflict into a nation-threatening monster ready to devour future Americans. Similar fantasies in the 1920s were instrumental in creating the Great Depression forcing Americans, and most of the developed world, into accepting major changes later in an attempt to save capitalism.

Americans must grow up and reach mental adulthood to match their physical maturity. That would require learning from the past and to refrain from repeating previous stupidities. But that doesn't appear promising at this time. When fundamentalist capitalism failed in the 1920s, much of the world looked to various socialist models in search of an economic system that would benefit the most while harming the fewest. When the Soviet system came apart in the 1980s, the world looked again to capitalism. But it is important the world not be allowed to regress to the capitalism that failed; it should be guided to a new and improved Democratic Capitalism. The nation, as well as the world, once again needs major changes within the parameters of capitalism and to succeed those changes must apply to government, to commerce and to the people. This book offers possible solutions to several problems—the national debt being the most important— and the solutions should be taken in totality because all are related and a solution to the most-important problem requires changes in all areas. Attempts to facilitate a solution to the nation's problems have usually been restricted to various schemes of tinkering with taxes and spending of the federal government. None of these schemes offer much chance of success, as this book intends to demonstrate, because they defy economic logic. Many solutions to our problems are offered by various experts or special interests, but they too propose merely tinkering with taxes and spending, which are bound to be ineffectual. And those experts and special interests usually rely on sacrifices by someone other than themselves to facilitate our rescue. There needs to be changes in taxes and spending but there also needs to be changes in commercial thinking and operations, business's relationship to the nation and government, changes in employees' relationship to their employment in addition to how they and their employers are taxed. Government needs to take on more responsibilities in some areas—if that eases the burden on the nation's corporations and small businesses and enhances quality of life for citizens—while government needs to be kept out of other areas. But government must be used; it is what makes us one nation and it cannot be dismissed, as many on the unrealistic right seem to want.

The modern left believes in using the government of a democratic republic in public relationships of mankind because there has been no other way—except rebellion—for all the people to participate on an equal footing with the privileged in the making of rules for society or to even control one's destiny. Those of the modern right have hated government—if they didn't control it—for that same reason; they felt their privileged positions would be diluted because of equality of rights and equal treatment for the lesser classes. This book tries to show that equality of rights can be accomplished without diminishing the position of those who view themselves as society's elite. It also will debunk the right's claim that it wants more freedom and less government in the lives of Americans or that the left wants more government and less freedom. The reliance on only government to solve society's problems is likewise dismissed; the book intends to show that government should create conditions for solutions through its rules; doing what is needed to solve problems must be by America's citizens and businesses.

The book is extremely critical of the economic fundamentalists on the right who have brought on our monumental debt with their outdated and flawed notions and whose policies of "only us" have created other serious problems to this nation.

The author—an honors graduate in business administration (with a journalism major) who had lived since 1980 mainly on earnings from investing before founding a small publishing firm—writes from the perspective of someone who understands commerce and has made the capitalist system work for him and who believes it should benefit all Americans, not just those with economic control or who have political connections and representation. And as a highly trained intelligence analyst with the United States Air Force Security Service and the National Security Agency, the author sees meaning where others only see words. Many Americans have little or no control over their futures and are underrepresented or not represented at all in the political sector. Only Democratic Capitalism offers them much hope. Fundamentalist capitalism offers them nothing.

Chapter 1. America Must Change

Not a One-Man Job

Shortly before Bill Clinton was sworn into office as President of the United States of America in 1993, a University of Washington professor published in a Seattle newspaper an op-ed article headlined "Can Bill Clinton Save America?"[1]

Of course, saving America is vital to all Americans—as well as to the rest of the world—but it may not be a job for one man; he can only offer leadership and insight for all Americans who must do their share to save the nation. It was, after all, the American electorate that indirectly brought on the conditions the nation needs to be saved from. Nor is it realistic to think that a president, who will not be in office long enough for the entire salvation, could do much by himself. The professor at Washington's Graduate School of Public Affairs was remarkably accurate in his foresight about the task facing the-then new president after 12 years of what he called "unreality" and he identified Americans' past reluctance to endure the sacrifices and work needed to rid the nation of the results of bad policy. He wrote that, "The American public that had been beguiled by [Ronald] Reagan's politics of unreality with its eternal optimism have come to see that his and their optimism were unrealistic overconfidence in what clearly had been a

---

1 "Can Bill Clinton Save America?" Walter Williams; *The Seattle Times*; January 17, 1993.

debt-ridden economic boom with the borrowed funds squandered on consumption, not on productive investments."

By raising government spending on defense and lowering taxes by a like figure—about $100 billion each—the Reagan administration gave the public a perception of prosperity, but the perils of such policy remained hidden far too long. The Reagan economic policy did put $200 billion into the economy annually while subtracting a relatively minor amount in interest payment on the debt early in his reign. But as debt accumulated later, interest payments ballooned. There was always money coming in to pay for government spending and that was an economic positive, which could make most Americans feel better off; and they were—for a while. But the economic problem is serious when the borrowing that financed the Reagan policies has to be repaid. Now, the phantom wealth has vanished, and on top of that the interest payments drain real wealth from the nation's economy. Apologists for the Reagan policy refuse to admit their mistakes, claiming that $3 trillion in wealth was created during the Reagan years while another trillion was added under the rule of Reagan's successor, George H. W. Bush. In fact, $4 trillion in "wealth" was added to the United States economy but it wasn't created; much of the $4 trillion was borrowed, some of it was inflation and population growth. By the mid 1990s about three quarters of a trillion dollars had come from foreign investors. This imported money, coming from the financially privileged in Western Europe (mainly West Germany) and Asia (mainly Japan and China) and the money borrowed from Americans who just had their taxes reduced in the Reagan Revolution that extended into the administrations of the two George Bushes, must eventually be repaid. That repayment poses the most serious economic threat to the United States since the Great Depression. Americans who feel they are being cheated now will be much worse off in the future unless they resolve to prevent disaster.

The errors of the Reagan years were duplicated in the administration of George W. Bush.

But figures left by Reagan pale in comparison to what Bush left. And the task Clinton faced to save the nation from Reaganomics was nothing compared to the challenge facing President Barack Obama in the aftermath of Reaganomics-anew courtesy of George W. Bush.

Many people feel they are overtaxed. They are, but the over taxation is a result of paying for past stupidities. The interest on the national deficit when the first Bush left office in 1993 was nearing $300 billion a year (it came down as interest rates fell under Clinton, but rose again to pass $300 billion because of accumulated debt) which required a tax payment of more than $1,000 per person for every person in the United States just to pay interest to the privileged elite who had their taxes lowered by hundreds of thousands—if not millions—of dollars yearly. The requirements to pay for the savings-and-loan debacle, then estimated at $500 billion, represented a debt of not much under $2,000 for every man, woman and child in the United States at that time, and the American public created that debt by electing a president and other politicians who continually told them that "honest businessmen" were being hampered by federal banking regulations and an economic miracle would occur if government just went away and left business decisions to business people. Since the savings-and-loan payoff was spread over 30 years, the annual payment is about $70 a year per person. For a family of five, that is $350 over taxation for the savings-and-loan debacle. The interest payment of more than $1,000 per person costs that same family more than $5,000 a year in over taxation for a total of about $5,500—and Americans voted for that.

When the second Bush left office in 2009 interest on the debt had ballooned to the $400-billion range and that was considered "low" because of historically low interest rates. Under "normal" rates interest payments would be close to unbearable and the burden on the middle class greater because of tax breaks to favored people. The fiscal year 2012 budget projected the interest payment to reach $474.1 billion.

In February of 1995 *USA Today* asked readers, "What do you think is the biggest waste in the federal budget?" Answers claimed such things as "bureaucratic paperwork," or "public assistance programs like welfare." Others claimed "entitlement spending of all kinds," "welfare and its branches" and "federal and state bureaucracies" that "don't work in the same capacity as people in private industry."[2]

Those answers may reflect the extent some America politicians have influenced the public because they all were derived from political slogans, not from reality. Money spent in all the above manners finds its way quickly into the economy to support business activity, and that isn't wasteful. That $5,000-plus per year from the budget of a family of five is the real waste

---

2 "Voices: What do you think is the biggest waste in the federal budget?"; *USA Today*; February 7, 1995

because it drains money from the economy to pay interest to the privileged, who use the income from interest payments to buy more debt instruments from the Treasury to drain more money from the economy in a continuing cycle of self-enrichment. That cycle of self-enrichment was created by the very people who tell the American public that government spending—including welfare, entitlements or the bureaucracy—is the root of all our problems. In the *USA Today* poll, no one mentioned the real waste: interest payments.

There is no question that the last budget surplus generated by the federal government before Clinton's four surpluses was in 1969, the final budget of Democratic President Lyndon Johnson (as modified by newly elected Republican President Richard Nixon) and the acceleration of accumulated debt was mainly under Republican and—even worse—conservative leadership; the same people who constantly harp about lower taxes and less spending. Since Clinton left office there have been no balanced budgets again under right-wing presidency of George Bush the Younger and it doesn't appear there will be another for a considerable length of time. The economic leadership by America's right has resulted in a tax burden on all Americans much higher than it might have been had Republicans never been elected president. And the Republican/conservative spending on interest payments (much of it to themselves and to their friends) is also higher spending than would have occurred had their silly economic notions never been implemented.

The University of Washington professor's article didn't foresee the rapidity the American public showed in renewing its pessimism. When Clinton unveiled his economic plan in February of 1993, 79 percent of Americans approved of it, according to a *USA Today*/CNN/Gallup Poll.[3]

About four months later, another poll showed disillusionment had replaced optimism as the American public perceived that nothing had changed. This is a disheartening occurrence demonstrating that Americans would tolerate irresponsibility for nearly three decades, if the irresponsible made them feel good, but would not tolerate minor changes if those changes did not eliminate all problems in a matter of months. Such an attitude was reminiscent of the early Nixon years when he sought to delete Johnson's "War on Poverty" programs because of his dislike of government acting on

---

3 "Post-election euphoria fades as many voters perceive few changes" by Richard Benedetto; *USA Today*; June 8, 1993.

behalf of those people at the bottom of the social order. The Nixon attitude was that three and a half years of Johnson programs had not eliminated problems that had been building for three and a half centuries, so War on Poverty programs were a failure. (That lie is exposed in chapter 3.)

The same irrational response occurred after the 2008 election of Barack Obama, who was charged with cleaning up the mess left by Bush the Younger. Bush left a national debt of $12 trillion, an annual deficit of $1.3 trillion, two wars, a plunging stock market, rising unemployment, nearly 50 million Americans without healthcare that was exploding in cost at an unprecedented manner. But with less than a year in office for Obama, the electorate turned angry over situations the voters indirectly voted for. Even though Obama's policies had halted the recession's economic plunge, and revived the stock market angry voters began electing the very type of right-wing politicians who had created all the problems in the first place. Some complained that Obama hadn't governed from the "middle" as they think he promised to do, but moved to the left. Those on the left complained that he had moved too far to the right.

Governing from the middle is the proper course to take when the nation is running relatively smoothly. When the nation is in crisis, governing from the left is the only viable course because the left is the only political faction willing to change for the better. Had the nation stayed in the middle and not veered too far to the right in 1980 with the election of Reagan, it would still have in place the New Deal programs that had prevented catastrophic economic problems for half a century.

Throughout history, governments have always represented the privileged classes of society, ever catering to their interests while oppressing the lower classes. Governments would protect only the elite class but never protect the lower classes from the upper classes, which would automatically keep a lower class in existence. The same order continues to exist today in those nations known as the Third World, the main reason those countries can't escape Third World status.

Americans must submit to changes after three decades of leadership by politicians who detest governmental action on behalf of the underclasses, but love to use government to benefit themselves. The public can no longer shrink in horror at taxation or government spending because taxing and spending are vital for economic strength. Americans can no longer pretend that they were victims in the creation of a national debt now well passed the $12 trillion Bush the Younger passed on. Americans can no longer accept the fairy tale that lower taxes and less government spending will solve the problems caused by the people who advocate such nonsense. And Americans can no longer accept the discredited notion that "big government" is the problem. America's problems arose from misuse of government; size of that government had nothing to do with creating the ills. Changes to solve the nation's problems must be significant; the country can no longer afford to tinker with taxing and government spending or running from problems by pretending they don't exist or, if they do exist, they are the fault of only the other political party. The minor changes advocated by President Clinton and enacted—where possible—also weren't the ultimate solution but are better than doing nothing or returning to the silliness that created the problems. The minor changes by Obama likewise will not solve all the problems, even though, over time, they will heal some of the wounds the political right inflicted on the nation.

The Washington professor did make some prophetic observations and posed pertinent questions. He asked where is the nation after 12 years of the Reagan era, what must be done to turn America around, is Clinton up to such a task and "...cutting through the discussion is a fourth critical question that asks whether the American people are willing to make the needed sacrifices. Presidential leadership can go only so far."

The same questions must be asked today only with stronger emphasis.

But it seems Americans may not be willing to make sacrifices, just as they turned a blind eye to the problems of the 1920s, which were addressed only when they became a full-blown depression, Americans today are turning a blind eye to the present problems and going again for fairy tales in place of sound economic solutions.

The professor added:

> "If America is to turn around its relative economic decline, it needs a big impact president—a leader with even greater power to mobilize support than President Reagan because the required message after the Reagan-Bush years will offer no easy way out.

> "The new politics of unreality even permits the hope of a worldwide recovery or a sudden unexpected jump in American productivity levels that began declining unexpectedly starting in 1973.

> "Looked at historically, the United States is the latest of the world superpowers to fall into relative decline. While America's relative

decline is not irreversible, time may be running out to take the steps needed for socioeconomic and political system revival."

Merely tinkering with taxes and government spending will not make significant improvements to America's declining productivity. And it was obvious by the 1994 midterm elections that turned Congress over to the political right Americans were in no mood to make any of the needed sacrifices; they were content to buy into the nonsensical rhetoric that all would be paradise if government were just smaller. Voters repeated that move in the 2010 midterm elections, with many blaming Barack Obama or the problems he inherited.

The Clinton administration had already begun a modest program to reduce the size of government. An administration plan in the summer of 1993—well before dissatisfaction got out of hand—called for a reduction in the federal bureaucracy of 252,000 jobs and $108 billion less in spending over five years. Within a year, the administration reported it had cut the federal workforce by 71,000 jobs and had upped the reduction target to 271,000 jobs, according to *USA Today*.[4] The newspaper said 98,000 jobs and more than 100 programs had been eliminated near the end of 1994 with an administration-estimated $3 billion in "savings." Years after the Clinton administration had left office, it was estimated that 373,000 federal jobs had been eliminated.

Another part of the "reinventing government" program was to cut "red tape," a derogatory term used to describe regulations designed to prevent bureaucrats from abusing their positions or treating citizens arbitrarily. In October of 1994, Clinton signed legislation to simplify the government's cumbersome procurement procedures. "There will be no more $600 toilet seats," he said. At the same time a bill was signed to reduce Agriculture Department agencies by a third, reduce Agriculture's workforce by 7,500 and authorize the Agriculture secretary to close 1,100 field offices. The bill to reform procurement was hailed as saving $12.3 billion over five years.

Such changes may be well and good, but they don't really address the problems of the nation. Immediately upon taking office Clinton did propose changes, such as lifting the bans on fetal research and gays in the military, eliminating the abortion gag rule, and proposed federal debt reduction and healthcare reform. But they also weren't the significant changes needed be-

---

4 "Report won't gather dust, says Clinton," Richard Benedetto; *USA Today*; September 8, 1993.

cause they were changes of degree not of kind, and which the American political class and the public were unwilling to accept. The nation didn't need minor changes; it needs a meaningful change in attitude. The nation doesn't need cosmetic changes in health insurance; it needs a complete new reality. The nation doesn't need simple tinkering with taxing and spending; it needs an entire new system that will cover the full scope of the American economy. Changes of degree won't do; monumental changes are necessary.

America needs changes along the lines of those brought about by Franklin Delano Roosevelt after capitalism failed in the 1920s. He was credited with saving capitalism with his far-reaching programs, but he did more than that. Roosevelt's actions brought into existence a different type of capitalism—after World War II—which reversed right-wing politicians' self-serving policies that had damaged the economy and led to the Great Depression. Roosevelt instituted unemployment insurance, Social Security, the Civilian Conservation Corps, Works Project Administration, the National Recovery Act, the Agriculture Adjustment Act, and he promoted workers' rights, all of which helped re-create and expand a consumer class, which is the most-important facet of a Democratic Capitalism economy. His opponents did not want the changes necessary to rebuild the consumer class, arguing that it would be "redistributing wealth," just as modern foes of Clinton and Obama protest what they call "social engineering" or claim they are being "punished" by any attempts to rebuild a consumer class battered by right-wing self-servers. Roosevelt brought about major changes that led to the most comfortable society—for those allowed to participate—in the history of the world (before tax tinkerers subverted its prosperity during and after the Vietnam Conflict). Clinton didn't made, or even suggest, significant changes. And neither has Obama after the destructive rule of George Bush the Younger.

When an American president proposes real changes needed to "save the nation," he (or she) should not give a hoot what right-wingers think, provided the American public sees through right-wing scams. Changes engineered by FDR in the midst of the Great Depression were opposed adamantly by the right, including conservative economists, but the United States emerged as the greatest economic, military and social power in the history of the world by adhering to Roosevelt's liberalism and rejecting the vested interests of the right. The success of the New Deal that the right calls "failures", are detailed in chapter 11.

When dissatisfied liberals rose up in opposition to the rule of Great Britain in 1776, the right was steadfastly opposed to anything that might disturb its moneyed interests. The liberals did opt for the change of independence from the mother country, which caused an estimated 10 percent of about 500,000 right-wing Tories in America to abandon the colonies to remain with the British. Since then, the right has opposed all major advances of the nation, including the Constitution, elimination of slavery, equal civil rights, labor rights, Social Security and unemployment insurance; and the right will oppose any major change in the future, even if that change is necessary to keep the United States in existence. The right is always wrong.

This book will propose the major changes needed. The changes needed include rejecting the right and its scams, alterations in taxation and government budgets, workable reforms to healthcare, Social Security and commerce. First, and maybe the most important, America must change how its prospective leaders gain power through elections. The benefits from these changes will not be quickly evident _ just as Roosevelt's reforms weren't immediately felt—they will make a better nation for future generations just as FDR provided for a better society for this present time.

REFORM BEGINS IN CONGRESS

Of all the changes needed, the most important may be reforming the election process at all levels of government in the United States. It should be evident to all persons that the special interests that pay for the elections of office holders will be those who will be served by the office holders. That should be evident from the past half century in which the tax burden at all levels of government slowly shifted from the commercial special interests to the individual taxpayers. Those same special interests then use their tax savings to pay for the election of politicians who will offer more tax breaks for business to do what business should do as a part of doing business. This leads to more shifting of the tax burden onto those who don't pay for the elections, the American middle class. Because incumbents have power to facilitate the tax shifting, they get the majority of the special-interest money regardless of political party or political philosophy.

The lesson is clear; if the American voters want to "take back the country," they first must take back the election process. This clearly means that the voters must pay for the elections.

All recent attempts to ease into such an arrangement have met with failure. A much-noticed attempt was made just prior to the midterm elections of 1994, in which voters expressed their anger with the system by voting into power the very political party—the Republican—that had steadfastly opposed election reform. It was reported a Republican leader informed special interests that the GOP (with the aid of conservative Democrats) killed the attempt at election reform specifically so those interests would be heard over all others in a Republican-controlled Congress. Kentucky Sen. Mitch McConnell claimed in a 1993 *USA Today* article that campaign financing by the voters would amount to a raid on the Treasury to subsidize politics as a welfare program for politicians.[5] Republican leader Bob Dole of Kansas claimed Republicans have a better idea which would ban political-action committees, reduce out-of-state contributions, prohibit mass mailings by incumbents, (most of whom used to be Democrats) among other issues; but those proposals are questionable on legal grounds. Both Republicans claimed that the poor taxpayer was overburdened by Clinton's tax-and-spend policies, without once mentioning that it was the Reagan Revolution that enacted borrowing-and-spending policies in a Republican Senate and conservative House that exacerbated the financial woes that began in the Nixon administration and that spending was legally done by the Republican Senate Dole led or the Republican House led by Newt Gingrich of Georgia. Nor did they mention that Clinton had actually reduced the size of government that grew under Republican administrations.

The proposals mentioned by Dole—except for congressional mailings—might have constitutional problems because any such law could regulate the behavior of American citizens in areas where the government has no authority to regulate. McConnell's position is the position wanted by the special interests that now control government.

The only reform that could have any impact in returning government to the people would be a constitutional amendment placing all elections under the authority of government, so that elections could be run much like government runs trials. Government would pay for the procedure. All pertinent

5 "Say no to welfare for politicians," Sen. Mitch McConnell, R-KY; *USA Today*; April 13, 1993.

information would be entered into "evidence" by any candidate bringing charges against another candidate and all charges would have rebuttals and cross-examinations which would be allowed or disallowed by an impartial judge, just as evidence is handled in any trial—criminal or civil. When an election advertisement is offered for public consumption, the rebuttal evidence would accompany it in the same advertisement. That might restrict advertisements to issues campaigns should focus on and perhaps eliminate the character assassination that now dominates all elections.

In such an arrangement, the federal Treasury would pay for presidential elections, the states would finance elections of senators, representatives and governors, and counties and cities would be responsible for state and local offices. This would require taxpayer financing; perhaps the federal elections would cost every American $1 a year (adjusted annually for inflation), far less than the thousands of dollars now paid to finance the interest on a national debt brought on by government controlled by special interests. A dollar or two at the state and local levels, likewise, would not be burdensome but would provide much more protection for the taxpayer than the habit of voting incumbents out of office wholesale in anger over what many politicians are unable to control. Political parties would be free to select their candidates for office. All parties—Democratic, Republican, Libertarian, Socialist or any other—must be allowed to participate equally with all other parties. With special-interest money presently paying for campaigns, only Democrats and Republicans have chances of winning, and the United States loses. While minor parties might not win many elections, their ideas will get exposure and their better ideas could be adopted by politicians who are elected. Franklin Roosevelt used many ideas from minor-party candidates in rescuing the nation in the 1930s.

These measures will give government authority to act in some areas to ensure fair and honest elections, but not to interfere with the citizens' rights to promote their favorite candidates. The measures might limit unnamed special interests from joining in television advertising designed specifically for character assassination. Voter suppression, either physical or psychological, could be treated as voter fraud and made a felony.

But rather than reform the election process to return political power to the people, many politicians and special interests advocate nonsensical, unworkable and possibly dangerous "solutions" such as the unconstitutional term limits, a balanced-budget amendment, or the line-item veto. (When the House of Representatives approved its version of the line-item veto in early 1995, large special interests were exempted. That bill would apply only to matters that might aid people. And when a line-item veto law was enacted, it was rightfully declared unconstitutional by the Supreme Court.) After the Supreme Court's illogical 2010 decision in Citizens United v. Federal Election Commission that turned corporations loose to spend any amount executive leadership wants, this may be the ideal time for an amendment that does what was just discussed.

The Soviet Union learned in the late 1980s that the nation couldn't be saved by mere tinkering with the system (as Mikhail Gorbachev sought to do), and neither can our nation be saved by tinkering. Whether Dole and McConnell, who always represented the Great State of Special Interests, would ever propose anything meaningful to return government to the people is questionable. And a balanced-budget amendment isn't needed; what is needed is balancing government tax collections with government spending. Something Congress has been unwilling to do under GOP administrations.

JUSTICE WANTED

Most Americans would agree the nation would benefit from having "real" families with two parents raising "normal" children. But government often ruins such traditional arrangements. Government promoting the exportation of jobs so that corporations can benefit from subsistence wages and from avoidance of healthcare expenses, retirement benefits, unemployment insurance and workers' compensation for employees is most destructive to America's working-class families, just as is the Republican/conservative "surtax" of several thousand dollars for each family to pay for the interest on the national debt. Welfare also destroys families when it requires separation of parents. But many politicians call for programs that are detrimental to the family while bemoaning the deterioration of the family. Refusal to allow full participation in the general welfare of the nation for all persons destroys the families of those excluded. The best remedies for the ailing family would be to bring back exported jobs and to allow all Americans to participate in the nation's general welfare.

In a just world, all persons would be required to live the life they impose on, or demand, for others. Anyone favoring slavery should be a slave, just as those wanting to exclude others (for such reasons as race, religion or gender) from the general welfare of the nation should themselves be excluded. A business executive paying employees poverty-level wages should also live on subsistence income. Closing a factory in the United States, leaving Americans unemployed merely to move jobs overseas to cheap labor sources, should result in unemployment for the closer or removal from the United States. Nor should anyone be offended if a practitioner of Gestapo management is subjected to harsh regulation by government. Police who terrorize minorities should themselves be terrorized. Prosecutors and police who convict innocent persons willfully with lies and fraud should serve the sentences they caused for others. (Errors are forgivable; fraud is not.) And those who wish for justice, fairness and opportunity for others should have those things for themselves. That is not likely to happen automatically anytime soon, but society can be prodded in that direction through the redoing of many facets of modern American life.

What must be challenged first is a tactic perfected by the American political right: the art of character assassination. When Clarence Thomas was challenged in his quest for a United States Supreme Court position, critical doubt was cast upon his character. Whether any of the doubt was valid or not isn't the issue. The issue was that his supporters did little to defend his character; they attempted to destroy the character of witnesses against him. The same character assassination met Clinton on his entrance to the presidency just as it permeates all political elections—most noticeably the 1994 mudfest. And that has only grown worse in the early part of the Obama administration

When the United States came to the aid of Jean-Bertrand Aristide trying to reclaim the Haitian presidency to which he was legally elected, the same character assassination came from the American right. The favorite charge of the right—"Marxist, Marxist, Marxist"—was leveled because of his program of attempting social reforms in what was considered the poorest, most violent and most corrupt nation in the Western Hemisphere. One attempt at character assassination came from *USA Today* columnist Joe Urschel[6] who wrote, "He [Aristide] has embraced liberation theology, a Marxist doctrine specifically opposed by the Vatican."

The question is, how could liberation theology be Marxist when Marx and his adherents were adamantly antitheology? Other arguments were likewise nonsensical, including:

---

6 "Aristide: No credit to the Catholic priesthood," Joe Urschel; *USA Today*; September 23, 1994.

"Following his election in 1990, his followers burned down the Catholic Cathedral in Port-au-Prince and attacked representatives of the Vatican.

"While in office, he tolerated and condoned brutality, and torture."

In the United States, at the beginning of our democracy, many of the leaders were slave owners and Congress early on passed the Alien and Sedition Act that was blatantly antidemocratic and unconstitutional. In this century, the followers of Reagan subverted the Constitution on several points during the Iran–Contra affair just as the followers of Richard Nixon resorted to subversion in the Watergate escapade and Bush the Younger's minions were worst of all with many anti-Constitutional actions. And in all cases, the American presidents tolerated and condoned this blatant subversion, but our right whined that Aristide wasn't as pure (by its definition) as the Jesus Christ he preached about. The assistance to Aristide was also attacked on the grounds that American troops would be there for years (proven wrong), the United States has no national-security interests in Haiti (the Constitution doesn't require that) and that Aristide leaves "a lot to be desired" (so do many American leaders).

Republican Rep. Chris Smith of New Jersey was quoted in *USA Today* as saying; "There are real questions I continue to have, like the fact that the administration did not get prior authorization for this. In a way, Bill Clinton has played Russian roulette with other people's lives."[7]

That was a strange position for a Republican to take because of the party's lack of concern for Reagan's unauthorized invasion of Grenada or his landing of troops in Lebanon, in which Americans did die. Another right-winger from the Heritage Foundation said Clinton's policy would "get some Americans killed for no good reason." But Bush the Younger did get thousands of Americans killed for no good reason in a war against Iraq that was never a threat to America just as thousands of Americans were killed on 9/11 because Bush ignored warnings of an impending attack.

Former ambassador to El Salvador Robert E. White wrote in an article for *The Los Angeles Times* that Aristide was overthrown by the military "not because of a few disputed offenses against democracy or human rights but because he insisted that the rich pay taxes and the military put an end to its drug trafficking."[8]

---

7 "Range of reaction: 'It's a disgrace' to' It's a smart move' "; *USA Today*; September 20, 1994.

8 "The drama of Haiti in three acts," Robert White; *The Los Angeles Times* republished in *The Seattle Times*; July 10, 1994.

CHAPTER 2. REJECTING THE RIGHT

To make the changes necessary to bring about a new and improved America it is vital to cool a national love affair with the destructive political force from the far right. This is not a reactionary nation—in spite of some recent indications—it was born in the spirit of 18th-century liberalism, a political catalyst that succeeded in establishing democratic republics to replace aristocracies, theocracies, monarchies, and other undesirable forms of government. That liberalization put the world on a more-peaceful and prosperous path—democratic republics don't wage war against each other and more people are allowed to participate in the wealth of a society—but the regressive far right gives all indications it still prefers those evil empires.

America's split from Great Britain was the most-progressive movement of its time; breaking from one's roots in quest of a new direction, is fundamental political liberalism. Writing liberal constitutions for the newly freed colonies led to creation of the national Constitution a few years later. That Constitution—the most-liberal government document in history—was hated by the reactionary Tories of the time (at least those Tories who had not abandoned the colonies to side with Britain during the war for independence), and modern American regressive Tories still detest the document, as this chapter will demonstrate. This nation was not "hijacked" by liberals, as Republican ex-Sen. Bob Dole of Kansas and others on the right claim, it was built by liberals leading the way for moderates and classical conserva-tives—far-Righties aren't the same as classical conservatives.

It is also important to improve the short-term memory of America's col-lective mind lest the nation re-experience problems brought about by previ-ous love affairs with the far right. Before the 1994 midterm elections Texas billionaire H. Ross Perot urged the nation to give control of the Congress to the Republican Party—the political party the far right has chosen to reside in. He said, "... give the Republicans a majority in the House and Senate and say, 'All right, now we're going to let you guys have a turn at bat'." The vot-ers did.

Since America began as a liberal nation, with input by moderates and responsible conservatives, the regressive right seldom has held power over the entire government; but when it did, bad things happened. The far right was barely a factor in the early part of the nation because of its opposi-tion to independence (Some Righties engaged in subversion at the time) and the adoption of the Constitution. In recent times, the right controlled both Congress (1925-1931) and the presidency (1921-1933) and the result was the Great Depression. The right again controlled Congress in 1953-54 under Republican President Dwight D. Eisenhower and the result was the greatest political witch hunt in our history; the Joseph McCarthy escapade that threatened to destroy constitutional freedoms. The right again took control of government in 1981, holding the Senate until 1987 under far-right President Ronald Reagan and maintaining a conservative majority in the House of Representatives. (The Republican Party didn't need a majority in the House, it could control with less than 200 members who would team with 40 to 50 conservative Democrats to influence the output.) The result: beginning of the greatest peacetime public debt in our history. And the right had total control of government from 2001 until 2007 with the result being the worst economic disaster since the Great Depression and a na-tional debt approaching that run up by World War II as it relates to Gross Domestic Product.

In addition to creating bad things, the far right has never produced a beneficial social program when it held power. Eisenhower's program to fill the nation with the Interstate Highway System was a great success, but Eisenhower was a moderate—the far right opposes spending government money on public works and many Righties think highways should be privately owned. GOP successes in social activities have always come with moderate or progressive leadership.

To the far-right failures of the Monster Public Debt, the McCarthy era and the Great Depression add crime, drugs, environmental damage and problems involving commercial deregulation.

The present system of "getting tough on crime" tends to isolate miscreants in a life of crime and creates new criminals to replace those criminals put into the new and more-expensive prisons. The refusal to attempt preventive measures only creates new criminals, which are needed for politicians to campaign with promises "to get tough on crime." The "War on Drugs" also serves to create new criminals. By not caring for environmental concerns and not trying to prevent environmental damage, the results have been expensive cleanup programs when preventative measures would have been less expensive. Mention of deregulation's failures brings to mind the savings-and-loan debacle that will cost America an estimated $500 billion (minus money recaptured in bankruptcy sales) when preventive measures under fair regulations could have prevented much of the damage. Deregulation also brought about the Enron scandal with scandals on several other corporations.

But probably the most disastrous far-right failure has been the trickle-down supply-side economics experiment that helped bring on the Great Depression and which created the monster public debt. Economic common sense should tell anyone that capitalism operates best on balance of supply and demand. If there is supply with little demand to absorb that supply, the economy falters. If there is demand with little supply to satisfy it, inflation runs wild. Entrepreneurship functions best when there is a need and an ability to supply that need. This is where the right goes wrong when it tries to satisfy only supply and when it calls for "less government" when government is trying to empower persons outside the economy with tools to participate in the economy.

It was an emphasis on supply side that turned economic problems into the Great Depression. Many economists trace the depression to Winston Churchill (then Britain's top financial officer) who tied the British pound to the gold standard in 1925 at a too-high value. That move weakened the British economy and shrunk the world's money supply. When the United States economy began to suffer with numerous worker layoffs and weaker consumer demand because of the smaller money supply, President Herbert

Hoover's solution was to aid business with the Reconstruction Finance Corp., a supply-side scheme that sent funds to industry to spur productivity, i.e. trickle down. Nothing went for consumption. Industrialist Henry Ford lectured workers to be more productive, frugal, patient and ambitious. It was all nonsense. Being more productive and frugal was counterproductive; frugality couldn't absorb the added production and when that production couldn't be absorbed, industry had to eliminate the worker-consumer. Some economic experts said the problem was overproduction (supply side) not lack of effort or initiative by the workers. More production accomplishes nothing without the means of consumption, but some modern economic tinkerers on the right still advocate and praise supply-side nonsense.

The right is so hung up on class distinctions it uses all its might to further divide society along class lines. It does that by the enrichment of a small group at the top of the commercial hierarchy, as Calvin Coolidge did in the 1920s. Never mind that some products that provided the enrichment killed and maimed, and destroyed the environment, the habitat of wildlife, and peoples' health and lives. The right, when it has political power, uses the state to further enrich the already rich—the Reagan debt—in order to widen the gap between the privileged and the excluded. Devious means are used in this class warfare; the Reagan ploy of increased defense spending on the world's best military coupled with lower taxes for the most wealthy so they might load up on Treasury bonds, bills and notes, thereby creating a conduit for what may be the most-massive redistribution of wealth from the middle class to the privileged class in the history of the world. That is, until George W. Bush did the same from 2001 to 2009.

Government has always used its spending power to benefit a few, such as spending in a favored area like the industrial-military complex. But the most-obvious method of benefiting the few was to control educational systems so the excluded would be deprived of skills and knowledge to challenge the privileged; i.e., using racial separation in the past; now advocating school vouchers so those who already have the most may tap government for more while leaving less for those who presently have the least. The criminal justice system has also been a tool to keep the underprivileged underprivileged

This preoccupation with class division is why the right has historically hated Franklin D. Roosevelt's New Deal and the Lyndon Johnson's Great Society. The FDR programs that reconstructed the consumer class, recognized labor rights and introduced Social Security, retirement benefits, minimum wages, unemployment insurance and some federal welfare programs prevented a Reaganomic depression in the 1980s and 1990s by keeping America's consuming ability relative strong. LBJ's civil-rights laws and affirmative actions that helped many of the disadvantaged move into the consuming class added to that strength. The United States suffered severe economic crises in the 1830-40s, the 1870s and 1890s and followed those with the Great Depression of the 1930s—four depressions in nearly a century. In the years since the advent of the New Deal, there has been no depression. Is that accidental? The right would rather have periodic economic crises—hence a fervent opposition to anything that would smooth out violent boom-and-bust cycles—than have the lesser classes narrow the gap with the upper classes. But, under Democratic Capitalism the upper classes will benefit from a lifting of the lower classes, as this book will show.

By emphasizing class, Righties are the most-blatant "social engineers" in American history, and that is why they try to pin that label on persons who try to break down purposely erected barriers in front of the have-nots. The term behavioral scientists use is "transference"; transferring to other people those qualities one doesn't want to admit in him/herself; i.e., the habitual liar will accuse everyone else of lying because he thinks lying is a normal activity for everyone. By relying on transference, Righties are inconsistent concerning any activity.

That inconsistency was shown in June of 1993 when the right was successful in blocking Clinton's nominee, black law professor Lani Guinier, to be deputy attorney general for civil rights. It seems she had proposed a supermajority requirement in some governmental areas. That is: require five city-council members out of seven to approve a project or ordinance that would affect a minority community. In that way, the logic was, at least one minority politician usually would have to be part of the deciding coalition should a city council decide to put a toxic-waste facility in a minority neighborhood rather than next to the country club. Righties portrayed Mrs. Guinier as antidemocratic and against majority rule. Dole opined, "I find it hard to believe a new Democrat like President Clinton would have nominated Mrs. Guinier if he had known about her far-left views." Dole's statement was nonsensical buffoonery.

What's hard to believe is the right couldn't see that this supermajority proposal is the exact same thing Righties propose for their pet issues. When a balanced-budget amendment to the Constitution is proposed, the right always demands a supermajority—often 60, 67 or 75 percent—be required to adopt any deficit spending. In the Republican right's Contract with America in 1994, there was a stipulation that 60 percent majority would be required to raise taxes. It is quaint the right would blast Mrs. Guinier for proposing what Righties want to write into the United States Constitution or establish by law. Since she and the Righties have the same philosophy on this matter their hatred of her must have been racial.

The right did it again, rising up in near-unanimity to oppose the nomination of Dr. Henry Foster to be surgeon general of the United States because during his career as a physician he had performed abortions; a perfectly legal endeavor. At the same time, the right was trying to allow prosecutors the authority to use in trial evidence obtained by illegal police activities, or more succinctly, criminal activity by government. This hypocrisy shows the GOP/conservative political bloc to be an evil movement detesting legal behavior by other people but endorsing crime if that crime serves the right's purposes.

In the first few weeks of the right's reign under the Contract With America, House Democrats tricked Republicans into voting on the admirableness of the Constitution's Fourth Amendment, one of the amendments requiring government to obey laws. The Constitution lost in the Republican repudiation, and the Righties couldn't recognize the issue voted on was from the Constitution. Late in 1995, the Republican Congress passed a bill to let the states remove interstate-highway speed limits established by Congress in 1974 and to allow states to establish whatever speed limits they desire. The Republicans ignored the Constitution's provision (Article IV, Section 3, paragraph 2) that says, "The Congress shall have Power to ... make all needful Rules and Regulations respecting ... Property belonging to the United States ..." That statement means only Congress can set speed limits on federal highways; such a constitutional authority cannot be given away to the states merely to satisfy a political position that's basically antagonistic to the federal government. Such actions show the level of appreciation the right has for the constitutional principles of the United States: None.

Dishonesty crops up in other issues, such as the hullabaloo concerning "family values." The family is deteriorating, the right claims, because of Lyndon Johnson's programs of the 1960s, even though those programs were largely undermined by subsequent Republican administrations. But no social change occurs so quickly, programs have little effect until succeeding generations are raised up under the new principles. Family values are such an example.

In his best-selling book, *The Closing of the American Mind*, Prof. Allan Bloom wrote this about declining values:

> None of this results from the sixties, or from the appeal to masculine vanity begun by advertisers in the fifties, or from any other superficial, pop culture events. More than two hundred years ago Rousseau saw with alarm the seeds of the breakdown of the family in liberal society, and he dedicated much of his genius to trying to correct it. He found that the critical connection between man and woman was being broken by individualism ... He wanted to rebuild and reinforce that connection, previously encumbered by the now discredited religious and civil regulation, on modern grounds of desire and consent.[9]

In other words, the family began to lose "values" hundreds of years ago and it did so because the church and government were losing the ability to intrude into peoples' lives and the "individualism" the right claims to champion was the primary catalyst for loss of "values." Recent adoption of no-fault divorce laws was another attempt to remove government from personal lives, but that allowed divorce rates to rise, which the right claims to hate. Out-of-wedlock births were placed on the doorstep of Hollywood in general, and fictional television character Murphy Brown, in particular, by Hypocright Vice President Quayle during the 1992 presidential campaign. History shows Murphy Brown had nothing to do with loss of values and Quayle didn't discover the issue.

The right claims liberals instituted a welfare system to make the downtrodden dependent on government, which makes social-service jobs permanent and strengthens a liberal fiefdom. By using the right's logic, one might conclude political conservatives pursue policies of exclusion (especially of minorities) to break down the family. By encouraging the moving of jobs to foreign lands, using budget tricks to provide Treasury income to themselves, fostering a lock-'em-up crime solution, undermining educational opportunities, withholding community services (called "pork"), and requiring

---

9   *"Closing of the American Mind"* ; by Allan Bloom; Simon & Schuster; ©1987.

fathers to abandon families on welfare, the right undermines the families of the underprivileged and then harps on breakdown of values in order to have campaign issues. Syndicated newspaper columnist, the late Molly Ivins wrote in 1994: "If anything about welfare can be held to destroy families, it is certainly the 'no man in the house' rule. And that wicked and shortsighted bit of legislation came, friends, from the right wing, now so busy blaming welfare for the destruction of the family."[10]

Complaining about welfare has created many misconceptions the right uses to serve itself. The argument is that welfare is a financial drain on the American taxpayer who can no longer afford to pay the bill for those who don't want to work. Many studies dispute those allegations. Yet many politicians had long campaigned on the issue, then made little attempt at reform once in office lest they lose a campaign issue.

But welfare programs have not been expensive in this, the world's richest society. By 1995, federal costs for the primary welfare program, Aid to Families with Dependent Children, were estimated at about $14 billion, twice the cost they were when Reagan took office. State costs were less than $12 billion, also about twice the cost. On a population of about 260 million, those figures break down to $54 a year in taxes per person for the federal programs and $46 for state programs. When all forms of welfare are figured in (including that which aids the middle and upper classes), the costs work out to about $400. Compare those costs to the more than $1,000 each person is taxed to pay interest on the Republican/conservative national debt. Money spent on welfare ends up in cash registers of America's small businesses that buy corporations' merchandise. By contrast, money spent on interest payments often is reinvested in Treasury bills, bonds and notes without ever passing through the economy. Welfare money benefits the economy; interest payments damage the economy.

When he announced his candidacy for the Republican nomination for the presidency in 1995, Dole told a New Hampshire audience that, "Middle-class families are forced to send too much of their hard-earned money to Washington," as he resurrected the Reaganomic theme that, "We can cut taxes and balance the budget" at the same time. Middle-class Americans do send much of their money to Washington and they do so because the Republican/conservative coalition prevented a surcharge on taxes to pay for

---

10   Molly Ivins; "Opinionline: Welfare plan keeps people on the rolls"; *USA Today*; June 15, 1994.

the Vietnam Conflict and that same coalition inflicted the Reagan economic fairy tale on the nation in 1981 when Dole was a leading power broker in the Republican Senate. It is those regressive Righties screaming the loudest about the national debt who were responsible for the Reagan raid on the Treasury when they held power of government in 1981-87, yet none has ever admitted any culpability. *USA Today* editorialized that average 1996 federal taxes were well below record levels and the load for all taxes paid—federal, state and local—were about the same as in 1981.[11] Dole then ran for president in 1996 on the promise to reimpose Reagan's failure, which would result in middle-class Americans sending even more money to Washington to pay for right-wing nonsense.

The argument that welfare creates permanent widespread dependency is also questionable. Some studies show about half on welfare stay no longer than two years; about two-thirds stay four years. Some people are on welfare for long periods of times and their children end up on welfare. But permanent welfare recipients are usually from the excluded class and have never learned how to be part of the included classes. A spokesman for the Cato Institute in Washington, D.C. gave the standard conservative line in a 1994 *USA Today* "opposing view" column saying, "Welfare contributes to crime by destroying the family structure and breaking down the bonds of community."[12]

A more-logical argument is that welfare—like crime, destruction of the family and the breakdown of the bonds of community—comes from the exclusion of large numbers of Americans from the general welfare of the nation, and that has been occurring for centuries. Society is paying for past exclusions, just as future generations will pay for present exclusions. There have always been and will always be some people who abuse a welfare system to benefit themselves, just as there have always been and will always be business leaders who abuse defense spending for illegal gain, college administrations who cheat on research grants and GOP/Righty politicians who manipulate the nation's tax-spend authority to benefit themselves and their friends. It's not a few welfare cheats who endanger the nation. The threat comes from Righties who made a wholesale raid on the Treasury and con-

---

11 "Public doesn't hear whole story about taxes, budgets"; *USA Today* editorial debate; August 16, 1996.

12 "Just abolish welfare," Michael Tanner; *USA Today*; July 27, 1994

tinue that raid for interest payments for themselves and for friends while trying to "reform" welfare for the have-nots.

A suggestion for welfare reform coming from the right was to end all federal programs and turn welfare entirely over to the states. That is short-sighted. The Constitution's Fourteenth Amendment is clear in that no state can make a law denying equal protection of the law to any "person," which means no state law can exist if it treats any class of persons differently from the treatment afforded other persons. Any state law would have to extend welfare benefits to any person who needs them, and that includes illegal aliens. This suggestion to turn everything over to the states, which would greatly increase the costs to state governments, came at a time when politicians in California, Texas and Florida, among other states, were whining about the cost of illegal aliens. The right claims that the states can do a better job of solving welfare problems than can the federal government, which isn't saddled with the same strict "equal" provisions of the laws that states must observe. Federal social programs also have never prevented the states from solving the problems that created a need for welfare.

Right-wing leader Newt Gingrich, R-Ga., proposed dismantling the "welfare state" with many of its functions turned over to private charities, but was not specific about how private charities are to handle the increased demand when they are already hard pressed to meet existing needs. Nor do Gingrich and other Righties admit that nothing stops private charities from aiding the poor. Nothing prevents states from doing likewise. And if private charities and state governments would have been capable of doing what Gingrich proposed, there would have been little need for the federal programs in the first place. But federal programs were started precisely because of the miserable records of states that often did things to create welfare dependency (such as racial segregation) but did nothing to solve the problem.

Some people on the right wanted to end welfare programs, telling everyone to fend for themselves; some on the left wanted no changes or wanted to create more social programs designed to train the disadvantaged for jobs, even jobs that may not exist. For any solution to work it would have to end exclusion of any group or person—civil-rights and affirmative-action laws try to do that—and it would have to address the problem of American corporations firing hundreds of thousands of employees while "downsizing" or closing plants in the United States to escape the obligation of paying livable wages, providing healthcare insurance or retirement plans for employees and obeying environmental regulations.

Another right-wing "solution," coming immediately on the heels of the Republican capture of Congress in 1994 was the idea to establish orphanages to take care of children born out of wedlock to mothers on welfare. Like most Righty solutions, this one would be ordained to fail. Orphanages would be much more expensive than cash payments and would have to rely on government's powers to tax and spend; a most-hated government function. Government certainly has authority to spend tax money to promote general welfare of the nation or of a state; that includes cash payments to indigent mothers or to support orphanages. The national government can tax and spend to build and operate orphanages, but it has no authority to take children from their mothers to place those children in orphanages. That is also true of the states. The Constitution says no person can be deprived of life, liberty or property without due process of law. A mother's liberty is at stake in this situation so there must be due process. The Fifth Amendment depicts due process as indictment (for serious crimes), trial, conviction and punishment. A child's right to be free from abduction by government (Habeas Corpus) is involved. Habeas Corpus means government cannot take bodily possession of anyone and hold that person without legal reasons, and those legal reasons are included in due process. Therefore a state cannot snatch a child from a mother, regardless of her financial situation, except for a crime; usually a crime against the child. Government rewriting rules to force a mother to relinquish a child (through threats of a financial cutoff) is a tactic one would expect only from autocratic regimes. The only American children who could be legally placed in government-run orphanages are those presently in foster care. It's clear that the orphanage idea would do nothing to ease the welfare problem but would cost billions of dollars more to operate and would involve more government intrusion into Americans' lives.

Late Sen. Daniel Patrick Moynihan, D-N.Y., was quoted in the October 1994 issue of *Reader's Digest* as saying, "A community that allows a large number of young men to grow up in broken families, never acquiring any stable relationship to male authority, asks for and gets chaos. Crime, violence, unrest, disorder—most particularly the furious, unrestrained lashing out at the whole social structure—that is not only to be expected, it is very near to inevitable."[13]

The conditions to which Moynihan referred are caused by exclusion—not a temporary short-term exclusion, but a systematic generational exclusion—they are not caused by welfare.

Family values have also taken a beating in conservative politics. A 14-year-old boy, who had refused to go home to the Ukraine when his diplomatic father was reassigned to a position in the Soviet Union, was granted political asylum by the administration of Jimmy Carter then was given permanent residency under Reagan. His parents wanted him returned home to the family. When the American Civil Liberties Union argued the parents' plea for "traditional family values," the right was quick to blast the civil-rights organization. In 1992, in a case involving a 12-year-old trying to "divorce" his mother, the right took an opposite stance and attacked the idea a child should have such legal rights.

The right confuses itself on the matter of family. In Asia, the family is the most important facet of society. A person's allegiance is first to the family, then to the village and the state; the individual is subordinated to the group. But the American right campaigns on family values (personal collectivism) and the desirability of the corporation (commercial collectivism) while claiming to love individualism (the basis of liberalism). In truth, we need both the collectivism of the community and the individualism of liberty.

The Hypocritical Abound

A hypocritical stand by the right that may have solidified its designation as the "Hypocright" could have been the constant criticism heaped on Hillary Rodham Clinton when she led the information-gathering effort for the Clinton administration's attempt at healthcare reform. The Hyprocright complained—even went to court—about the task force gathering information and developing proposals to overhaul the healthcare field in America. The biggest complaint was about the closed-door process of gathering information from private citizens about problems and other nightmares in which they were victimized by the system. Right-wingers adamantly demanded all work should be done in public.

---

13   "The Ominous Rise in Illegitimacy," Daniel Patrick Moynihan; *Reader's Digest*, October, 1994.

There could probably be good reason for conducting information gathering in secret, such as keeping special-interest spokesmen from monopolizing the informational input and protecting some people from recriminations should their stories be made public. A person's medical condition, if made public, could lead to elimination of a job, loss of insurance coverage, ostracism by the community or other forms of undesirable repercussion. It was a common occurrence when the AIDS epidemic was causing a subtle panic to hear of afflicted persons having their insurance coverage canceled—when insurance companies found a loophole—or having the premiums repeatedly raised so the premiums would always cost more than the cost of treatment. Those persons who have suffered adversely at the hands of an insurance company trying to cut expenses would understand the secrecy arrangement. Government's first priority is to protect the people, not a corporation.

When a federal judge ruled in 1993 that the task force could not hold fact-finding and fact-reporting meetings until the sessions were opened or notifications they would be closed were posted, Republican leaders were delighted even though the ruling would not do much. Republican Dole was quoted as saying, "We believe in the open forum. Let the sun shine in." Another Republican was quoted by USA Today saying: "My feeling has always been that they would be better served themselves if this thing was opened up. It's a political embarrassment."[14]

The right's hypocrisy was shown by such statements after years of Quayle's Council on Competitiveness secretly meeting to rewrite federal regulations. The Knight-Ridder News Service in 1992 reported of Quayle's council that it

> [overturned] regulations governing everything from air pollution to airplane noises. It has blocked 59 provisions of the Clean Air Act ...
>
> It has knocked out provisions for recycling standards, fought to let polluting firms increase toxic emissions without public notice, scuttled acid rain regulations and sought to keep millions of acres of wetlands from the clutches of the Environmental Protection Agency.[15]

---

14 "Task force on health hit on secrecy," Judi Hasson; and "Ruling doesn't apply to units of task force," Judy Keen and Judi Hasson; USA Today; March 11, 1993.

15 "Quayle council actions now ensnarled in law"; Tim Weiner; Knight-Ridder News Service published in The Denver Post; July 24, 1992.

Such actions were taken in secret and no public records were kept. Quayle was quoted as saying he was "eliminating excessive, burdensome and unnecessary regulations" that result in multimillion-dollar bills for business and require tons of paperwork. Quayle's explanation was nonsensical. The Clinton administration hoped to end such skullduggery with an executive order in October of 1993 that banned secret contacts between administration officials and special-interest spokesmen and required public disclosure of regulatory review.

But in the early days of the George W. Bush administration, Vice President Dick Cheney convened an Energy Task Force where he met with executives from the fossil-fuel industry to consider regulations and oversight of that industry. All the proceedings were conducted in secrecy. There was silence from Republicans on this matter, even from those who had howled at Clinton's secret information gathering.

Throughout the history of the nation the United States Supreme Court and other courts have been telling governments at all levels they can't make laws, regulations or rules unless they have good reasons and proper authority to do so. The Constitution says in Article I, Section 8, paragraph 18 that Congress's lawmaking power refers to laws that are "necessary and proper." That same rule has been applied to the states by state constitutions or by Supreme Court decisions. A case in point was a 1994 decision in which city officials in Oregon tried to force a small business to set aside a portion of its land for public use not related to the firm's business activity in exchange for a building permit to expand the store. That wasn't proper, so the state action was nullified by the court. In the Plessy v. Ferguson case (1896) the court said government cannot make laws merely to annoy or harass, all laws must be necessary. The court ruled that use of power must be reasonable and "extend only to such laws as are enacted in good faith for the promotion of the public good, and not for the annoyance or oppression of a particular class."

Most modern political campaigns are fraught with silliness of two primary issues the nation has come to expect from Hypocrights: lower taxes and too much regulation of business and society. The Republican/Hyprocright alliance since the Nixon administration has caused the need for high taxes to pay interest on the debt started by the decision to pay for the Vietnam Conflict through borrowing, rather than taxes, and expanded by Reagan economic theories that were made worse by George W. Bush. Regulations should never be campaign issues because any regulation, whether on businesses or individuals, can be challenged in any courthouse, at any time, by anyone affected by the regulation. Regulators would have to prove their actions were necessary and proper, and if there is any merit to the challenge the regulation would be set aside. If regulations aren't negated after an un-biased court proceeding, that should be evidence that they are necessary. Quayle, as an attorney and longtime government official, should know that.

Corporations maintain legal staffs to challenge regulations. Chambers of commerce, or like organizations, could represent small businesses. But, the Hypocright never uses this proper method, it forms cabals to meet in secrecy and subvert properly enacted rules while complaining about other people meeting in private—the difference was that Mrs. Clinton's meetings did not involve laws, regulations or any other rules, it was only information gathering. The right may not use this proper method of legal protection in order to keep "overregulation" as a campaign issue.

The Hypocright often resorts to clichéd postures, whether on purpose or for lack of knowledge, about our constitutional system. From the begin-ning of a non-Republican administration in 1993, propagandists of the right have sung the same silly song. Conservative newspaper columnist George Will argued in May of 1993 that the Clinton administration was engaged in an "aggressive and comprehensive power grab" with the "motor-voter" law which would make it easier for people to register to vote by doing so when they renew driver's licenses or when in welfare offices. The "power-grab" argument also was made by many on the right concerning the health-reform effort. In the same month, Will complained that Clinton "has a breathtak-ing agenda for expanding supervision of American life" and complained in November of 1994 that "Their (liberals) real agenda is increasing regulation of society."[16]

A comparison of agendas in the Liberal-Hypocright debate reveals a dif-ferent conclusion.

Liberals will resort to regulation of commerce and the power to tax and spend to provide for the general welfare (both in Article I, Section 8 of the United States Constitution) for the basis of most of their programs. Since the powers are there and clear to see by anyone who can read, there is no "power grab." The federal government has the authority to regulate

---

16   "The president grabs for power" and "It's only Clinton who needs a crisis," George Will; *Washington Post* Writers Group; May 23 and 30, 1993.

the registration and voting process for political office, and state officials are "bound by Oath or Affirmation, to support this Constitution ... " (Article VI) and that means administering federal standards, when required to do so. So the motor-voter law is no power grab. Regulation of commerce is not "expanding supervision of American life." Neither is a legal tax.

Compare those three uses of power by liberals with what the Hypocrights do, in addition to using the taxing and borrowing provisions of the Constitution to enrich themselves and their backers. It's the right clamoring to put government into the spiritual lives of Americans by using public schools to conduct religious services. (The right constantly argues that public schools are incapable of delivering a decent education to children, but then wants the same schools to provide spiritual guidance.) The right wants government to regulate reproduction through abortion laws; and when those laws fail in court, Hypocrights try to regulate the speech of pregnant women, their healthcare providers and advisors with other laws. The right is adamant in its desire to regulate other persons' speech, especially of homeless persons publicly begging for handouts. The right has been consistent in its desire to regulate Americans' patriotism or lack of patriotism with such things as flag-burning laws or a constitutional amendment. The right wants governmental control of some Americans' love lives through regulation of sexual preference, especially when it comes to homosexuals. It was right-wing politicians who regulated personal relationships in the past by outlawing the marriages of blacks to whites (mostly in the South), Caucasians to Asians (mostly on the West Coast) or other mixed-race unions. The Hypocright has regulated matters of thought with silly laws and actions that punish people for thinking differently from the majority (i.e., the McCarthy era and its resultant blacklists).

The right would regulate associations or gatherings, as it did during the civil-rights struggles of the 1960s—even going so far as implying that the Constitution's provision for equal rights is communistic. The right loved it when a Virginia judge used the power of the state to intrude into the family to take a child from his mother because she was born a lesbian. And the right wants to regulate how we die; an example is the state of Michigan's regulation and imprisonment of Dr. Jack Kevorkian who became famous assisting people who decide themselves they want to die. This state intrusion gained widespread approval by Hypocrights. (The state's power to control medicine may be restricted to regulation of commerce, so it is questionable if it has jurisdiction in noncommercial matters such as suicide, assisted or otherwise.)

In 1993, a Righty politician in Oregon claimed she wanted to fight crime by having government compel all Oregonians to have a gun and ammunition in the home, just as Kennesaw, Georgia, did 12 years earlier, even though governments usually do not have powers to force citizens to take such actions. The right supported sheriffs in some Western localities in 1996 when those law-enforcement officers challenged the Brady Law's requirement that sheriffs conduct background checks for criminal records of would-be gun buyers. Sheriffs challenging the provision claimed they were not employees of the federal government so they didn't have to enforce federal laws (the sheriffs apparently didn't know about Article VI). Prior to this situation, the right argued for years that local school administrators enforce federal immigration policies by denying education to children of illegal immigrants even though such action would subvert the Constitution's principle of equal protection of the laws for all persons that the Fourteenth Amendment requires of all governments below the federal level. Right-wingers in Congress and in state legislatures have tried legislation telling states they don't have to recognize marriages of gay persons from other states even though the Constitution says in Article IV that, "Full Faith and Credit shall be given in each State to the public Acts, Records, and judicial Proceedings of every other State." (A simple law can't authorize state governments to subvert this constitutional principle.) The right misused government by having National Guard troops and police and sheriff departments act as goons to try to deny labor rights and livable wages to the working-class people—many of whom were killed in the process—earlier in the 20th century. The worst misuse of government power was forcing segregation of the races in society following the Civil War in order to deprive millions of people—mostly black—the opportunity to participate in the general welfare of society. Most problems of the modern nation can be traced to such misuse of government authority.

There are differences in the regulatory thrust of the left and the right. The left uses powers that are in constitutions—federal and state—while the right tries to use powers that haven't been given to government or have been specifically prohibited by constitutions. The other difference is money. The left will use money in its programs to "do for" people, the right will not. The right will intrude into personal matters to "do to" people, the left will not. The liberal wants to provide needful social programs through regulations and taxation. The right will not regulate in matters concerning money—or gun control—but uses government to regulate private matters. This is why Hypocrights sent American troops to die in Granada for economic concerns but wouldn't risk them in Haiti for democratic philosophies.

As shown, the argument that the right wants limited government and the left is for big government is a lie. The Tenth Amendment of the Constitution reserves for the people powers not given to the national government or to the state governments. Intrusion into the peoples' private lives is the real "power grab," because power over personal lives is what the Tenth Amendment reserves for the people. Limited government means the state is limited to using only those powers given to it by its constitution—that's liberalism. Using the state to intrude into private lives—a Hypocright custom—is true big government. When Republicans constantly cry out that they are for "smaller government," they are trying to evade the truth that it is the GOP right that is the purveyor of Big Brother government.

There is a difference between a Hypocright and a classical conservative, such as late-Sen. Barry Goldwater of Arizona. The Hypocright would regulate religion, reproduction, speech, patriotism, marriage and other love lives, thought (especially political thought), association, dying, racial relations or participation in public life, and property ownership such as the demand that people buy and keep guns. A true classical conservative would regulate none, and neither would a true liberal. Goldwater, the father of modern conservatism, is like a preacher whose children continue sinning even though he lectured them from birth on virtue. Hypocrights were sired by Goldwater, but they have gone bad by ignoring his lectures on limited government.

Liberalism has been under attack since the Vietnam Conflict for logical reasons. Liberals have always insisted on resorting to their "highly developed intellectual abilities" to reason with the American people. What liberals failed to notice soon enough during the period of increasing conservative political acceptance was the disintegration of the educational system, which greatly reduced the number of people who could reason. That suited the conservative movement just fine because people who can't reason are always open to emotions. Young people just out of inferior schools have been voting conservative because the right's political message was the emotional, but unrealistic, lower taxes. Liberals tried to appeal to reason on the mounting public debt by advocating real government income from taxation to ward off financial disaster. That may be reasonable but it doesn't please the emotions and is usually rejected. The 1984 presidential campaign was a prime example when Walter Mondale appealed to logic about confronting the mounting national debt and the need to pay it off through taxes. Reagan went after the emotions of just be happy and the debt will take care of itself. Reagan won in a landslide.

Hypocrights do not know what they want. They claim to want smaller government, but seek regulation of things government isn't authorized to regulate: that's bigger government. They want to lower taxes and to return power to the states, but returning powers to the states would increase taxes to meet the Fourteenth Amendment demand that state laws apply equally to all "persons," which means everyone, including aliens—illegal or otherwise—would be eligible for needful social programs, and that would increase state spending.

By having states handle most public business, Righties would empower the Equal Rights Amendment they defeated in the 1970s and 1980s; the Fourteenth is an Equal Rights Amendment. Feminists need only assist Righties in moving most power back to the states and they would have the equal rights Hypocrights detest.

UNDERSTANDING A RIGHTY MIND

There is a method of reading between the lines to see what a Righty is really saying.

TV Guide quoted right-wing publisher Brent Bozell as saying in 1993 that Picket Fences was the "most-liberally biased" show on television while Northern Exposure promoted feminist rhetoric and homosexuality. "Television folk are 'unabashedly abusing the airwaves to indoctrinate America'," Bozell said. [17]

To understand a Righty's mind one must pay attention to the words he (or she) uses to attack others. Words like "indoctrinate," "promote" and "biased." Such usages suggest that the right views the nation's communication apparatuses (movies, television, radio, newspapers and magazines) as vehicles of indoctrination and would use them that way when they have control. When the right fails to detect a conservative bias in the nation's

---

17 Brent Bozell quoted in "TV's 'Most Liberal' Programs?"; *TV Guide*; July 3-9, 1993.

media, the assumption is made that there may be a liberal bias when there is no bias either way; but the complaint does reveal how the right views the roll of the media. Righties have long complained left-wing professors brainwash college students to create more liberalism among the educated. That long-standing contention indicates that Righties view education as a means of political indoctrination and their argument shows how they would use education if in control. But the argument falters when a curious person wonders why right-wing professors can't rescue students from liberalism. The truth is that liberalism is a byproduct of intelligence, not training or indoctrination, and liberal dominance in advanced degrees only means that more-intelligent persons obtain these degrees.

A logical person could see that "Northern Exposure" reflected—not promoted or indoctrinated—the views of a wide range of Americans or movements: liberal, conservative or moderate; political and apolitical; white, black, Indian; environmental or commercial interests, and the arts. The main character, Dr. Joel Fleischman, reflected the relentless pursuit of status. Maurice Minnifield represented the money-seeking business conservative who was enamored with his own importance. Holling Vincouer typified the rebel who succumbed to the lure of entrepreneurship and accepted family values late in life after giving up his liberated lifestyle. Ruth-Anne was the small-business owner struggling to succeed on her own rugged individualism, as was bush pilot Maggie O'Connell. The reformed bad boy's point of view was represented by Chris, the disc jockey; just as Maurice's one-time love, Sgt. Barbara Semanski of the Alaska State Police, represented the law-and-order crowd. Adam, the gourmet chef, former espionage agent, world traveler and on-and-off newspaper columnist, spoke for everyone who was just a little bit hacked off about life. The homosexual characters— the town's two female founders and two men running a bed-and-breakfast establishment—were presented as ordinary human beings.

Picket Fences took a similar path. The main character and two of his compatriots were no-nonsense law-and-order types, like the black district attorney. Judge Henry Bone was a stickler for legal protocol, much like the conservative bunch on the U.S. Supreme Court, which he used in the quest for justice, like any liberal member of the court. They lived in a city with normal but exaggerated societal problems.

Cicely, Alaska, (Northern Exposure) was Everyville, USA, while Rome, Wisconsin, (Picket Fences) was Anytown, America. It's possible a Righty could not grasp the Northern Exposure humor, such as a Grosse Pointe feminist Democrat or a Jewish Republican spawned in a New York City academic environment. The Hypocright may be disturbed because he and his fellow travelers don't care for a nation that contains all races, all nationalities, all faiths, all creeds, all colors, all political views, and all social classes. The United States is like the biblical tree that grew majestic from a mustard seed to allow room for all birds of the sky—including the raven, the wren, the cardinal, the canary and the snowy egret—to find refuge in its branches. America is a land where all persons should live equally with all others without fear of attack; many on the right only want to attack other Americans.

EXPLANATION OFFERED

All this explains the Rush Limbaugh phenomenon.

The Rush Limbaugh Television Show went on the air in mid-1992 after it became obvious President Bush was in political trouble. The Limbaugh show ran in syndication for four years and ended only when Limbaugh felt he wasn't getting proper air times at many stations, was produced by Roger Ailes, who at the time was identified by *USA Today* as a "GOP strategist." Ailes, a longtime Republican official had a great strategy: political propaganda disguised as entertainment and now as news, as the head of Fox television news. So Limbaugh's television show was a program with no relationship to entertainment, information, enlightenment or communication and there was no exchange of views on any issue. The show contained only harangues of political propaganda presented as talk-show entertainment. The program was a fraud; it was bait and switch, it was an electronic monte game, it was three walnut shells and a pea presented to America by the people who brought the nation a Reagan Ponzi scheme (more about that in chapter 3) disguised as economic policy. And it wasn't very truthful. In viewing and listening to Limbaugh a person is ever reminded of Sergeant Schultz, the rotund, know-nothing tool of fascist masters on the old television program Hogan's Heroes.

In defending the Reagan regime, Limbaugh claimed (Feb. 16, 1993, program) Reagan had to overcome a Democratic Congress in 1981 to enact his economic program. As already shown, Reagan went into office with a Republican Senate and a conservative House—so conservative that every Reagan budget was reduced before passage—and held that advantage for the six years in which most of his economic policies were enacted. Representatives reflect the districts from which they come and to vote the way those districts voted in presidential elections. Reagan captured most districts in 1980 and an overwhelming majority in the 1984 landslide, so he controlled the House regardless of party affiliation. He could get his programs passed with fewer than 200 Republicans because he had the support of conservative Democrats who had historically been the majority of Southerners. In that Congress about 100 Democrats came from Southern conservative states. Only 25 conservative Democrats were needed to give Reagan a majority.

Limbaugh said (June 24, 1993):

> "Let me tell you something folks. Tax rates went down. How many times do I got to say this? Reagan assumes office; top marginal rates, 70 percent—thank you Jimmy Carter—1989, Reagan leaves office, top marginal rate, 28 percent. We really reduced tax rates; but guess what, we nearly doubled revenues generated by the tax system in the country. The rich are paying an even larger percentage of the tax burden than they ever have. This is a lie (Clinton contention that the rich aren't paying their fair share). This is right out of the liberal handbook. It's a cliché. It's a lie. It's class envy.

> "It's exploitation. It's designed to do nothing more than make you hate the rich. To make you resent the rich."

Unfortunately that speech left out one important bit of information—how much the privileged class extracted from the tax system after spending the Reagan years loading up on Treasury bonds, bills and notes. The true tax load will be the difference in taxes paid and interest received, and the right never mentions that. (Incidentally: the top tax of 70 percent was established under John F. Kennedy, not Jimmy Carter, and 70 percent was a reduction from the 91 percent left by Republican Eisenhower. The right also never mentions that under these high rates "loopholes" were established whereby the rich could escape taxation by investing in worthwhile endeavors like housing projects; exploration for oil, gas and minerals; manufacturing, or any of many other beneficial activities. When such loopholes are removed as tax rates fall, the most beneficial place to invest money becomes the U. S. Treasury. Government then grows to address societal problems once handled by the private sector. An example of failed Righty policies resulting in bigger government.)

Another instance of Sergeant Schultz know-nothingism was the criticism of the Clinton debt-reduction plan as the exact same thing as Bush's 1990 plan, which Limbaugh claimed didn't work, therefore Clinton's 1993 plan wouldn't work. But Clinton's plan did work, and the Limbaugh criticism wasn't honest. Bush's 1990 plan raised tax revenue by eliminating many deductions on the middle class, thereby reducing the money this consuming group had to spend with small businesses. That reduced small-business profitability and a recession followed; the recession that cost Bush his presidency. Clinton's 1993 plan raised most of its revenue from high incomes that weren't used to purchase consumer goods; consumer spending is done with first-earned income, not tail-end earnings. High incomes weren't affected by Bush's 1990 plan. A tax that wouldn't negatively impact the economy is one that targets money, items or assets which do nothing to advance economic growth, and an income that does the least for the economy is interest income from the Treasury, which goes back into the Treasury to buy more debt instruments. By taxing money destined to buy debt instruments, Clinton's plan didn't damage the economy as Republican plans always do. Within a year, the economy was so strong that the Federal Reserve Board was raising interest rates to prevent inflation. That's the truthfulness about differences of the two debt-reduction plans.

Many people, deceived by the Hypocright rhetoric, bemoaned the Clinton plan. A business owner called the Limbaugh show claiming he would have to fire his employees because of the Clinton debt-reduction effort and because of taxes, workmen's compensation and other obligations, salaried workers were making more than he was as an owner (Democratic Capitalism as promoted in this book would solve that glitch, if there was such a glitch). Many employers apparently didn't fire their employees; employment increased by millions after the Clinton plan was enacted, because a reduction in the deficit freed up money for investment in the economy rather than for the purchase of Treasury bills, bonds and notes.

In his silly tome called *The Way Things Ought to Be*, Limbaugh showed his link to Sergeant Schultz by writing that "Reagan's presidency, coupled with the longest sustained economic boom in modern history, invalidated almost everything liberals stand for, believe in, and have spouted for decades. Virtually every important cornerstone of liberalism was shown for what it is: wrong."[18]

---

18   "The Way Things Ought to Be," Rush H. Limbaugh III; Pocket Books; © 1992.

But comparing principles of liberals with thoughts of Hypocrights shows otherwise. Liberalism brought the United States independence from British rule (conservatives, led by Benedict Arnold, opposed it); the United States Constitution and the Bill of Rights; an end to slavery and the preservation of the union; labor rights, unemployment insurance, Social Security and industrial-retirement rights, all important for a strong consumer class; civil rights, and what may dig at the Righties the most, integration of modern baseball.

By contrast, the right was anti-independence, anti-Constitution (and still uses the same 1787-88 arguments to oppose constitutional principles), proslavery and for the breakup of the union, for segregation and against civil rights, anti-labor (i.e. the working middle class), and the right detested Social Security, minimum wages and unemployment insurance (Hypocrights claim to this day all were bad ideas), but were for the states' rights that produced slavery, American apartheid and other evils, and for the economic Ponzi scheme called Reaganomics.

"I believe in the individual, in less government ... societies which are founded on restraining the government rather than the individual are optimum...," Limbaugh wrote. Yet in the same book and on his broadcast programs Limbaugh advocates—as most Righties do—government involvement in religion, regulation of procreation, regulation of speech (especially speech of pregnant women and homeless beggars), regulation of patriotism and regulation of homosexual behavior and regulation of everybody's marriages. When Righties talk about "shrinking" government and about "personal freedom" they speak of less involvement in government programs that benefit the have-nots, not about less governmental intrusion into personal matters of religion, reproduction, patriotism, speech, and our love lives; and their "freedom" is only freedom for the haves to avoid their responsibilities to the democratic republic.

About political opponents—i.e. liberals—Limbaugh wrote, "They do think it [the economy] is a zero-sum game, that there's only so much to go around and it has to be shared more fairly."

That's not what liberals think (it is typical of right-wing propagandists to distort the views of others and then use that distortion as a club to beat on foes during political harangues); liberals think everyone should be allowed to participate, and what must be shared more fairly is opportunity. Civil-rights and affirmative-action laws were created to eliminate race, religion, age, gender or sexual orientation, nationality or any other minority status as reasons for disqualifying persons from employment, education or other social comforts. When everyone is allowed to participate, the nation will benefit from an expanded and healthier economy where there's enough for everyone. Liberals think that when everyone is able to participate fairly, government services can be reduced, or phased out, for true smaller government. Advocating smaller government without solving problems caused by exclusion is irresponsible.

So like Sergeant Schultz, the Limbaugh catch phrase should be, "I know nothing."

Righties are consistent in their inconsistency. As their anti-America refrain grew ever louder in the late 1980s and early 1990s, many persons began to consider a return to the "Fairness Doctrine" on radio and television broadcasting. But, since the right dominated those media, the call from them was that the doctrine requiring time we provided for a counterargument would violate their right to "free speech." The Fairness Doctrine, when it had been the law of the land, never censored speech, never dictated what opposing speech must say and never punished anyone for anything they said.

Not all talk-show hosts were so adamantly opposed to the doctrine; Larry King wrote in his *USA Today* column: "Every responsible broadcaster I know likes the Fairness Doctrine because fairness is what the USA is all about." [19]

But, for the most part, those who adamantly oppose the Fairness Doctrine are the very same folks who advocate government regulation of speech when it concerns reproduction. They support the power of government to compel physicians or family planners to lecture women on aspects of abortion women may not want to hear; or to prohibit other speech the physician might feel important. They support government action forcing women to tell the male who impregnated them of their desires and to get the male's permission for an abortion. They want government to compel teen-age girls to seek out fathers they may have never seen to tell him of a pregnancy. They want government to regulate speech of homeless people to prevent them from asking for handouts while on public property—remember, the airways are public property—and many Righties want governments to compel pledges of allegiance to government. Reactionaries have always

---

19   "The late-night wars and daytime drama," Larry King; *USA Today*; September 7, 1993.

wanted government to regulate speech of others, but they do not want any government regulation that would open up channels where others could freely speak to counter the Righties' prattle. The Fairness Doctrine would not have impeded speech of reactionaries, only opened up opportunities to speak for those who opposed the politics of the talk-show hosts.

Government power to regulate commerce and to govern the use of public property is well established in the United States Constitution, so government has power to institute the Fairness Doctrine. Government can regulate medical practice because it is commerce, but government has no power to regulate speech of pregnant women or of teen-age girls. The state cannot regulate the speech of people just because they are homeless or speak on public property. Government has no power to regulate speech by compelling vows of allegiance to the state. Hypocright talk-show hosts want un-American regulations imposed on others but howl about constitutional conditions on themselves.

When Righties don't get their views endorsed in news stories of America's newspapers or of electronic broadcasts, they claim there is a liberal bias in the press. But that is not the case. Like any workforce in America—except for Wall Street firms—newspaper and television news operations are stocked mainly with people from the working middle class and that tends to be Democratic. News operations, like most callings considered to be dependent on educated and intelligent employees, attract those qualities which are considered liberal. But the hierarchies of most newspapers and electronic media are Republican—some moderate, some conservative, a few liberal—and that is reflected in editorial policy and on editorial and op-ed pages where Republican publishers and editors fill their opinion pages with material reflecting their personal beliefs.

There is a shuttle between government and the press. Government jobs will usually be political payoffs to loyal soldiers and press jobs will usually be as columnists or editorial writers to give publishers' political biases an air of legitimacy. The press defends the practice by claiming the politician-journalist is needed because he/she has many important contacts in government.

A rundown of people published most often shows a strong conservative bent by those who came from political positions. William Safire of the *New York Times* was a Nixon administration politician as was Patrick Buchanan, who also served Reagan and who continued to be a politician in his quests for the GOP presidential nomination. George Will was an administrative assistant to a conservative politician before he was a "journalist." Columnist Mona Charon came from Republican politics, as did the late Tony Snow of *The Detroit News* and *Gannett News Service*, and so did syndicated columnist Jeanne Kirkpatrick. Bombastic John McLaughlin came storming out of GOP politics, as did Linda Chavez. David Gergen went from Republican politics to news magazine, to Democratic politics to academia. A few, such as Bill Moyers, Chris Matthews, Pierre Salinger and the late Tim Russert came from Democratic politics.

Virtually all major newspapers and many medium-sized operations have former politicians in various positions of control of operations or editorial policy. When Jimmy Carter became president, politician/journalists from the Nixon/Ford administrations expounded on his "weaknesses and failures" just as politician /journalists from the Carter reign revealed any Reagan incompetence. Reagan journalists labeled anything by Clinton to be a failure, even before he introduced any proposals. Buchanan opined one month after Clinton's inauguration that the President's then-unapproved budget plan proposed "the greatest single government seizure of wealth and income in American history."[20] Buchanan ignored the Republican/ Hypocright debt that seizes more than $1,000 a year from every person in the nation and turns it over to those who stocked up on Treasury instruments during the Reagan/Bush regimes.

Many politician/journalists are not concerned with fairly informing the public; their concern is spoon-feeding America a particular propaganda line funneled to them by their controlling political party with no journalistic ethics considered. And these politician /journalists tarnish real journalists who are concerned with informing America. Journalism is held in low esteem by the American public and this reliance on the politjourns is one reason why.

The American press—including the electronic media—has failed the nation on the public debt. There has been an almost-fanatical concern about what politician is cavorting with which bimbo even though bimbo-cavorting has little to do with how competently an official does a job. The less-responsible journalists question political candidates about whether they ever smoked marijuana. A never-addressed issue is how much income

---

20 Patrick Buchanan quoted in "Opinionline: Clinton's plan: 'Sheer audacity' "; *USA Today*; February 22, 1993.

each politician derives from the Treasury after spending the past three decades (especially the 1980s) loading up on Treasury bonds, bills and notes. The first question any reporter should ask any office seeker—incumbent or challenger—is "how much income do you derive (never use the word "earn") from ownership of debt instruments supporting the national debt?" Politicians ashamed of their freeloading will not answer. The second question should be "how much do your campaign contributors derive?" One reason the press does not pursue this line of reporting may be that many overpaid publishers, editors, TV anchors or producers have also spent years accumulating Treasury instruments to further enrich themselves at the expense of the working middle-class taxpayers who don't have the excess cash necessary to freeload off government.

Complaints about a "liberal press" usually target the hardworking and moderately paid reporters and copy editors, not the highly paid and privileged politician/syndicated columnists or the executive leaders. The politjourns have their positions because of political connections and biases. Reporters and copy editors have their jobs because they are intelligent, educated and competent. The nation's press has historically supported Republicans; in the 13 presidential elections in the half century starting in 1940 newspaper endorsements have been overwhelmingly for the Republican candidate in all but one election—the 1964 contest when Lyndon Johnson was backed by 42 percent of newspapers compared to 35 percent for Barry Goldwater. Endorsements were virtually even in 1992.[21]

Attacks on the press is employed by the right because its propaganda is unlikely to fool an educated and competent journalist, so the media need to be neutralized in order to sway the public. So, when a Hypocright rails against a liberal bias in the press, he or she just may be complaining about a literate press, not a liberal press.

The Hypocright attacks on the working-class commoners of America may have been behind the complaints about Clinton avoiding the draft during the Vietnam Conflict. Ever since the first federal draft during the Civil War, loopholes have purposely been written into the law so some people could avoid service. Those loopholes usually favored the privileged. During the Civil War, the rich could hire someone from the lower classes to serve for them. The privileged had the money to pay the price; the poor

---

21 "More newspapers elect not to choose candidates," Pat Guy; *USA Today*; October 26, 1992.

didn't have money and needed money, so they fought while the well-off privileged stayed safely at home. In the South, well-off white men would send their black slaves to fight for the Confederacy in their place. During other drafts, the privileged could hide out in colleges or through political influence (i.e. getting into a noncombat National Guard unit or being appointed to a "vital" government job). Many men were exempt from the draft because they had too many dependents needing their support. When ordinary Americans tried to hide their ages or disabilities to enlist in the armed forces during World War II right-wing macho hero John Wayne, who often talked about love of country, remained a civilian. Neither he nor Reagan, who spent the war making movies for the Army, fought for their country in that war; slapstick comedian Soupy Sales did. Both Wayne and Reagan had one dependent child too many to be eligible for combat (each extra child was adopted) and neither volunteered.

Then came Clinton. This son of a common salesman avoided the draft using intelligence when the system had been designed for the privileged to avoid service based on their status in society. Clinton used student deferments to avoid military service, but so did Hypocright politician Phil Gramm (senator from Texas) who stayed in college until he received a Ph.D. then took a teaching position to gain another deferment. But Gramm stressed that he supported the war while Clinton opposed it. That means Gramm wouldn't fight in the war he approved of (he could have enlisted had he truly supported that war just as other right-wing supporters of the war could have enlisted) but would let others go fight and possibly die in his place. Clinton wouldn't fight in the war he disapproved of and didn't want others to die in a conflict that had no significant national security concern for the United States. Both men avoided military service legally, but Gramm did so hypocritically; that's an issue about character.

Nothing demonstrates the hypocrisy of the American right better than the Reagan administration. That regime, like previous Righty administrations, constantly harped on themes of patriotism and law and order. Reagan demonstrated his concern for obeying law by firing thousands of air-traffic controllers for striking illegally in 1981. He told the strikers that laws must be obeyed. Governmental obedience to law is the primary principle of our democratic republic, but the Reagan administration repeatedly broke the law with such escapades as unauthorized military attacks on Libya and Granada and the mining of the harbor at Managua, Nicaragua. But it was the Iran-contra subversion that best proved the hypocrisy. Administration lackeys took it upon themselves to "steal" United States property to sell to Iran, a terrorist state, then divert the proceeds to arm reactionary forces in Nicaragua. The United States Constitution says that only Congress can dispose of U.S. property, no U.S. money can be spent except under authority of law and "Receipts and Expenditures of all public Money" must be made known in published form, which wasn't the case when US money from the sale of US missiles was sent to antidemocratic Nicaraguan contras. Reagan, then the chief law-enforcement official in the United States, claimed to be ignorant of all these crimes. Not only was the Reagan administration possibly the most crime-infested regime in history, it may have been the most subversive; slightly worse than the administration of Richard Nixon, who built his political career on themes of patriotism and law and order then destroyed his presidency with acts of subversion and crime.

Righties, if unchecked, will eventually destroy all they claim to protect. McCarthyism claimed to be protecting "freedom" from "communism" but was itself the greatest threat to American liberty in the 20th century. When Righties use government to intrude into religion, reproduction, speech or human relationships, they destroy more liberty. In commerce, corporations destroy their liberty by creating the need for more government involvement. When government becomes more involved to protect Americans from the effects of corporate irresponsibility, the conservatives are responsible.

The right is wrong in its contention that entrepreneurship blooms if people have a desperate need to succeed, i.e., poverty. Entrepreneurship doesn't automatically come from want because all people have their own abilities and no one has all abilities. Persons with entrepreneurial skills will become entrepreneurs no matter what their financial situation. Those without entrepreneurial abilities won't become entrepreneurs regardless of the necessity. Bill Gates and Paul Allen didn't found computer software giant Microsoft and guide it to success because of poverty and the need to escape their stations in life. They came from Seattle, Washington's comfortable class and had no financial need to be entrepreneurs. Gates and Allen created Microsoft's success because there was a demand; thanks to development of the personal computer. Steve Jobs and Steve Wozniak, who weren't poverty stricken either, founded Apple Computer, Inc., and relied on development of the microprocessor chip by Intel engineers. All these innovators knew what they were doing, and there were profits to be made. Demand requires advancement by society; no one person is responsible for creating demand. Creation comes from ability enhanced by education or training. Profitability comes from demand-side economics, not from supply-side madness. All the supply imaginable is worthless if there's no demand for the products. Microsoft was established in 1975, Apple in 1976, when the top tax rate was 70 percent, disproving another right-wing lie that tax cuts are important to innovation.

A study released in the summer of 1995 said that those children working at jobs while still in high school were more likely to come from well-educated middle-class families, not from the downtrodden, which refutes common notions. The study indicated that persons who show initiative are those who have been taught and encouraged to exercise initiative. A spokesman for the institute that sponsored the study said, "Parents who have reaped the rewards of their work ... tend to inspire their children to follow in their footsteps."[22]

Parents of the excluded class, likewise, would inspire their children, but to inspire them to also expect be excluded. This problem can't be overcome by telling government to get out of the way so the downtrodden can pull themselves up by their bootstraps.

Many people who constantly use the bootstrap cliché often put their opinions into books once they leave public life. They usually have to hire competent ghostwriters to write their books, they don't have the talent to create a book just as most people don't have the ability to create a business, but might have employee skills that must be accommodated and rewarded.

Righties always claim a "quota" is being used if there is an effort to attract more people from a minority class or group. That is, if a business is cited for having too few blacks or women in its workforce, Righties claim any effort to increase those numbers amounts to a quota because the effort involves number counting. But the Righties are frauds for they want to keep all homosexuals out of the military. That quest for zero representation is a quota, a quota of none. Exclusion of blacks from decent public education, which continues to happen in some areas, is a quota, and the quota is none. Country clubs that exclude blacks, women or Jews are practicing a quota system, and the quota is none. Corporations that hire one or two minority workers for high-profile, low-effect positions are using a quota system, and

---

22   "Middle-class students most likely to work," Tamara Henry; *USA Today*; August 21, 1995.

the quota is tokenism. Righties have been the most quota-conscious group of all time, but anytime they can level a quota charge against others they charge after that issue like a Republican pursuing a dollar bill.

When government, which must represent the interests of the entire nation and of all its citizens, pursues inclusion of all minorities in the commercial system, Righties detest that government. And they misrepresent concerns about government. *Reader's Digest*, a vehicle for the right's viewpoints and which often prints articles hostile to America's constitutional principles i.e., articles that imply our Supreme Court judges do not know what they're doing on church–state and criminal justice controversies but right-wing writers and editors have an expertise on constitutional issues that has eluded our best judges, attorneys and professors), did that in May of 1994, with the statement: "When Administrations in power undertake to solve more social problems, the people trust government less. When Washington looks to private solutions, the people trust their leaders more." [23]

The *Reader's Digest* statement is not true. Less trust of government comes when government advances special interests to the detriment of the people, i.e., Reagan's manipulation of the tax system to further enrich the already rich or the savings-and-loan debacle. Americans trust government less when it engages in crimes, such as Nixon's Watergate escapade or Reagan's Iran-contra corruption. People distrust government when politicians are self-serving and when government fails to solve problems; they want government to find solutions. Crime is an example; the people want more government in the fight against crime. The people do not look to the private sector even though the private sector mainly commerce) helped create the crime problem with centuries of excluding many groups of people.

A valuable insight into the characters of Hypocrights came after the bombing of the Alfred P. Murrah Federal Building in Oklahoma City April 19, 1995. President Clinton said in a speech that it was time for "purveyors of hatred" to tone down their harangues on America's airways. The President said in remarks to the American Association of Community Colleges in Minnesota that, "We hear so many loud and angry voices," and that they spread hate. His statement brought immediate defensive reaction from the right. Limbaugh called Clinton's talk "irresponsible."

---

23   "Do We Trust Government?"; *Reader' s Digest*; May, 1994.

Other conservative talk-show hosts were quoted in *USA Today* on April 25, 1995,[24] as saying:

> "If they can tie us to Oklahoma, they don't have to deal with us, all they have to do is invoke the mad bomber title and cast us aside."—Neil Boortz

> "He's dead wrong. [He] has what is a very sorry perception of talk listeners as sheep, people who are weak and uneducated and it's the reverse. They're the people who read the news, who watch C-SPAN, who are plugged in."—Blanquita Cullum

> "It's unfair because they're trying to cast this as only right-wing talk show hosts. It's not about right-wing hosts, it's about individuals."—Armstrong Williams

> "Clinton is attempting to use the mass murder ... to further his agenda, to turn the tide among the bulk of Americans who are fed up with government."—Ken Hamblin

Chavez followed the next day in *USA Today*. The headline on her column said "Stop slandering 'right' for bombing." The subhead read, "Blaming conservative rhetoric for the tragedy in Oklahoma City is offensive, ridiculous and wrong."

What all these Hypocright spokesmen missed was that Clinton never mentioned conservatives or the American right wing; he said nothing about Limbaugh or his cronies. The argument that Clinton referred to "only right-wing talk show hosts" was ludicrous; there was no mention of talk-show hosts—right wing or otherwise—nor any mention of the mainstream media. But all these people felt an overwhelming need to defend themselves. Their defenses should then be construed as confessions; there's no other reason for them to defend themselves against charges never made. The right has long argued that depictions of sex and violence in movies and on television has led the nation down a path to promiscuous sex, illegitimate births, welfare and to "out-of-control" crime and that Hollywood is leading the parade to ruination. People who explained the Los Angeles riots following the acquittal of four police officers in the Rodney King-beating case were vilified by the right and accused of fomenting violence, and warnings that more riots would occur if the excluded class continued to be excluded were dismissed as threat making.

---

24 "Clinton hits airways 'hatred'," Robin DeRosa; *USA Today*; April 25, 1995.

But then right-wing statements such as, "Clinton better have plenty of bodyguards with him when he comes to North Carolina," are dismissed by Hypocrights as mere joking, never viewed as threats. The right argued for decades that Marxist literature must be censored or banned and communists must be jailed for their thoughts because their mere presence in society would subvert American minds. Righties then brazenly claim their incessant anti-America, anti-democracy, anti-Constitution harangues do nothing to influence actions of their extremist followers, whether it's formation of anti-America "citizens' militias" or the Oklahoma City bombing.

Righty leader Newt Gingrich reacted to the 1994 deaths of two young boys, drowned by their mother in South Carolina, by implying it was President Clinton's fault, somehow tied to the mood of the nation under Democratic control of the nation and Clinton leadership. Gingrich conveniently ignored another mother who shot her three children near Eugene, Oregon, in the mid-1980s, under right-wing Republican control of the nation and Reagan's leadership. Facts subsequently brought to light in the trial of the South Carolina mother showed that sexual molestation by her stepfather—among other abuses—might have been more influential in her crime than was political leadership of the nation. And the molester was a pillar in both the local South Carolina Republican Party and the right-wing Christian Coalition, the two groups that have provided the strength needed to keep Gingrich in public office. The murders occurred in a conservative, God-fearing "family values" clan that the right says America must "get back to." Another possible factor in driving the mother to murder was the rejection by a boyfriend who cited her children as reasons he did not want a permanent "traditional family values" relationship after having a sexual affair with her, an affair begun by him using his father's position as the town's leading business owner and primary employer, the privileged class that provides the election funding to Gingrich so he can prolong his political career.

When the Federal Bureau of Investigation made an arrest in the notorious Unabomber case in early 1996, Righties were quick to blame their favorite targets to explain the perceived behavior of suspect Theodore Kaczynski. Dole took a shot at Harvard University, implying that institution was responsible for the suspect's anti-technology convictions because Kaczynski had received his bachelor's of science degree at Harvard more than 30 years earlier. Other Righties blamed the University of Michigan, where Kaczynski earned his Ph.D., or the University of California at Berkeley, where he taught mathematics for a brief time. A few blamed his family life, although it was a relative who did the detective work that led to the arrest. Chavez used her *USA Today* column to blame the environmental movement for the Unabomber. She targeted the most-committed environmental group, Earth First!, claiming that its publications, teachings or leaders had planted suggestions in the mind of the Unabomber that led to 18 years of bombings that killed three people and injured 29. Chavez wrote, "The Unabomber may well have taken his inspiration from the writings of Earth First!'s radical fringe."[25]

There are errors and inconsistencies of thinking in the Righties' contentions. Chavez made the most-glaring error. She rightfully put the formation of Earth First! as 1980, two years after the Unabomber's reign of terror began—so even by Chavez's calculation Earth First! could hardly be a source of his inspiration. And, it was shown that Kaczynski had a wide range of reading matter, especially publications appealing to scientific or technological readerships. Kaczynski also abandoned a promising teaching career at the University of California to move to Montana's wilderness about 15 years before the first bombing incident, indicating his anti-technology psyche was well established years before Earth First! came into existence. That was proven later by Kaczynski's writings in which he penned the statement that, "I act merely from my desire for revenge." He added, "I believe in nothing, ... I don't care even believe in the cult of nature worshipers or wilderness worshipers." Kaczynski's writing—made public just before his May 4, 1998, sentencing—was written in 1971, seven years before he began his bombing and nine years before Earth First! was founded.

When liberals or moderates cite deprived social conditions as the reasons for most crime, Righties yelp the loudest, claiming welfare or a lack of morals and of family values as the causes of crime. The right then claims that each person is the only one responsible for his or her actions. But in the Unabomber case, Righties saw the opportunity to attack educational and environmental concerns so they abandoned their standard pronouncement of "individual responsibility" in order to hit at those things progressive and to blame anyone or anything except the bomber. Many of those Hypocrights blaming progressive sources for inspiring the Unabomber are the same people who claimed their years of incessant harangues against American government had no influence in inspiring the bombing of the federal office building in Oklahoma City. That is inconsistency to the extreme.

America's Righties have strange allies in their application of doctrine. Reaganites applying Darwinism's survival-of-the-fittest theory to econom-

---

25 "Want motive for Unabomber? By Linda Chavez; *USA Today* Counterpoints; April 10, 1996.

ics is an example. People who succeed in business are a "superior" breed and must not be encumbered by such things as laws, regulations, taxes or democracy that threaten the survival-of-the-fittest few. With no retardation of the superior, Righties think, society would eventually be composed of only the best (that's why propagandists for the right, such as Limbaugh, claim taxes on the wealthy are punishment for success). Anything helping the lower classes of humanity such as education, training or aid, only elevates the least fit to a position they haven't earned, Righties think, and that weakens what the superior created. Adolf Hitler also misused Darwin's theories to produce the Third Reich. Anything that would diminish the superior (Hitler's idea of a master race) had to be relegated to an inferior position or eliminated (the Third Reich's Final Solution) if it was viewed as a threat to the superior.

CHAPTER 3. HYPOCRIGHTS APLENTY

FAILURES AND CON GAMES

Hypocrisies and inconsistencies of the right would be amusing if right-wing politicians didn't try to implement the right's foolishness as governmental policies once in office. Only two things can happen when a Righty policy becomes law: the policy can fail with dire consequences, or a scam evolves.

Righty mischievousness is legendary. Righties in commerce brought slaves to America; Righties in government protected the ownership of slaves. When the left finally rid the nation of slavery, Righties instituted sharecropping, a form of slavery based on debt impossible to pay, and Righty politicians protected that evil until the left secured national protection of labor rights and fair contractual conditions. Righties in commerce have historically excluded women, blacks and other minorities—and still try to do so—and Righties in government abetted that exclusion until the left enacted civil-rights and affirmative-action laws to protect the right of all people to participate in the general welfare of the nation.

The right has constantly assailed these laws by claiming they promote reverse discrimination or quotas or special rights. Righties have historically excluded minorities from education; some Southern school districts closed their public schools and opened tax-funded white-only private schools after the United States Supreme Court ordered equal educational opportunities for all American children in 1954. The news media have found Southern schools that now place all white students in "advanced" or "college-preparatory" programs while putting all blacks in classes that lead the opposite direction. Those black children with the intellect and drive to succeed in college and the professions are at a disadvantage when testing for college admission because they were aimed toward manual-labor areas. The only function of such "tracking" is to subvert the lives of all blacks.

The Citadel, South Carolina's public military college, went to great lengths in 1993-95 trying to keep out a first female member of its Corps of Cadets—who lasted only one week because of harassment after finally being admitted under court order. Citadel spokesmen and conservative politicians argued that the South's "heritage" and "tradition" should allow them to ignore the principle of equal protection of the law for all persons in South Carolina, even though the United States Constitution required that equality under state laws since 1868. The school then had to sell some assets given to it as gifts to pay its legal bills. The Virginia Military Institute lost its case before the United States Supreme Court in 1996 after basing its years-long battle on the familiar right-wing argument that ignoring the Constitution for nearly 130 years justified its exclusionary practices. McCarthyism was from far-right political fanatics, abetted by right-wing employers nationwide—especially in Hollywood—who fired employees or blacklisted potential employees for no reason other than accusations made by some far-right extremists. Often persons fired or blacklisted were guilty of merely proposing adherence of the Constitution's principle of equality under law for all persons.

Right-wing arguments are usually nonsense. The Constitution says clearly in the Fourteenth Amendment that no state law can deny equal protection for any person and the federal courts have consistently upheld that provision. In the 1980s, the right defeated the proposed Equal Rights Amendment that would have put the same restriction on the federal government regarding sex. Any "reverse discrimination" or "special rights" under any state law would be negated by most courts, and those not thrown out at lower levels would surely be voided by the United States Supreme Court. The Supreme Court has already ruled quotas illegal in cases from California, Virginia and Colorado. But the political right seldom goes into court to prove—in fair exchange of arguments before an impartial panel—that civil-rights and affirmative-action laws create reverse discrimination or promote special rights. After Republican victories in the 1994 elections, the right politically attacked these laws after decades of ignoring court remedies. That is because the right knows its arguments would have little merit in a fair court setting; so fighting is done politically, not legally.

The far right has never instituted a successful social program in the United States and has consistently opposed those programs from the center and the left that have been successful. The right's failures were mentioned in chapter 2. The right's most-obvious recent scams have included Reaganomics and the savings-and-loan scandals, yet more scams are proposed under the guise of social policy. And Righty scams center around one thing: money.

The scam that has done the most damage, takes up the most time by policy makers and which this book addresses is the national debt. Debt has been with the nation for most its entire history but it has always been manageable. The debt was largest following World War II, but the war had created the mechanism to overcome the huge debt that in 1946 was above 121 percent of the Gross Domestic Production (GDP). The debt declined as a percentage of GDP each year until 1980, according to the *Statistical Abstract of the United States* (issued since shortly after the Civil War by the Department of Commerce)—Jimmy Carter's last budget—where it was 32.58 percent of GDP, before beginning a steady rise under Ronald Reagan and George H. W. Bush to more than 55 percent in 1990. Bill Clinton inherited a debt-to-GDP ratio of 65.35 percent in 1993 and held it steady despite the Reagan-Bush carryover, reaching 66.57 percent in 1995. It then began a steady reduction (to 56.97 percent in 2001) by four years of surpluses that he turned over to George W. Bush, who then blew up the debt until it was above 65 percent of GDP by 2007. By midyear 2010 the debt was $13 trillion on a $15-trillion GDP.

Bringing the debt down from 121 percent to 32 percent occurred because American factories were not damaged by war and merely needed retooling to shift into peacetime production to satisfy the demand for consumer goods caused by years of deprivation. This enabled the United States to secure its position as the world's industrial leader because other advanced nations suffered considerable damage to their industrial infrastructures. Germany and Japan were hit the hardest; Western European nations likewise suffered heavy damage to their ability to produce.

Because of its advantage, the United States was able to create wealth at a faster pace than other nations, thereby escaping the ravages of the debt created by the war. But that also created a problem that now hurts America. Those nations with the most war-related damage—Germany and Japan— were compelled to rebuilt entire factories (usually relying on American funding) with all the modern machinery and tools available, and that ultimately gave them an advantage over U.S. factories. Inefficient American firms were forced out of business or corporations moved manufacturing operations overseas to compete with modern foreign factories and to feast on lower labor costs. This hurt the American economy.

When the Vietnam Conflict began to sap the economy, the dilemma became whether the nation would pay for the weaponry needed for conducting warfare or would meet social needs of a nation that still had millions of excluded people—the "guns or butter" debate of the 1960s. Rather than face the problem directly and pay for the war—a surcharge on taxes for that purpose was proposed during the Lyndon Johnson administration—the anti-tax coalition in government had the influence to prevent a pay-as-you-go approach and to force the war to be financed with the national "credit card." This same scam was resurrected by the younger Bush to fund his wars of choice against Iraq and Afghanistan.

Over the years, taxes on corporations have been lowered because of the American disadvantage in competitiveness and the tax burden has been shifted onto the consumer class, which left less disposable income for consumers to spend on the corporations' products resulting in another tax reduction for business and another transfer of the tax burden to the middle class. In 1965, as the Vietnam Conflict was expanding, about 34 percent of income-tax revenue came from business ($25 billion), about 66 percent from individuals ($49 billion). Over the years of Republican administrations sending tax bills to Congress, the burden on business had been reduced to about 19 percent in 1994 ($131 billion) with individuals paying 81 percent ($550 billion), yet calls still went out from the right to further reduce business taxes. Before, and just after, World War II, the ratio was 53-47 (individuals paid the 53 percent). Inflation, not heavier tax burdens, account for those higher dollar figures. In 1964, a new Ford Mustang cost $2,500; the average price for the same automobile in 1994 was $20,000. This tax shifting continued unabated under Ronald Reagan and the younger

Bush until the tax split is closer to 90-10 by 2010 and the cheapest Mustang cost more than $25,000 while the ritziest model was above $50,000.

The competitiveness disadvantage coupled with the tax shifting created an ever-expanding deficit until Reagan swept to an election victory in 1980 on an anti-debt platform. He promised that his economic theories would result in a balanced budget by 1984. But that promise turned out to be the scam that has caused the most damage to the nation and threatens to inflict more damage if Reaganomics practitioners in Congress succeed in restricting reforms and rely on budget gimmickry or a return to "trickle-down" economics. (Author's note: this paragraph was written during the Clinton administration and has proved to be valid as the Bush-the-Son administration brought back the "trickle down" fallacy.)

In the 1980 presidential primary campaign, Reagan opponent George H. W. Bush termed the Reagan theories "voodoo economics," but was forced to defend the policies when he became Reagan's vice president. That apparently hampered Bush's efforts to deal with the mounting debt when he became president in 1989. But Reaganomics was not a mere case of silly economic theories, as the term "voodoo economics" would suggest. Many economists have viewed Reaganomics as a calculated raid on the national Treasury to enrich those who needed little further enrichment. It was another scheme for gaining wealth without working for it and without incurring risk. It was no different from welfare fraud, income-tax cheating or the padding of an expense account, except Reagan made it legal.

Reaganomics was similar to a Ponzi scheme in which investors are rewarded with high dividend payments coming from newer investors who were lured by the high dividend returns paid to the original investors. Those high returns lure more new investors, who are paid with money from even newer investors until there are no more new investors and the schemers have left town.

Reagan's policy was to cut taxes across the board—the wealthy received hefty tax cuts, the working classes received slight cuts—while raising spending on defense by a like amount; about $100 billion per year. That created a $200 billion deficit on top of the deficit that was gaining momentum from the Vietnam Conflict, which resulted in the need for the U.S. Treasury to issue more notes, bills and bonds to finance government. Borrowing by government would be financed by the same people and investment firms that had taxes reduced the most under Reagan. But to make up much of the shortfall, Reagan got Congress in 1982 to restore much of the taxes that had been cut for the middle class and raise the payroll tax on working middle-class taxpayers in 1983 but not enough to cover the $200-billion hole he created, thereby making the deficit much bigger.

Income-tax rates are imposed on the last income a person receives, not the first income, and tail-end income for a high-income person is usually far beyond what is necessary for living expenses. Early income for a business is used to operate the business such as paying salaries and wages and meeting all business-related expenses that are deducted from tax obligations. It is the final income of both businesses and individuals that is taxed, and that tax money is used to provide for the "general welfare" of the nation as the United States Constitution specifies and which maintains the conditions by which businesses and individuals are able to enrich themselves legally. Paradoxically, Social Security and Medicare taxes are levied against first-earned income which higher incomes escape; often making the percentage of income taxed considerably higher for working-class Americans than for those persons with larger incomes.

When Reagan's policies reduced the top tax rates—say for the last million dollars of an income—from 70 percent to 50 percent, the high-income taxpayer saved $200,000 annually, which could then be used to buy Treasury instruments. When the top tax rate was subsequently reduced to 28 percent, that taxpayer had $420,000 extra yearly for the purchase of Treasury instruments. In 1981, yields on Treasury bonds were around 15 percent and gradually declined until they were about 9 percent at the end of Reagan's term. By accumulating Treasury instruments throughout the Reagan and the first Bush presidencies, a wealthy investor could increase wealth by both savings in taxes and extraction of interest payments from the Treasury. Multibillion-dollar Wall Street investment firms were the big winners, and their executives who paid themselves millions of dollars in salaries and bonuses were responsible for much of Reagan's campaign financing that got him elected.

This scam, of course, has to be obscured by propagandists, and that is the job of Rush Limbaugh. On his May 19, 1993, television program, while showing a picture of President Bill Clinton speaking on the tax situation of the nation, Limbaugh said:

> "Stop the tape. Stop the tape. We did not cut taxes on the rich. Now get this, and get this for a final time. We lowered taxes on ev-

erybody; less on the rich. The rich ended up paying a larger percentage of the overall tax burden than they ever have. But they did it at lower rates.

"Now if you want to be punitive about the tax code; if you're a Democrat like Clinton and you think the tax code is to punish people, then you care about what their rate is. But, if you want to get money out of them, you lower rates. And we did, and we doubled revenues. The number—the amount of money collected by the federal government from tax rates, from income taxes—doubled during the 1980s.

"And the middle class, they did not get a tax increase. And everybody's incomes went way up, and I don't know how you can call creating 19 to 20 million new jobs running the country into the ditch. It just didn't happen."

But, during that time, the population of the United States rose from 226 million in 1980 to 249 million in 1990 (more than 10 percent; more than 12 percent when considering the entire 12-year Reagan-Bush regime) and inflation continued with more than a 70 percent increase in the cost of living during the Reagan–Bush years. Those two factors would produce an increase of more than an 82 percent in tax money flowing to the Treasury without any alterations in the tax laws. Tax revenues over those 12 years rose from $599 billion to $1,090 billion, an 82 percent growth, not the doubling Limbaugh claimed. So, basically there was no growth in tax collections because of Reaganomics and Reagan's plan had cut the taxes of the wealthy by billions of dollars in 1981, then raised the payroll tax on working Americans by billions in 1983 but not enough to address the deficit created by tax cuts for the wealthy. When Limbaugh said, "the middle class, they did not get a tax increase" he lied because the payroll tax on workers was definitely a tax increase that hit the middle class the most. That tax, in effect for three decades now, has extracted several trillions of dollars from the working middle class.

In addition, Reagan/Bush spending rose faster than tax collections, which would boost tax collection because this deficit spending put hundreds of billions of borrowed dollars into the economy to be taxed. The tax bills of the privileged, who could take advantage of the risk-free investment in Treasury bills, notes and bonds also increased because of added wealth created by accumulated money that once would have gone to taxation and by the money paid by the Treasury as interest on Treasury instruments. Middle-class taxpayers got little benefit from the Treasury other than what was available through mutual funds or similar small investments.

And Reagan didn't produce "19 to 20 million new jobs" during his two-term administration. The total was about 16 million, a ratio far less than that produced in Jimmy Carter's one term (see chapter 11).

(Please note the usage of "we" throughout Limbaugh's statement. That should be considered to be a confession by Limbaugh that he is a propagandist for the right, not a disinterested commentator on social issues. And note that he considers paying taxes to provide for the protection and general welfare of the nation, as the United States Constitution specifies, as punishment. Caring persons probably should pity Limbaugh and other Righties for their torment of living in the most-envied nation in the history of the world; a nation other persons risk their lives to reach so they can toil and be punished by taxation. In 1995, more than a million persons applied for United States citizenship so they could be punished for the rest of their lives and their descendants would also be tormented forever. That was five times the number who sought to be punished in 1991, the midst of the elder Bush's kinder, gentler nation.)

Statements from Limbaugh and other right-wing propagandists appear to be valid, but amount to fairy tales because they do not disclose the amount of money flowing out of the Treasury and into the coffers of those who imposed Reaganomics on the nation. The only true burden must include the amount of taxes paid, less the amount of money extracted from the Treasury. It may be possible for some people to accumulate enough Treasury instruments over the Reagan/Bush years (and later) to extract sufficient wealth from the Treasury that they have little or no drain of money regardless of how much they pay in taxes. And right-wing propagandists will never admit to that.

How the raid on the United States Treasury was accomplished can be demonstrated by a fictional investor who put all of his/her tax savings into Treasury instruments during the Reagan/Bush administrations. We will use only the last $1 million in income, ignoring earliest income because it is spent supporting an accustomed lifestyle. The money a person or business spends in the economy comes from this earliest income. The illustration begins after the top tax rate was cut from 70 percent to 50 percent in 1981 when the interest rate was 15 percent and descends one percentage point per year until it hits about six percent.

In 1982, the first full year at the lower rates, that lower tax rate saved a high-income taxpayer $200,000 per each $1,000,000, which could be placed into Treasury instruments at the 15 percent return. After a 50 percent tax on the interest payment the money was worth $215,000 that would be coupled with another $200,000 tax savings for 1983 to be invested at 14 percent. That yielded more than $29,000 after taxes that were added to another $200,000 tax savings for 1984 and invested at 13 percent. This would continue until the top rate was reduced in two steps (38.5 percent in 1987) to 28 percent in 1988, and stayed there until it rose to 31 percent in 1991 during the Bush administration. By the end of the Bush administration, money accumulated because of the lower tax rates coupled with money extracted from the Treasury would have grown to more than $4,125,000, from an original $1,000,000, which would produce an annual tax bill of almost $1,280,000 at the 31 percent rate. Of that $4,125,000 total, $1,540,000 was extracted from the Treasury by the investor, and that figure will continue to grow into perpetuity unless all government debt is paid off. The money extracted from the Treasury as interest income and the taxes not paid but used to invest in Treasury debt instruments didn't circulate in the economy to create wealth; it was taken out of the economy. The invested amounts, that once would have been tax revenues, will have to be returned to those who escaped the previous taxation on that last $1,000,000 of income. While it's clear that the Reagan tax cuts may have increased the total taxes paid by the privileged because they were paying taxes on the money extracted from the Treasury, and with money extracted from the Treasury, it is also clear the cuts increased the amount the Treasury must pay out in interest and jeopardized the nation because trillions of borrowed dollars also need to be repaid. An alternative was to use the savings from the tax cuts to load up on tax-free municipal bonds to the extent that the income from such investments far outstrip the amount of taxes paid on taxable income.

It's worth noting that two Pulitzer Prize-winning reporters said in their book *America: What Went Wrong?* that they were unable to locate those 19 million to 20 million new jobs.[26] Critics of the book said it was because millions of people no longer had to file income-tax returns. But persons excused

---

26 "*America: What Went Wrong?*" ; Donald L. Barlett and James B. Steele; Andrews McMeel Publishing; © 1992.

from filing returns were those with poverty-level incomes or no incomes, which would mean a huge increase in the number of Americans in poverty during the Reagan/Bush years. Many low-income workers would still file income tax returns to be eligible for the Earned Income Credit. Tax returns also would not be the best place to find new-job statistics; that would best be found in payroll-tax payments, which do not require tax returns. The U.S. Commerce Department placed the number of hard-core poverty at 26 million Americans in 1979 and 36.9 million in 1992 and Bureau of the Census statistics indicated that more than 50 million would have been in poverty by the 1990s had government benefits—such as the Earned Income Credit many Righties want to scrap—not lifted many above the poverty line. One study indicated that more than 40 percent of the population suffered declines in real income during the 1980s, so it's not true that "everybody's incomes went way up" during the 1980s, as Limbaugh claimed.

It is also worth noting, according to the *Statistical Abstract of the United States*, that at the end of Republican Dwight Eisenhower's reign, 39.9 million Americans (22.25 percent of the population) were in poverty. Poverty was steadily lowered throughout the "dreadful" 1960s under the administrations of John Kennedy and Lyndon Johnson until it was 12 percent (24 million) in 1969, only to have an uptick under Nixon, a low point of 11.4 percent under Carter and then a steady rise under Reagan and Bush to 15.1 percent (37 million and a 33 percent increase) in 1993. After Bush left office, the poverty rates dropped significantly under Clinton to the historic low of 11.3 percent that he handed off to the Bush the Son. Cutting America's poverty rates nearly in half during the Kennedy/Johnson years is considered by Righties to be a "failure" of Great Society programs and increasing poverty by a third under Republican presidents (Reagan and Bush the Elder) is "success." Apologists for Reaganomics always measured success by how many millionaires were created, not by how many persons were able to share in the nation's general welfare by rising from the bottom of the economic pile. And, as shown, many persons with high incomes left largely untaxed could extract enough money from the Treasury to add millions more to their holdings without creating a cent of wealth for the nation.

Another failure of philosophy from the right that will plague the American middle-class taxpayer for years is the debacle of the savings-and-loan failures of the 1980s. The right used its leader, Reagan, to lecture about its philosophy that honest businessmen would lead us to an economic paradise if government just got out of the way and let the marketplace work. Reagan's administration dampened the regulatory zeal of federal bank examiners, and the $500-billion bill to rescue depositors was the result. But, to add insult to injury, "honest businessmen" who fleeced the savings-and-loan industry were then able to fleece taxpayers, who finance the rescue, to enrich themselves even further.

How this GOP scam worked is best explained by looking at a fictional character, who would plan a multimillion-dollar housing development or commercial center. This fictional developer would either take over a savings-and-loan business (regulators wouldn't protest) or had a cozy relationship with savings-and-loan executives. The developer would purchase a ranch or other acreage for several million on credit (we'll say $20 million) and finance it through his or his friend's savings and loan. He would require construction funds (say, $30 million). The developer, paying himself or herself or relatives six- or seven-figure salaries, would begin work on the development. Roads would be carved out with earth-moving equipment (usually rented) but not much else would progress and the developer would walk away from the project (with the money) and the savings-and-loan firm would foreclose on the defaulted loan, getting a $20-million property with a few dirt roads on it for its $50-million investment. When the savings-and-loan firm became insolvent, the government would take it over and cover the losses with the Federal Savings and Loan Insurance Corporation. Reclaiming money from persons who legally fleeced the business was impossible, only persons who were convicted of committing crimes would be held financially responsible.

Insiders benefited when costs of rescuing depositors grew more expensive than federal insurance programs (financed by member saving-and-loan firms) could handle. Then, government had to finance the majority of the losses by issuing more government debt instruments. The developer, who bought the ranch, financed it far in excess of its value and walked away with the borrowed money, could come back and purchase those debt instruments to continue living off the taxpayers while never losing any of the absconded millions—if he hadn't been convicted for his efforts.

It's obvious that Reaganomics the right loves to praise was only a Ponzi scheme designed to fleece American taxpayers and to further enrich the already-rich who finance the obtaining of office for Hypocrights. The savings-and-loan fiasco was an example of the nonsense of Hypocright arguments—in this case the claim that unregulated commerce would benefit the nation. Such scams and failures do not deter the right from promoting more con jobs and sure-to-fail schemes.

The late Supreme Court judge Oliver Wendell Holmes often said there was no legal barrier (other than constitutional prohibitions) to states acting as laboratories to test theories of social policy before imposing new ideas on the nation. Oregon has long had the reputation of trying new and innovative approaches for combating social ills, then having other states or the nation adopting its successes. But the state experience that might be of utmost importance to the nation is the California Experience of the 1980s and 1990s, but it featured failures, not Oregon's successes.

The political right has long maintained that an economic paradise would blossom if government just got out of the way and let American genius flourish. But the right usually means government "getting out of the way" only constitutes less taxes and spending and less regulation of commerce. Government "getting out of our lives" does not include to the right such things as keeping the state out of religion, nor does it mean less regulation of reproduction, speech, personal relationships or patriotism and personal property, such as regulation the never-dead flag-burning amendment would authorize. And the right continues to tell America it wants "limited government" or "smaller government" without specifying what that entails except for lower taxes on our aristocracy and less commercial regulation, the very things that caused our economic problems.

What the right really wants is government that is limited to serving only the needs of the nation's aristocracy and corporations and to limit what it can do for ordinary Americans. Limited government, if carried to extremes, would mean no laws about Social Security or Medicare, no unemployment insurance or workers' compensation protection, no minimum or livable wages, no safe working sites, no protection of the environment, no public education, no safe drinking water or uncontaminated food. It would resemble the system our Founding Fathers rebelled against more than two centuries ago.

When Founder Alexander Hamilton wrote on the topic he said, "By a limited Constitution, I understand one which contains certain specified exemptions to the legislative authority; such as, for instance, it shall pass no bills of attainder, no ex post facto laws, and the like."[27] The "like" would include habeas corpus. And those are the specific prohibitions that were ignored in the second Bush administration's "war on terror" and gladly accepted by the Republican/conservative Congress. They should be forced to be specific about their concept of "limited government."

A Georgetown University Graduate School of Government professor told his classes years before the deregulating Reagan Revolution that a regulation exists to combat an evil that is present in the system, and when that regulation is removed the evil it addressed comes back. Evils came flooding back under Reaganomics and again under George Bush the Younger.

THE CALIFORNIA EXPERIENCE

The savings-and-loan fiasco demonstrates the nonsense of the right's less-regulation arguments. The California Experience shows the bankruptcy of the right's most-cherished philosophy that government spending always hampers economic development because it takes money from the individual (who would spend in a more-rational manner than would any government) and wastes money with foolish and wasteful government spending.

The father of the modern American conservative movement had a concept that continues to influence Hypocright thought. In his 1988 book, *Goldwater*, the late Republican senator from Arizona Barry Goldwater, said on page 389 that, "Federal, state and local governments have never created a single job in this country."[28]

On page 392 of the same book Goldwater said no president can "stop Reagan's increased defense spending without jeopardizing big weapons systems, sharply curtailing the military's combat effectiveness, and wiping out tens of thousands of jobs."

The two Goldwater statements are diametrically opposed. If less government spending would eliminate thousands of jobs, government spending created those jobs in the first place. But if government had never created a job, as Goldwater claimed, a reduction in spending wouldn't affect any jobs.

---

27 "A View of the Constitution of the Judicial Department in Relation to the Tenure of Good Behavior," Alexander Hamilton; *Federalist Papers*; Number 78.
28 *"Goldwater,"* Barry M. Goldwater, with Jack Casserly; Doubleday, © 1988.

The statement that government doesn't create jobs is nonsense. Without government involvement, the United States would not have the computer systems that provided many of the new jobs in the expanding economy of the Clinton years. The Internet, or World Wide Web, and other areas of computer-based communications were born because the Pentagon developed and maintained a computer network for decades before private-sector concerns could take advantage of the technology. Huge successful dot-com firms such as Google, Yahoo, eBay, Facebook and Amazon would not exist without government spending to develop the Internet. Microsoft and Apple would have a much smaller presence without government spending because much of their success is tied to the Internet.

It was the United States government that put satellites into orbit to support the advancements in communications in the present-day world. These government functions have led to the creation of millions of jobs in the private sector where none would have been developed by private enterprise acting alone because both the Internet and communication satellites required years of unprofitable development by government spending before profits could be made in the private sector. The private sector doesn't do basic scientific research; government does or funds universities to do so. Only when that research provides pertinent knowledge does the private sector get involved to develop products based on the government research.

The federal government created millions of jobs in the automobile industry and related businesses by initiating the federal highway system in the 1920s. When automobiles and trucks had access to paved highways for easy travel, travel became common enough to enable roadside businesses to begin to succeed and goods to be shipped to market. That economic activity also created the wealth needed for members of the working class to become owners of automobiles, turning that commodity into an ordinary possession no longer a luxury item just for the wealthy. That enlargement of automobile ownership created millions of jobs in automobile manufacturing and in such things as mining, steel making, glass making, rubber and tire manufacturing and government spending got it going. Private enterprise did not pave the highways that provided the stimulus from which the automobile industry led the United States to become the top industrial power in the world. Defense spending also developed the technology necessary for defense contractors to participate in the civilian economy when military spending was beginning a steady decline in the late 1980s. Goldwater's statements only showed that the right is not consistent in its propaganda, and when the nation acts on that propaganda bad things happen.

After the collapse of the Soviet Union and its allies in the late 1980s and early 1990s, the United States had the opportunity to test the right-wing tenet that less government spending would create an economic paradise. It was the perfect time to reduce government spending because the massive expenditures of the Cold War were no longer needed. It was called "the peace dividend." But California, one of the states that depended most on federal government defense-related spending, was one place where reduced federal spending had an impact on the state's fiscal condition. California could serve as a laboratory where the right's basic philosophies could be observed in action. At the time when Cold War spending could be reduced, the nation was experiencing an economic recession that seemed to go on and on, although its severity was not deep. But reductions in defense spending in the aerospace industry and for military bases turned the California recession into a near-depression which continued to drag on well after the rest of the nation had recovered.

In a 1994 segment entitled "Jobs, America's Most Wanted," *NBC Nightly News* asked, "does government create jobs?" The segment said that 1.4 million aerospace workers had lost work since the government reduced spending in that industry and the figure was due to rise to 3 million by 2000. If government spending had not created those jobs, reduced government spending would not have eliminated them. Companies suffering from spending cuts then sought incentive funding from the United States government, the news program said. Hughes Aircraft sought funds to enter television manufacturing. Other companies went to video games. Corporations that suffered from reduced spending in Reagan's so-called "Star Wars" programs sought to convert to high-density television. These companies sought funds under the Constitution's provision in Article I, Section 8, paragraph 1, that authorizes Congress to tax and spend to provide for the general welfare of the nation and the companies requested the money because their executives knew that government spending would create thousands of jobs to replace the thousands lost because of reduced government spending.

During the 1992 presidential campaign debates, Clinton claimed that 200,000 persons nationwide had lost their jobs in the defense industry because of reduced spending. California's Commission of State Finance reported shortly after that 126,000 jobs were lost in California since 1988 with 81,000 more to be gone by the end of 1997. Defense spending in California had been reduced under Republican administrations from $60 billion in 1988 to $51 billion in 1992 with the projected spending pegged at $37 billion in 1997. Base closings announced in 1995 were to eliminate more than 42,000 California jobs along with almost 33,000 in Texas, 12,400 in Utah and several thousand more in other states. The Labor Department estimated in 1993 that nearly 600,000 manufacturing jobs nationwide would disappear by 1997 because of reductions in defense spending. Labor estimated that aircraft manufacturing would lose 57,000 jobs by 1997; research and testing services, 47,000; wholesale trade, 70,000; restaurants, bars and other retail, 33,000; temporary-help services 60,000; construction, 35,000; shipbuilding and repairing, 35,000; and guided missiles and space vehicles, 37,000. Such figures show that government spending had directly created hundreds of thousands of jobs in defense and those jobs created hundreds of thousands more because of the disposable income of defense workers, contrary to what Goldwater and other far-right ideologues claim. Goldwater was only correct in saying reduced government spending would eliminate thousands of jobs.

These figures show that reduced defense spending spreads into nondefense areas and affect areas that receive no federal defense money. California fought a 1992 battle to cut $11 billion from the state budget after cutting it $14 billion in 1991, but still had a shortfall of more than $7 billion in 1993. It wasn't until 1995 that California officials spoke about optimism for an economic recovery in the state. When that recovery came it was fueled in a large part by federal government spending on such things as disaster relief and conversion of defense plants to civilian use.

As seen, reduced federal spending turned the recession in California into a near-depression in which the entire state suffered because there was less money circulating in the state's economy—not more, as the right's arguments always claim—and that reduced the money the California state government received in taxes. The state's lower spending in its budget then further reduced the amount of money flowing through the California economy, resulting in more lost jobs.

But reduced spending in California by the federal government was only part of the state's economic problems. Other right-wing philosophies contributed. Since World War II, California had been a magnet for people from all over the nation seeking a new life in a state with more desirable aspects than any other state. This migration into California pushed real estate prices to some of the highest levels in the nation because the demand was constantly outstripping supply. Californians added to this problem with the self-serving Proposition 13 that was advertised as a restriction on property taxes but which merely shifted the tax load from longtime real-estate owners onto owners of newly sold or newly developed real estate.

Business formation was adversely affected by these two developments. As some businesses quit operating (retirement, bankruptcy or other reasons), new business formation was needed to maintain the same level of commercial activity. But new businesses often wouldn't form because of real-estate costs (purchase or rental) coupled with property taxes on new purchases or new construction that were several times higher than on property just a few years older. Older property could then bring higher rents because of high rents on newer property. Often entrepreneurs couldn't afford to begin a business in California because of results of tax protests, national budget cuts eliminated many consumers, high real-estate costs and state budget reductions that eliminated more consumers. National firms seeking to expand operations in the Southwest often found it advantageous to locate in Arizona, Nevada or Mexico rather than California. Businesses begun in California usually had few options about location but would have operating expenses that were higher than expenditures for older established competition and would often fail when they couldn't compete because of higher costs.

By the early 1990s, unemployment in California had surpassed 1.5 million persons—more than 10 percent of the workforce—with 95,000 jobs lost in construction and almost 140,000 jobs in aerospace gone, according to the U.S. Labor Department and the California Employment Development Department. *USA Today* reported that the state had lost 830,000 jobs between mid-1990 and early 1993.[29] Such losses of high-paying jobs caused many companies to flee the state for more-economical sites.

---

29 "Growing woes in the Golden State," Haya El Nasser and Jonathan T. Lovitt; *USA Today*; March 9, 1993.

When Righties discovered that California's economic problems came mainly from their pet theories put into practice, the right changed its tune to claim all problems were the result of regulations that were put into place to protect the public or employees. California regulations often are more stringent—because of damages caused in the past by unregulated activities. But those regulations didn't cause such economic damage during the years of California prosperity and wouldn't cause economic damages that quickly. A fast shutoff of money causes quick economic damage, as happened with sharp Republican reductions in government spending.

Because of reduced spending, the state's welfare caseload rose by more than 200,000 in one year to reach the then-record high of 3.7 million, the state reported. The increase in welfare was caused by reduced economic activity, not laziness of workers. Persons going onto welfare could have been employed in jobs created and maintained by disposable income from those persons employed because of government spending. A few displaced workers might also turn to crime for income, at a time when the nation seemed to be paranoid about high levels of crime. Reduced budgets were cited by law-enforcement people statewide as the reason many criminals had to be released from jail and why others wouldn't be prosecuted. Los Angeles County Sheriff Sherman Block told *USA Today* in 1993 that he would have to release incarcerated persons, close some county jails and lay off sworn deputies.[30] Other jurisdictions claimed that their prosecutors would have to do with fewer assistants so they would not be able to prosecute minor offenses such as shoplifting. Nationwide, libraries have had to cut back on hours, halt purchases of books or close entirely because a lack of money brought on by draining money from the economy to provide risk-free investments (Treasury notes, bonds and bills) for the most-privileged Americans (Reaganomics).

Rather than admit that Hypocrights' economic theories (less government spending) and programs (Reaganomics) were responsible for the nation's and California's experiences, the right started blaming immigrants. The attack on immigrants resulted in California voters approving the constitutionally dubious Proposition 187, that intended to deny social services to illegal immigrants even though the Constitution's Fourteenth Amendment says a state cannot deny equal protection of its laws to any "person"

---

30   "'No room at the inn,' so inmates will walk," Sally Ann Stewart; *USA Today*; May 12, 1993.

within its jurisdiction. The animosity raised by propagandizing for this measure caused two of the largest groups in the excluded class to come to odds with each other. Blacks, most excluded from the nation's wealth for four centuries, tended to support Proposition 187 because illegal Hispanic immigrants were blamed for taking available resources that might benefit blacks and for undercutting wages on all jobs. Hispanics, a big part of the excluded class for two centuries, feared they would be further victimized by the anti-immigrant fervor. (Not all Righties favored Proposition 187; those who truly want less government intrusion into private lives opposed the measure.)

Hypocrights were constantly wrong on the California Experience. Less government spending didn't create an economic paradise they promise; regulations didn't cause the states depression and immigrants weren't responsible for any of the problems. The California Experience resulted from putting into practice those things Hypocrights want to apply to the entire nation.

MORE SCAMS PROPOSED

The right is never shy about proposing one scam after another, ever thinking no one is paying attention and there is more money to be had. As seen, Reaganomics was only a scheme to redistribute wealth from the middle-class taxpayers to the privileged-class investors who have been loading up on Treasury instruments since deficit financing overwhelmed the nation. The savings-and-loan bailout by government served the same purpose, benefiting the same privileged-class investors who purchased more Treasury debt instruments, which will draw funds from the middle class to pay interest for years then will draw more funds from the middle class to retire the original borrowing.

Among the latest "money for us" schemes proposed by the political right are a "flat tax to get the country moving again," which will be dealt with in chapter 5, and school vouchers, which the right claims will improve the public-school system by providing competition from private schools.

When the voucher question went to California voters in 1993—it was soundly rejected as it was later in other states—the right argued that a $2,600 voucher for parents to send their child to any school they wished would make the public schools more accountable and the competition to attract the better students would force public education to improve. The

Righties argued that public schools were doing a lousy job of educating America's youth, though experts nationwide disputed that contention. Opponents of the voucher system argued that taking $2,600 out of the state education budget for every child in private schools would drain money from public schools, making them even less accountable and less able to educate.

(It's strange that Righties claim competition from private schools will improve public schools but don't extend that argument to advocate that competition from public television and radio should likewise improve private-sector television and radio. Righties would rather blame the nation's ills on television, movies and on rock 'n' roll and rap music. If competition from public radio and television hasn't improved private radio and television, why should Americans think that competition from private schools would force public schools to improve?)

Right-wing proponent George Will used his syndicated newspaper column to stump for the California measure, but was refuted by Albert Shanker, president of the American Federation of Teachers. In letters to the editors in newspapers running Will's column, Shanker said that parents couldn't send their child to any private school they wanted because it was the schools who chose, not the parents.[31] The argument that public schools would have to cut down on their "bureaucracy" was likewise questioned with the argument that those nations consistently beating the United States in student performances also had much-more-extensive bureaucracies than the United States and had more federal control of education than does the United States.

Then *Money* magazine, hardly an advocate of liberal or government causes, reported in 1994 that its findings showed that public schools could hold their own with private schools, when student-body makeup was similar. Logic would indicate that a private school taking mostly children from the privileged class or those with desirable academic habits would appear to be superior to a public school that had to accept children from all classes and with all attitudes.

Vouchers offering $2,600 for a private school charging $10,000 to $20,000 or more in tuition would be of no value to the poverty stricken in the excluded class. Parents, who don't have enough income to eat healthfully, afford decent housing or adequately clothe themselves or their children

---

31 Letter to the editor, from Albert Shanker; *Seattle Post Intelligencer*; September 12, 1993.

also don't have money for that part of the tuition in excess of the voucher. They couldn't even afford transportation costs to send a child across town to neighborhoods where private schools are located—few private schools locate where the disadvantaged live. The poverty stricken could only sell their vouchers, probably at a greatly reduced rate, to those who already had the children in private schools, further benefiting those who don't need governmental assistance. (America introduced a voucher system in pollution-control programs. Rules soon were adopted to allow nonpolluting industry to sell their vouchers to polluters, allowing the polluters to avoid any effort to eliminate pollution. That also would happen with school vouchers.)

The voucher proposal seems to be another scam for extracting government money for those parents who could easily afford private schools while reducing the money available to educate children in disadvantaged positions in life. We find that the push for school vouchers is only a "money-for-us" scheme and not a true movement to improve education when we compare it to Righty actions regarding another problem—healthcare. Every family and every child in the United States has access to public education. That education varies from excellent in affluent suburbs to adequate in working middle-class areas to poor or inferior in areas of poverty or of minority populations. The same situation is present regarding healthcare insurance—it is excellent for those of affluence, adequate for the majority of the population and nonexistent for persons in poverty. In this area, where close to 50 million Americans have no healthcare protection, no Hypocright politician or spokesman of Righty causes has ever proposed a voucher system so the have-nots can obtain health insurance. When such proposals were made in the Barack Obama healthcare-reform proposal, the right rose up in protest claiming it would bankrupt the nation. Righties have proposed healthcare savings accounts, which would only benefit those with incomes high enough to pay for health insurance in the first place. In the right-wing world, healthcare coverage is restricted to people of means; those who have been excluded will remain excluded.

Public education is often disrupted by worries—founded and unfounded—about violence which has been abetted by Congress's refusal to properly use its Second Amendment authority to link gun ownership to its power for arming the militia (i.e. National Guard). This misuse of power over the centuries resulted in arming of most hoodlums in America and they disrupt schools for all other children.

The right would always use its arguments that "money wouldn't help." Reagan espoused that trite conservative argument in 1983 when he was presented with a report saying that American education was mediocre. He said:

> I think most parents agree it's time to change course. We must put education forward again with common sense as our guide. We must put the basics back in the schools and the parents back in charge ... Our high standards of literacy and educational diversity have been slipping. Well-intentioned but misguided policy-makers have stamped a uniform mediocrity on the rich variety and excellence that had been our heritage.

But, he added, bigger federal budgets "are not the answer."

A report in 1995, detailing results of college admission test scores prove Reagan and other Righties totally wrong. The American College Testing Program's report indicated a national average of 20.8 points out of a perfect 36 for nearly a million high school juniors and seniors taxing the exam.[32] All Southern states, which have historically spent less on education than have the other states, fell well below the national average. That shows money plays a significant role in the quality of education. The Southern states are also where right-wing politics are strongest, where conservative politicians and commercial leaders have excluded the greatest number of citizens from the general welfare of society and where the economy is weakest.

The lowest score of 18.8 came from Mississippi. Other scores were 19.1 in South Carolina, 19.4 in Louisiana, and 19.6 in North Carolina. Washington, DC, where the school system is comprised predominately of students from the excluded class, scored 18.9. Because the tests were for students intending to attend college, many blacks—the group historically most excluded—wouldn't be included in the Southern states' results, indicating that low spending and conservative control may be as responsible for poor education as exclusion. States that have historically excluded their Hispanic populations also were below the average. So these low scores came from only the college-bound students. California, with the nation's largest Hispanic population, was just barely above average; it had not blatantly excluded Hispanics before Proposition 187 was passed.

The highest-scoring states were Oregon at 22.6; New Hampshire, 22.3; Washington 22.2, and Minnesota at 21.9. These four states have several

---

32 "ACT scores of minorities rise," Tamara Henry; *USA Today*; August 17, 1995.

things in common: they fund their public schools well (at least better than the South), they do not have a history of racial exclusion of many of their citizens, they have healthy economies and they are not hotbeds of reactionary conservatism (New Hampshire has responsible conservatism). Similar results were registered in the 1995 Scholastic Assessment Test. Of states where the SAT is the dominant admissions test, Oregon scored at the top; New Hampshire was second. Washington and Minnesota weren't included because the SAT was not the dominant test, but Washington would have been second had 50 percent of its high-school seniors taken the test instead of 48 percent. Only nine percent of Minnesota seniors took the test, but they were among the highest scorers in the nation. (Editor's note: the author of this book was educated in the Oregon state public school system.)

There's always a reactionary ready to attack all things decent and progressive in the United States. When voters in Texas defeated a measure for equal funding of all Texas public schools in 1993, Austin radio and TV talk-show host and syndicated newspaper columnist Jack Chambers rejoiced in a *USA Today* column saying:

"I'm proud of my fellow Texans. Last Saturday, voters said 'No!' to a constitutional amendment which would have legalized socialistic school funding.

"A state district judge had ruled that the legislature must revise funding so that 'property-poor' school districts would benefit from a redistribution of tax dollars raised from 'property-rich' districts. (A typical example of the judiciary trying to assume legislative powers.)

"This system was appropriately nicknamed the 'Robin Hood' plan, since it stole from the rich to give to the poor. The concept is based on two faulty premises: (1) that more dollars will improve education, and (2) that it's the government's right to redistribute wealth."[33]

Such tirades should be considered anti-America, and there are several idiotic aspects to it. Texas fell well below average in both scholastic tests, possibly a result of its unequal funding. School districts that have adequate money at their disposal score high in scholastic testing, those with inadequate funding do poorly. There is no need for a Texas constitutional amendment because the Constitution of the United States already calls for equal protection of the laws for all persons within the jurisdiction of Texas, and

---

33 "Reject school socialism," an Opposing View column by Jack Chambers; *USA Today*; May 6, 1993.

that includes equal protection under school-financing laws. That constitutional command of equality applies to both "property-rich" and "property-poor" districts. States obeying this command of equal treatment aren't redistributing wealth; they are adhering to the Americanism of the Constitution. Judges who tell state legislators to heed the United States Constitution's command of equality under the laws for all persons are not "trying to assume legislative power," they're telling anti-America politicians to begin obeying the supreme law of the land. If money is not an answer, why are Righties so intent on keeping most of it in those school districts that benefit the privileged?

PHILOSOPHY OF FAILURE

Scams by the right and disasters of programs the right has imposed on the nation are not the only Hypocright failures. The most bankrupt of all Hypocright failures is its far-right philosophy. Often a Righty action will result in the opposite of what the right claims will occur. That happened with Reagan's promise that his economic plan would balance the federal budget by 1984, but his actions resulted in the huge national debt the nation now combats after George W. Bush added to the problem with his imitation of Reaganomics. Reagan's war on drugs was advertised as the only responsible approach to illegal drugs but has resulted in an out-of-control problem leading to a tripling of the prison population. His subversive Iran-contra program in which his administration sold weapons to Iran in order to finance a civil war in Nicaragua would have returned that Latin American nation to its ousted fascist dictators and, had Reagan succeeded, it would have ended any hope of developing a Nicaraguan democracy.

Illustrative of Hypocright failures is its economic arguments. The right has long argued that tax cuts will spur the economy and a resulting economic growth would produce more taxes than would have been generated had taxes not been cut. Reagan pushed through his first big tax cut in 1981 and the economy immediately slid into a recession. By November of 1982 more than nine million Americans were unemployed, and that figure would rise to 11,543,000 by the beginning of 1983. Democrats picked up 26 House seats in the 1982 election, which caused Republican leaders to persuade Reagan to accept tax increases to fight his expanding deficit. Those tax increases were followed by an economic expansion that lasted through the Reagan presidency and made him one of the most-popular presidents of the century in spite of his tax proposals doing the exact opposite of what he claimed they would do.

Political conservatives are the most-inconsistent beasts ever created by God. Ever since the Vietnam Conflict—which began our budgetary problems—conservatives have argued that growth of the economy would pay off the mounting government debt so tax increases were not needed. Taxes were continually cut—mostly on upper incomes—on the argument it would create wealth that would generate even more taxes to pay the debt. The debt continued to climb; so more tax cuts were offered on the same argument that always proved false.

But, when economic growth under Clinton, following tax increases, replaced the stagnation under the elder Bush, the conservative bankers and economists running the Federal Reserve Board raised interest rates to retard growth. Raising interest rates would hamper efforts to reduce the debt because it would increase the interest payments on money government has to borrow because of Reagan's trickle-down failure. So, who is right, the conservative politicians who claim growth from tax cuts would solve all conservative-caused problems or conservative bankers who feared too much growth after tax increases would fuel inflation? Most reasonable persons might side with the bankers.

Another deception, perpetuated on the American public during the 1994 healthcare-reform battle, was the argument that common tax-paying folk shouldn't pay taxes to support health insurance for the needy. (Chapters 9 and 10 will show how the some of the needy subsidize health insurance for well-off Americans.) But the middle class already pays for health care for the poor who use hospital emergency rooms for treatment, plus it also pays for many of the privileged. A corporation provides top-of-the-line health insurance to all its million-dollar-a-year executives then deducts those costs from its taxable income—if it still pays taxes—and those lost taxes have to be recovered by higher taxes on the middle class, many of whom have no health insurance themselves. If a corporation has been given enough tax bribes so that it pays no taxes, the middle class covers those insurance costs in two ways; as taxpayers paying the taxes the corporation does not pay and as consumers paying higher prices for the corporations' products. This double taxation on the common folk appears to be what Hypocrights in the Republican Party want and that's what has been achieved since Nixon began his presidency in 1969.

The right argued that if some businesses were required to provide health insurance for their workers (who often were driven into bankruptcy when a major medical bill hit their families) businesses would be forced to lay off those workers, costing the American economy thousands of jobs. The right was strangely silent about the approximately 200 million Americans who had health insurance through their employer or their providers' employment at the time of the Clinton effort for reform. If healthcare reform that requires businesses to cover workers not now protected would eliminate jobs, then the present system whereby most persons are insured through employment has already cost the nation tens of millions of jobs. The same economic principles would apply to persons already covered through employment as would apply to those workers the right said would be unemployed if they were to become covered.

The same deceptive argument was presented about the minimum wages paid to millions of American workers. It was argued by the right when the issue came up in the mid-1990s that an increase in the minimum wage above the $4.25 level would force thousands of employers nationwide to fire workers because business couldn't afford higher wages, the same argument raised during Bush the Son's administration when it was raised from $5.15. But the rise in the minimum wage in the 1990s also accompanied Clinton's great economic expansion that produced 22.75 million new jobs (See chapter 11).

The right-wing argument against the minimum wage implies that American business owners or leaders are fools. Competent business executives employ a workforce big enough to perform the tasks the business needs to perform.

Businesses do not employ 10 or 20 percent more workers than they need merely because minimum wages are at near-poverty levels. Competent business executives seek a balance between the expense of employment and the wealth such employment creates. Employment would be decreased when the income generated by the workforce does not justify its cost. And a competent employer would not reduce the ability to generate income if the expense of the work force rises slightly nor would he or she be enticed into employing more workers than needed simply because minimum wages are kept low. Many jobs disappear because of technological advances, and maintaining near-starvation wages for millions of workers will not stop technology. The technology that allows one person in a booth to control two-dozen gasoline pumps at a self-service gasoline station is why hundreds of thousands of low-wage jobs have disappeared in that industry. Decent pay for decent work didn't eliminate any of the jobs. Oregon, which has outlawed self-service gasoline stations has lower gas prices than both Washington and California, both of which have only self-service.

The right also conveniently ignored the fact that a higher income for low-income employees would also provide more disposable cash to be circulated in the economy and those businesses, mostly fast-food establishments, providing much of the additional disposable income would also receive much of that money from additional business. Single mothers would use an increase in minimum wages on their children by spending the extra cash with local small businesses. Teenagers serious about their futures would put some of their income away to pay college expenses. In all three instances the economy will benefit, and there would be less need for government assistance in the latter two cases. An increase in disposable income on low incomes would be more beneficial for the economy than a tax cut on high incomes because members of the privileged class would not put tax-reduction money into the everyday economy; they would put it into Treasury instruments or the south of France.

One startling fact about the right stands out: it does not practice what it preaches. After Republicans took over Congress in the 1994 elections, the talk by the right was about reducing the federal budget, but the right refused to reduce spending in areas that benefit the right. The classic example is defense spending.

While the California Experience shows that slashing defense spending can have dire consequences, that shouldn't be taken to mean it would be beneficial to throw more money into the system just to enrich a particular politician's state or district.

Most defense spending is in southern areas because the weather is more conducive to continuous military training. So, in matters of defense spending, conservatives in Congress ignored what the administration, the Pentagon and defense analysts said was needed. In June of 1995, the House voted to spend $9.5 billion more than President Clinton and Pentagon officials determined was necessary. Some Republican senators—the moderate variety—complained that the House spending had little to do with defense requirements. The Republican Senate trimmed that overspending to $7 billion. The spending bill still contained 20 B-2 bombers the Pentagon said it didn't want, in addition to billions for a helicopter carrier ship the Navy said it wouldn't need for years, twice the number of Navy fighter planes requested, $300 million more than was sought for research and development of a missile defense system and $1.5 billion for a submarine the Pentagon didn't request.

When Clinton had tried to open up the military for all Americans to serve without discrimination—his "gays in the military" posture—he received opposition from the majority of generals and admirals. The right then harped on the need to "listen to the experts," though military officers aren't generally considered experts on sexuality or civil rights. But, in matters of properly arming the military, where generals and admirals are bona fide experts, the right refused their advice. The right's calls for increased military spending went out at a time when the nation was presented with news story after news story of wasteful actions by military officials, such as spending hundreds of thousands of dollars to fly privileged officers on military aircraft to such events as football games at the military academies. The right had also squandered more than $500 million since the advent of the Reagan administration by cleansing the military of homosexuals—who were never accused of any wrongdoing—then training replacements for them. The argument for unrequested spending was the tired and unproved claim that the defensive capabilities of the world's most-powerful nation had suffered "a decade of decline."

A more-logical argument is that most defense spending is done in states represented by conservative politicians and they are not about to cut the pork that feeds conservatives. That welfare was vetoed near the end of 1995. And when Republicans started to slash defense spending in California in Bush the Elder's administration—under plans drawn up by Defense Secretary Dick Cheney and Joint Chiefs of Staff Chairman Gen. Colin Powell—serious problems ensued, which they blamed on Clinton who inherited the program.

Many persons have argued that the United States should invest in helping to create and preserve democratic republics in as many lands as possible because such nations do not wage war against each other. But the right has often destroyed democratic movements in other lands, claiming that anything that provides for the privileged class to allow the excluded classes to share in the general welfare of a nation is "Marxist."

Such hypocrisy has not gone unnoticed, even by some people who are proud to be called conservative. One "conservative" not ashamed of that label is Kevin Phillips, publisher of the American Political Report and author of "The Politics of Rich and Poor: Wealth and the American Electorate in the Reagan Aftermath", who wrote in a *USA Today* column in the spring of 1995:

> The Contract with America—which isn't a Contract with America because voters didn't know about it or accept it—is beginning to resemble a Sun Belt savings and loan association circa 1989. It's not a failure, but it's getting closer.
>
> The problem is that Gingrich and Co. took a 10-point campaign manifesto and handcuffed their postelection governance to its dubious mix of reforms, gimmicks and con jobs. Now categories 2 and 3 are catching up with them ...
>
> The pledged middle-class tax cuts are headed for the chute. The line item veto has been repackaged so that appropriations bills are sent to the president in hundreds of separate pieces, which may not stand up in court.
>
> Term limits have just been defeated in the House because top Republicans—despite gallons of crocodile tears—don't want to go back to Spokane or Syracuse any more than the Democrats did ...
>
> Companies and trade associations in the nation's capital are being told that (a) they should give money only to Republicans and (b) if they cooperate, they'll get to help redraw the nation's laws.
>
> Lobbyists who duly pledge their hearts, wallets and Rolodexes get to be part of the various teams and task forces that determine legislative strategies, pick the current regulations to be torpedoed, and write the speeches for the various congressional Newtoids."[34]

But Phillips, who was a conservative long before "conservative" was another way of saying "greedy and evil," wasn't the only GOP disciple to see through the Hypocright facade of failures, deceptions, con games, Ponzi schemes and scams. Republican mayors Rudolph Giuliani in New York City and Richard Riordan of Los Angeles endorsed Democrats in 1994 elections because the leading Republicans seemed to embrace Hypocright political

---

34 "Newt's formula for failure," Kevin Phillips; *USA Today*; April 3, 1995.

fairy tales. Some observers interpreted the endorsements to mean that the mayors were putting needs of their cities above partisan party politics.

But maybe big-city voters have been doing themselves a disservice by usually electing Democratic mayors, which prompted Republican governors and presidents to neglect needs of the cities. Most cities are in a precarious position; they attract money to a metropolitan region but the suburbs benefit from that wealth. A newspaper is a prime example. It brings in millions of dollars annually from national advertising, then pays high salaries to editors, publishers and columnists who take that income to the suburbs where they patronize suburban businesses and pay taxes to suburban governments. Average income for people living in the city—many in the excluded class—does not provide the same amount of disposable income to fund city government: i.e. persons who daily commute to the city and extract its wealth are gainfully employed; many of those who reside in the city every day and use city services are not wage earners.

Republican pollster Frank Lutz warned the GOP that it was out of touch with mainstream America a few months before the party took control of Congress. (An ominous sign in that election was that many winners received fewer votes in victory than the losers did in defeat in the same districts in 1992.) Lutz told the Righties that Americans are "pessimistic" and they "need a vision for the future," which the party must satisfy to be successful. But, he added, many Americans think the "Republican party of today has no vision for tomorrow."

A Republican speechwriter for presidents Reagan and Bush, Douglas MacKinnon, told the GOP in a 1993 *USA Today* opinion piece that it must reach out to black Americans if it is serious in its claim it wants to "build a country that will serve all its citizens."[35]

Former Washington governor and U.S. senator Daniel J. Evans also had harsh words for his party in a 1993 newspaper article when he quoted another local Republican stalwart as asking of the GOP:

> "Is it the party whose candidates and spokesmen say 'no new taxes,' then proceed to borrow against our kids' and their country's future faster than any Democrat Party has ever raised taxes? The one that argues to keep government out of business and private lives, then insists on forcing government into our bedrooms? The one that would force kids to pray in school, to God knows whom, but won't fund their schooling? The one that tells the poor, the homeless, the

---

35 "GOP must reach out to blacks," Douglas MacKinnon; *USA Today*; July 1, 1993.

sick and the disabled that 'the free market will save you, sooner or later?

"... Or does one work to save and reconstruct the party of Lincoln, who took the first and hardest shots, literally, at institutionalized racism and slavery ... the party whose president and congressional majorities created the first forest resources protection on public lands, created the first national parks, the first workmen's compensation programs ... the party whose congressional leaders advocated the first federal aid for housing and for public education? [These successes were the work of progressive—often called "liberal"—Republicans.]"[36]

But with the giddiness of the GOP congressional election victory in 1994 much of this sound reasoning was seemingly discarded as Hypocrights dragged the Republican Party back to its sure-to-fail, self-serving, regressive legacy of the Reagan years.

When politicians think merely cutting government spending would reduce the national debt they do a major disservice to the nation. Should budget cutting eliminate one well-paying job to save money paid an employee, that job—especially if it's in manufacturing—would eliminate two or three other jobs in the economy. Seattle economists estimate that one well-paying Boeing job generates 2.8 other jobs because of the disposable income it brings into the Puget Sound area. If one Boeing job is lost to reduced government spending, those jobs it created would also be lost. If all those workers had paid 25 percent or more of their income in taxes to all levels of government, that tax income would be lost to those governments. The net result of less spending: government saved little or nothing and three or four families were hurt. Then factor in expenses to government for unemployment compensation, Social Security, retraining costs, welfare and increased costs of crime and the consequence could be that government loses money because of simple-minded cuts in government spending. The program of reduced spending undertaken by the Republican 104th Congress was aimed at programs the right detests; programs that mainly benefit the under classes. Reduced spending was not evident for the corporate welfare programs the right created for itself and to enrich the privileged class. It is only a fairy tale that the federal budget can be balanced merely by less spending. It will

---

36 "Revival: A manifesto for the GOP"; by Daniel J. Evans; *The Seattle Times*; May 16, 1993.

never happen without serious consequences. We only have to look at the California Experience and to use logic to know that.

These problems that arose under the Reagan administration were made much worse under the George W. Bush administration (2001–2009), but when the Obama administration attempted to reverse course in 2009, the right rose up against "deficit spending" that it had constructed during three decades of mostly conservative rule. Once again, the right claimed reductions in government spending and lower taxes on the wealthy would solve all problems even though those were the cause of the problems. And the American public seemed to be deluded once again, voting into power the right that was the cause of the deficit spending. Obama was attacked in 2009 for a deficit of more than $1.3 trillion in the first year of his administration even though that deficit budget was a carryover from the Bush debacle.

Chapter 4. Our Dreaded Taxes

Rhetoric Never Right

There is a mantra from the political right that raising taxes will destroy the United States economy and cutting taxes will create a growth so spectacular that we will all be living in an economic paradise in no time.

They are full of it. But they keep trotting out that some old canard whenever there is an election or when they want to fiddle with the tax codes to make taxation even less fair than it already is. It is also disheartening to read the mainstream media regurgitate the GOP talking points as if they are Gospel Truth and refusing to accept arguments that disprove the GOP's lies.

Kevin Hassett, director for economic policy studies at the conservative American Enterprise Institute and adviser to the 2008 Republican presidential candidate, John McCain, has said, "What really happens is that the economy grows more vigorously when you lower tax rates. It is beyond the reach of economic science to explain precisely why that happens, but it does."

But it doesn't.

And that is the secret behind lies, propaganda, scams of all sorts; the rhetoric must always be more palatable than reality.

Let us examine how taxes and economic activity relate to each other.

After Ronald Reagan went into office in 1981, he engineered massive tax cuts through a conservative House and Republican Senate where the top rate for the richest Americans went from 70 percent to 50 percent, which was followed by the then-worst economic recession since the Great Depression. Unemployment hit 10.8 percent, the highest since 1941 when the world was still in the Great Depression.

As Reagan's recession roared on, he proposed other major tax shifts. In 1982 he restored much of the taxes that were cut for the middle class, but not the wealthy, and got much higher taxes in 1983, especially the payroll tax paid by the workers of America, and raised the gasoline and cigarette taxes, and the economic growth that followed was dubbed by the right as the "Reagan Miracle," and Reagan is portrayed by the right as an economic genius.

After Reagan and Congress lowered the top rate from 50 percent to 38.5 percent in 1987, his Miracle ran out of steam, and he rushed through another reduction in the top rate to 28 percent in 1988. But those tax cuts didn't halt the slowdown as the nation drifted into recession under George Bush the Daddy and deficits exploded. Taxes were raised in Bush's administration with the top rate rising to 31 percent to address the deficit, and the economy began a slow expansion.

Bill Clinton took over and said he found a budgetary mess worse than anticipated, so sought and got tax hikes out of Congress. The nation then went on the greatest sustained economic expansion of America or any nation in history and it lasted until beginning to slow in 2000. Franklin Roosevelt's New Deal recovery from the Great Depression had gaudier numbers, but his recovery was not sustained for eight consecutive years, as was Clinton's.

George W. Bush took over in 2001 when growth was slowing to a crawl, but still positive, so he obtained tax cuts from a doctrinaire-but-economically-illiterate Congress as an economic cure-all. We went into another recession and we were officially in a recession by September 1, 2001, before the 9/11 attacks the right claim caused our economic problems.

This short history shows that after every major tax cut since 1981, the economy fell into recession, and after every major tax increase, the economy rallied, the exact opposite of what the right claims would happen. Those economic rallies produced tens of millions of new jobs; contrary to the right's claims that tax increases would kill jobs. It should be clear that Hassett knows nothing about what he was talking about and shouldn't advise anyone on anything.

It isn't just modern times where tax cuts produced the opposite of what conservatives promise. At the end of World War I the top tax rate stood at 77 percent for incomes over $1 million. That was lowered to 58 percent in 1922. The 1923–24 recession followed. The top rate was lowered again, to 25 percent in 1925. The 1926–27 recession followed. The top rate was lowered again, to 24 percent in 1929, and everyone knows what followed. And as the Great Depression gripped the nation, Herbert Hoover won tax cuts and spending cuts from Congress to no avail as the downturn roared on unabated.

Now we examine how the conservative economics philosophy shifts to match the times.

After Reagan got us into the 1981 recession the standard line from the right was that presidents don't have any influence on the nation's economic performances, the economy will experience growths and retractions purely on its own due to the "business cycle."

When the Reagan Miracle was steaming ahead, conservatives praised Reagan as a master economic wizard, which can only be interpreted to mean presidents have great control over the economy.

Bush the Daddy had no influence on the economy during his recession, the right said, but was an acceptable steward of the economy when recovery began.

Clinton, of course, had absolutely no control on the economy, the right howled, and the great expansion merely coincided with Clinton's term.

An elected California office holder and Republican party official opined on the progressive Dave Ross radio talk-show in Seattle that wise small-business owners making sound business decisions caused the spectacular growth under Clinton, not the President's policies. Why those same small-business owners couldn't, or didn't, make sound business decisions during Reagan's huge recession or Bush the Daddy's recession was left untouched. In a column in Seattle's *Post-Intelligencer*, a former official of the previous GOP administration was quoted as saying that Clinton's proposed tax increases would destroy the economy and plunge the nation back into the recession it was just beginning to crawl out of. The exact opposite happened.

Think Progress.org cited those GOP complaints as the same we heard during 2010 arguments about letting tax cuts expire, as they were scheduled to do. The organization said:

> Republicans, however, want to renew all of the cuts, and have been apoplectic about Obama's plan, claiming that it will kill jobs and cripple small businesses. "This is about stopping a job-killing tax hike on small businesses during tough economic times," said Sen. Orrin Hatch (R-UT). "You can't raise taxes in the middle of a weak economy without risking a double dip in the recession," said House Minority Leader John Boehner (R-OH).

> If these warnings about double-dip recessions and job-killing tax increases sound vaguely familiar, that's because they are. TaxVox yesterday pointed to a couple of quotes from Republicans in 1993 employing very similar rhetoric as today's Republicans, with then Senate Minority leader Bob Dole (R-KS), claiming that "half the tax increase because of the rate increases is going to be paid by small business and they're not rich," which is the same false argument employed by today's Senate Minority Leader, Mitch McConnell (R-KY).

> Here is just some of the rhetoric employed by Republicans in 1993 to fearmonger about Clinton's tax increases:

> *Rep. Newt Gingrich (R-GA), February 2, 1993*: "We have all too many people in the Democratic administration who are talking about bigger Government, bigger bureaucracy, more programs, and higher taxes. I believe that that will in fact kill the current recovery and put us back in a recession. It might take 1 1/2 or 2 years, but it will happen." (Congressional Record, 1993, Thomas)

> *Rep. Bill Archer (R-TX), May 24, 1993*: "I would much rather be here today supporting the President and I would do so if his proposals could expect to increase jobs and the standard of living for Americans, but I believe his massive tax increases will do just the opposite." (Congressional Record, 1993, Thomas)

> *Rep. Bob Goodlatte (R-GA), July 13, 1993*: "Small businesses generate the bulk of this Nation's new jobs. And they will be the hardest hit by the Clinton tax-and-spend budget. Because, when you raise taxes, you kill jobs." (Congressional Record, 1993, Thomas)

> *Rep. Christopher Cox (R-CA), May, 27, 1993*: "This is really the Dr. Kevorkian plan for our economy. It will kill jobs, kill businesses, and yes, kill even the higher tax revenues that these suicidal tax increasers hope to gain." (Congressional Record, 1993, Page: H2949)[37]

---

37 "FLASHBACK: in 1993, GOP Warned That Clinton's Tax Plan Would 'Kill Jobs,' 'Kill The Current Recovery' "; Think Progress.org; August 10, 2010.

And Republicans claimed (in another article in the *P-I* by former Ohio GOP representative John Kasich[38], elected Ohio governor in 2010) that it was a GOP Congress that created the Clinton economic expansion, especially the reduction in the annual deficits that eventually turned into four years of surpluses, by "holding his feet to the fire" on budgets, even though every Republican in Congress had voted against his first budget that began the downward spiral of deficit spending. Kasich, trying to take credit for Clinton economic successes, wrote that, "It took a government shutdown [showdown] to make it clear to President Clinton that I and others in Congress would stop at nothing less than fiscal responsibility. Less discretionary spending, savings in entitlements, lower interest rates and capital gains tax cuts, which provided incentives for economic growth, were the drivers of our success."

To recap, Clinton inherited a $290-billion deficit from Bush the Daddy which was reduced to $255 billion the first year and then to $203 billion in the second year, the very budget every GOP member of Congress voted against, and which former Rep. Dick Armey (R-TX) called a "big-government boondoggle" that "will never work." (Armey was an economics professor who didn't merit tenure and who wholeheartedly supported the Reagan and Bush tax cuts that now threaten the nation's well-being.) Clinton's budget in the next term of Congress again reduced the deficit by billions, down to $107 billion in fiscal 1996 after being $164 the previous year. In July of 1997 the GOP Congress saw the direction things were going and joined the parade to finally adopt a bill designed to balance the budget by 2002, then turned around and claimed credit for everything when the budget was balanced years earlier than hoped.

When George W. Bush came into office with annual economic growth slowing to below the two percent range, after being close to, or well above, six percent at times in the middle of Clinton's growth period, he engineered more tax cuts through the Republican Congress, and the nation slipped into recession (apparently those wise small-business owners stopped making sound business decisions again) when additional spending on the nation's infrastructure to prevent bridge collapses or sewer explosions might have staved off the recession. Tax cuts do nothing for the economy when

---

38 "No end in sight to spending spree," John Kasich; *Seattle Post-Intelligencer*; February 4, 2004.

those who got the cuts just turn around and buy Treasury bills, bonds and notes or Italian villas with the money shielded from taxation.

And with the certainty that the sun rises in the east, the right changed its argument again to claim anew that the President has no control of the economy. Like all recessions, the end came, sort of, and slow-and-modest growth occurred as the economy struggled to recover in 2003. When the economy seemed to be healthy in mid-decade even though it was not creating jobs, Bush maintained, and his supporters concurred, that the President indeed controls the economy and the huge tax cuts for America's aristocracy were the reason for the economy growing. But, those tax cuts were still in effect months later when the economy slipped into recession in 2007 and imploded into a near-depression in 2008 and didn't show signs of recovery until late 2009.

Of course, always ignored was the huge borrowing the right did, and when the borrowed dollars were placed in the economy, the right claimed the additional dollars as growth; an asset not a debit. In short; Enron business practices.

The business cycle does, indeed, drive the growth or retraction of the economy without any political input. But, what a president and Congress do will impact how far in either direction the cycle goes. When the economy drifts toward recession, Republicans always do the wrong thing and the drift continues into recession. That is why every Republican administration since World War II has ruled over a recession after giving us two recessions and the Great Depression before the war. Democratic administrations tend to do the correct thing because they have stayed recession-free, save for the one under Jimmy Carter which was the shortest and mildest of them all and was caused more by the oil boycott from the Iranian revolution than by policy, and the short Harry Truman recession brought about by low industrial activity as the nation shifted from wartime to peacetime production.

The only consistency detectable in conservative economic arguments is that the right is always wrong. Conservatives ought to pick a philosophy—the President does or does not influence the economy—and stick to it.

When the administration of Barack Obama began to get serious about job creation at the beginning of 2010, the President proposed a spending freeze for three years on discretionary spending beginning in 2011 and Senators Charles Schumer (D-NY) and Orrin Hatch (R-Utah) proposed a tax break for businesses hiring an unemployed American who had been jobless for 60 days by forgiving the payroll tax for that year. In a *New York Times* article, Schumer said, "A $60,000 worker hired on Feb. 1 will save a business about $3,400 in taxes, while that same worker hired on May 1 will save it about $2,500."[39]

Both proposals would do little. A spending freeze while population and inflation continue to grow amounts to a spending cut, and as repeatedly shown, spending cuts most often do the opposite of what they are intended to do. And Robert Reich, of the successful Clinton administration, said that in some of his many writings. A tax break for businesses to hire unemployed workers also would fail. A business taking on the salary or wages, plus healthcare costs, would spend more to employ one unnecessary employee than any tax break would save, creating a net loss for the employer. Under the Schumer-Hatch proposal, a business would lose $56,600 in salary, plus the cost of healthcare and other benefits, for just one unnecessary employee. And a business that needed to hire a necessary worker, even if the tax breaks weren't in place, would claim that credit resulting in a larger government deficit with no employment bonus.

When Obama released his record-high budget that included some spending cuts and tax increases in 2010, it was greeted with the same GOP arguments that greeted Clinton's first budget. *The Washington Post* cited then-House minority leader House Minority Leader John Boehner, R-Ohio, saying:

"Just three days after talking to House Republicans about the importance of fiscal responsibility, President Obama is submitting another budget that spends too much, taxes too much and borrows too much ... Filled with more reckless spending and more unsustainable debt, the president's budget is just more of the same at a time when the American people are looking for Democrats in Washington to listen and change course." [40]

Republican National Committee Chairman Michael Steele speaking for the GOP added, the Post said:

> In a statement Monday, Steele said Obama's budget "will double down on his liberal agenda, growing the deficit by record proportions and killing jobs by raising taxes on small businesses." He said

---

39 "A Payroll Tax Break for Jobs," Charles E. Schumer and Orrin G. Hatch; *The New York Times*; Jan. 25, 2010.

40 "Budget analysis: Obama trying to balance his vision with nation's needs," *The Washington Post* reprinted in *The Denver Post*: February 2, 2010.

the GOP would "present a common-sense budget that will reduce the deficit, grow the economy and create jobs, giving voters yet another reason to vote Republican this November and return balance and sanity to Washington."

Of course, in the 20 years of the Reagan-Bush-Bush control of the White House and Republican near-continuous control of Congress, the growing deficit and debt were Republican creations and no such common-sense budget was ever proposed, no deficit was ever reduced, the economy only grew on the back of borrowed money and job creation was miserable. How much the GOP and Democrats create jobs is shown in chapter 11.

Rep. Mike Pence, R-Ind., the chairman of the House Republican Conference, said in a *Salon Magazine* report:

> "The budget the administration released this morning is just more of the same old failed fiscal policies that gave us record spending, record debt and no job growth over the past year. This course is irresponsible and unsustainable." [41]

Pence neglected to say that the "irresponsible and unsustainable course" was laid out by his party, Ronald Reagan and the two George Bushes. And what "failed" the previous year was an inheritance from the younger Bush.

THE LIBERTARIAN SOLUTION

To combat our economic problems, libertarian Texas GOP Rep. Ron Paul, who ran for president in 2008 partly on economic issues, proposed elimination of the federal income tax and repeal of the Sixteenth Amendment and to reintroduce the Constitution as it applied in the 18th Century. That would be foolhardy as will be shown by examining tax collections in the 18th and 19th centuries.

Until the 20th Century, taxes were collected from duties, imposts and excises and a tax the federal government imposed on the states according to their populations as specified in Article I, Section 2, paragraph 3, of the Constitution and again in Section 9, paragraph 4. The feds taxed the states and the states taxed individuals and businesses any way they wished.

If done today, using figures available prior to Bush taking office and screwing up the nation, we would get a scary picture for some. We use population and income figures from 2000, the last time the nation had near normalcy in its taxing-and-spending priorities.

---

41 "White House blames Bush for budget woes"; *Salon Magazine*, February 1, 2010.

The tax burden would be about $10,000 for each man, woman and child in the nation for a federal budget that has come to hover above $3 trillion dollars. Under the original system taxes not collected through duties, imposts and excises would have to come directly from individuals or businesses the states would tax. Connecticut's population of 3.41 million almost mirrors Oklahoma with a population of 3.45 million (population figures from the 2000 census). Both states would pay about $34 billion dollars in all forms of taxes to the federal government, but Connecticut's annual per capita income of $40,702 dwarfed Oklahoma's per capita income of $23,650 (2000 figures).

The cheese-nibbling, wine-sipping gentile folk of Connecticut would get a tax break because they could easily pay—would pay much less than now—for taxes. Our beer-guzzling dust-kicking Okies would get slammed, required to pay much more than they now pay. Good ole boys from Mississippi would be worse off, the worst of any state in America. With a per capita income of $20,900 they would be taxed twice as heavily as their fellow Americans in Connecticut. In fact, most Southern states had per capita incomes below the national average of $29,469 while most non-Southern states had incomes at or above the average, many in the mid-$35-thousand range or above with New Jersey at $37-thousand and the District of Columbia at $39-thousand.

Under Obama's first budget passing $3.8 trillion those figures would be more than $12,500 per person; with both Connecticut and Oklahoma owning about $42 billion. But that budget contained spending to combat Bush's recession and shouldn't be repeat expenditures.

The federal income tax instituted in 1913 actually benefits residents of the conservative low-income states of the South because it prevents their people from paying a higher percentage of income in taxes than inhabitants of the well-to-do states. Low-income conservative states are also the ones where businesses are most likely to have low taxation—manufacturers being lured into the area by huge tax breaks and the promises of lower wages in a nonunion workforce—meaning individuals would have a higher tax burden on lower incomes. These figures on per capita income should also demonstrate that huge business tax breaks and low wages do not produce a healthy economy.

It is strange that the people who hate the income tax the most and call for reverting to the method of taxation of early America are the ones who would be hurt the most. Connecticut's per capita income was almost 50 percent higher than the income of Paul's fellow Texans, but Texans keep returning Paul to Congress where he argues for the elimination of the Sixteenth Amendment and the income tax to return to the taxation that would hurt the well-being of all Texans.

Paul and his minions think their ideas can save American. They are mad fools.

TAX-REFORM SCAMS

Paying taxes of any sort is one of the least-pleasant activities any American can experience including those levelheaded taxpayers who know that taxation is an important and necessary function of a civilized nation.

Our Founding Fathers knew that well. When listing the powers of Congress in Article I, Section 8, of the United States Constitution, the power of taxation was the first one they named proving wrong the claim by anti-tax propagandists that the US was founded on anti-tax sentiments.

Since the beginning of the nation, there has always been a movement to escape taxation by some that would result in transferring taxes to someone else, all of which are fraudulently labeled "tax reform."

The most damaging and harmful tax movements of late have been the cutting of taxes for the nation's aristocracy and transferring the tax load to the working middle class or taking on massive debt through borrowing to meet society's needs. That began in earnest in the Reagan presidential administration and has been carried to its ruinous extreme by the recently departed George W. Bush administration.

When not cutting taxes on themselves, anti-tax proponents dream up new and more-novel plans to make the tax codes more unfair for others and more beneficial for themselves.

One tax scheme was proposed by magazine publisher Malcolm Forbes, who ran for president in 2000 with his only platform proposal being a flat tax on income. Forbes, a multimillionaire, earned his great fortune by two strokes of genius: 1) being born and 2) waiting for Daddy to die.

Forbes failed to mention that under his flat tax, that left interest and dividend income untaxed, he could have had his $500-million fortune stashed away earning only five percent for an annual tax-free income of $25 million. It apparently slipped his mind that he should have mentioned that fact or the fact that the "death tax" on inheritances never prevented him from becoming extremely wealthy for doing nothing.

Other "tax reformers" periodically offer the nation a sales tax of 23 percent up to 34 percent to replace the income tax, payroll taxes, capital-gains tax, inheritance tax and all other taxes. Proponents call the proposal "The Fair Tax" but like all sales taxes, the burden would fall more heavily on the middle class and less so on the wealthy. What proponents always forget to mention is that, while the working American is busy all year long at the job and paying the steep sales tax, the proponents, who could be reaping a small fortune from their investments, could well be off on a yacht stopping in all the Caribbean locations, which, surprisingly, wouldn't have the US sales tax in force. Or they could just settle down in the Italian villas their vast fortunes purchased and, surprisingly again, they wouldn't be paying the US sales tax.

Others propose a "value-added tax" which would have the same effect. Under this plan, a sales tax based on the added value of a commodity is added to the cost of that item at each stop in its development or movement through the economic system. An example would apply to the lumbering industry that framed the author's formative years. A tree has no economic value standing in the forest. When it is harvested and sold to a lumber mill, a tax is added. After the log is sawed into lumber, another tax is added when that lumber is sold to a distributor for a price that also recoups the initial tax. Another tax is added when the distributor sells the lumber to a lumberyard, which adds another tax when sold to a customer, either a contractor of an individual. If sold to a contractor, another tax is added when the lumber used in construction, is sold as part of a building. This total tax is paid by the end user, which is the individual, not the business or corporation. And the elite sailing the Caribbean on a million-dollar yacht or taking life easy at an Italian villa pays no US tax on investment earned in the United States.

As an example of the scam of national sales or value-added taxes, is an American actor educated and trained with American tax dollars who may receive $20 million American dollars to film an American movie for an American producer in Vancouver, BC, or Toronto, Ont., (no US taxes there) to be played in American theaters with American moviegoers paying $10 American (oops, that might be the cost before several layers of "value-added taxes" were heaped on), then the actor and the producer could take their American loot to their Riviera villas and never pay a cent in American taxes while an American earning $20,000 annually as a sewer worker (i.e. Ed Norton of "The Honeymooners") pays all the taxes. That is promoted as a "fair tax" by those backing the scam.

No person should ever take advice on wealth building from someone who inherited great wealth and no nation should base its tax laws on the proposals of one who would greatly benefit from those laws.

Others who benefit from the US economy simply make no bones about their desire to escape US taxation. Halliburton, the giant oil-services corporation once headed by former Vice President Dick Cheney, has abandoned its Texas birth place to run off to Dubai to escape US taxes all the while feasting on American defense contracts, many associated with the war on Iraq.

The Boston Globe reported in March of 2008 about another scam perpetrated by an American corporation under the headline:

> Shell companies in Cayman Islands allow KBR to avoid Medicare, Social Security deductions[42]

The Globe said:

> Cayman Islands - Kellogg Brown & Root, the nation's top Iraq war contractor and until last year a subsidiary of Halliburton Corp., has avoided paying hundreds of millions of dollars in federal Medicare and Social Security taxes by hiring workers through shell companies based in this tropical tax haven.

> More than 21,000 people working for KBR in Iraq—including about 10,500 Americans—are listed as employees of two companies that exist in a computer file on the fourth floor of a building on a palm-studded boulevard here in the Caribbean. Neither company has an office or phone number in the Cayman Islands.

> The Defense Department has known since at least 2004 that KBR was avoiding taxes by declaring its American workers as employees of Cayman Islands shell companies, and officials said the move allowed KBR to perform the work more cheaply, saving Defense dollars.

> But the use of the loophole results in a significantly greater loss of revenue to the government as a whole, particularly to the Social Security and Medicare trust funds. And the creation of shell companies in places such as the Cayman Islands to avoid taxes has long been attacked by members of Congress.

42 "Top Iraq contractor skirts US taxes offshore," Farah Stockman; *The Boston Globe*; March 6, 2008.

Under Democratic Capitalism's method of taxing the corporation's profits as well as the profit of its employees, this scam could not occur.

In sharing of income taxes between individuals and corporations (not including collections such as fees and minor taxes) individuals in the United States paid 53.2 percent of income taxes while corporations paid the remaining 46.8 percent in 1940, according to the *Department of Commerce's Historical Statistics* produced by the Bureau of the Census. In 1945 the division was 52.9 individuals to 47.1 corporations. Tax laws have been altered ever since with businesses getting more and more tax breaks while the individual taxpayer picks up more and more of the tax load each year. In 1950 the split was 60.1–39.9; in 1960 it was 65.5–34.5; in 1970 it was 73.4–26.6. The shift picked up steam under the Reagan–Bush Revolution so now the burden has shifted so much that the 53–47 split is about 90–10. In 2011, *The New York Times* reported corporate taxes accounted for only 6.6 percent of all tax revenue. Of course, with individual taxpayers picking up more and more of the burden they have less to spend in the economy, which means less income for business and that prompts politicians to offer a new tax break for businesses while millions of Americans go into debt just to survive.

Tax cuts are less beneficial when a corporation, that already pays little in taxes, gets a tax reduction to spur job creation. A business leader will hire only enough workers to produce the product or service being sold, and not a single worker more, regardless of tax status. If a tax decrease would result in hiring, those untaxed corporations would have absorbed the "surplus" unemployed long ago because they have already received the ultimate in tax cuts. A corporation will only retain the tax savings, which makes it easier to buy up a smaller competing business, which could be shut down to eliminate competition, or merged with the larger firm, which would produce numerous redundant jobs. That job redundancy would be eliminated by firing hundreds or thousands of employees. We have been sold this "bill of goods" for decades now and it has never panned out. The results invariably have been the opposite of promises, just as the Reagan, Bush and Clinton tax manipulation recounted earlier produced results opposite of promises of economic paradise or warnings of doom.

And tax scams that have been made possible by the nation's tax codes open the doors for other scams; the most notable being the Enron collapse.

The giant Texas energy trading company had many important connections to lawmakers, being the closest with George W. Bush before and during his reign as governor of Texas and as president. Enron, like many other influential corporations, managed to use those connections to free itself of tax obligations at all levels of government.

This free ride allowed the company to report money received as income and profit even though that income would be liabilities if taxes were applied as they were before the conservative revolution. Enron would list dollar figures in contracts to be fulfilled as income or sell bonds or stock and list the money from each transaction as income inflating the balance sheet "profits," which jacked up the stock price because debt was hidden in subsidiaries that did no business. It would borrow money and do the same, and the stock came to be rated by brokerage firms as potentially a "hundred-dollar stock." Had Enron been heavily taxed on its phantom "profit" there likely would have been no scandal and no collapse.

Many apologists for Enron CEO Kenneth Lay—known as "Kenny Boy" to Bush—excused Lay's crimes on which he was later convicted by claiming him to be an ignorant dupe who knew nothing of the company's illegalities. The fact that he drew hundreds of millions of dollars from the company in wages and bonuses, because of his exalted status as the "smartest man in the room" and competent leader who couldn't be lost to the company because of his value was of no consequences to the "dupe" argument. The apologists cited Lay's purchase of Enron stock late in the company's life as proof to support their claim of his innocence.

They are fools. Lay was in on the scam and played it well. Here is how it could work, if as news reports said:

Lay would name his cronies to the board of directors. As payback for their lavish unearned income, the board members would give Lay stock options—reported at $659 million in 2001 the year Enron collapsed—that he could activate if the stock price increased or ignore if the stock declined. Listing money from stock and bond sales and money borrowed from financial institutions and figures from unfulfilled contracts as income and profit caused the stock price to soar.

Lay could then exercise his option and buy a million shares at $10 a share—the price when the option was extended—when the phony stock price hit $50 a share. (Figures are used to demonstrate the scam, not to represent reality.) He could immediately borrow $50 million in cash from the company and put up as collateral his million Enron shares, which could be used for stock options in the future. There was never an intention of repaying the loan, leaving Lay with a $40 million profit and the company with a million shares of stock that would eventually become worthless when the company died; killed in part by the very scams that enriched company leaders. It was advantageous for executives to exercise all options on the falling stock before it become less "valuable" and to borrow on the stock at virtually the same moment as purchasing it. The nation's brokerage houses continued to tout Enron as a $100 stock going through a "correction" following the 9/11 terrorist attacks, the same story executives told their employees who had their retirement hopes tied up in Enron stock that they were forbidden to sell. It took several months for the Enron stocks to become worthless, providing executives plenty of time to clean out all options at huge profit.

Had Lay sold those million shares on the New York Stock Exchange, he would have paid several million dollars in a short-term capital-gains tax, but since this cash went to Lay as a loan, he paid no taxes whatsoever. Lay had one loan of $94 million that he "repaid" with Enron stock. [43]

Thousands of others lost their jobs, careers and retirements. Shareholders lost their investments. Former Republican Texas Senator Phil Gramm went public to claim he and his wife, who served on the Enron board of directors and helped facilitate the collapse by ignoring the ongoing scams, lost hundreds of thousands of dollars because of the collapse. But what he downplayed was the Gramm loss involved the compensation his wife would have received to continue serving on the board had the company not collapsed. How much, if any, personal Gramm money was invested was unmentioned.

These are some of the ways the nation is being scammed by tax manipulation and few people are capable of seeing this grand theft being perpetrated so they continuously vote into office the politicians who make these scams possible and inevitable. And the zeal to reform the corporate community to combat corruption following the Enron collapse has dissipated.

But we saw that in the 2008 presidential campaign no one offered a solution to this national injustice that could, and possible does, easily occur in any corporation. Neither of the final two Democratic candidates mentioned it and the Republican candidates offered to make permanent the tax laws

---

43   "Enron Could Force Kenneth Lay to Repay $94 Million Loan"; *CFO.com*; November 26, 2003. "Enron creditors sue Ken Lay and wife," Eric Berger; *Hearst Newspapers*; February 4, 2003.

and deregulation that made scams possible and proposed more tax cuts and deregulation to make them easier and more abundant in the future.

Many Americans think they are being taxed to death; but it is not with tax collections; it's with scams labeled as "tax reform

Chapter 5. Taxing Problem

Dishonesty About Taxes

Each year, about the first week in May, some tax-watchdog group issues a statement saying that American wage earners had worked the first four months plus a few days of the fifth month just to pay taxes to various governments and would now start earning money for self. This fairy tale of the so-called Tax Freedom Day is a monstrous lie. As explained in earlier chapters, income taxes are not imposed on first income. First earned income is tax free—except for Social Security and Medicare taxes—either through deductions, exemptions, dependents, expenses or credits. Later incomes are taxed.

If these tax-watching groups were honest they would announce in the fall that the wage earner is embarking on earnings for government income taxes after working eight or nine months for self. Even more honest would be to announce in March that the wage earner had earned all of his/her tax-free income and was now embarking on a course where the first five-plus hours of the work day earned money for self and the final part of the working day would earn taxes for all governments.

But complainers about taxes are never totally honest. Those politicians who imposed the Reaganite and Bushite raids on the Treasury to enrich themselves and their friends are the same politicians who scream loudest about the lack of a balanced budget. And they blame that imbalanced budget on taxing and spending. Such is the lie. Taxes didn't cause the deficit or the debt. Spending didn't cause the debt or the deficit. The adverse financial condition of the United States is totally the result of mismanagement of the nation's wealth by the right.

Hypocrights often use a catch question of, "What country ever taxed itself into prosperity?" The answer they constantly refuse to acknowledge, is the United States, but could also include most of the industrial nations of the world; advanced nations have high taxes, impoverished nations have low taxes. Foreign nations and their maximum tax rates in the 1990s when the United States was last prosperous: France, 56.8 percent; Spain 56 percent; Germany, 53 percent; Japan, 50 percent; and Great Britain 40 percent. In the United States the maximum tax rates have varied from 28 percent into the mid-30 percent range since the Reagan tax cuts.

The Bureau of Economic Analysis reported in the spring of 2010 what might indicate Americans the least taxed among all developed nations. *USA Today* said "Amid complaints about high taxes and calls for a smaller government, Americans paid their lowest level of taxes last year since Harry Truman's presidency, a USA TODAY analysis of federal data found.

> Some conservative political movements such as the "Tea Party" have criticized federal spending as being out of control. While spending is up, taxes have fallen to exceptionally low levels.

> Federal, state and local income taxes consumed 9.2% of all personal income in 2009, the lowest rate since 1950, the Bureau of Economic Analysis reports. That rate is far below the historic average of 12% for the last half-century. The overall tax burden hit bottom in December at 8.8.% of income before rising slightly in the first three months of 2010.[44]

The United States has never recaptured the prosperity it had under high taxes when those high tax rates also included many carefully crafted "loopholes" to steer money into needful areas. Prosperity began to unravel with tax cuts for corporations accompanied by shifts of the tax burden off the upper class and onto the middle class. That tax tinkering, accompanied by borrowing to finance the Vietnam Conflict, set the debt on its upward course and the situation was only exacerbated by Reaganomics; then made far worse by Bushonomics and George W. Bush's wars of choice in Iraq and in Afghanistan.

---

44 "Tax bills in 2009 at Lowest level since 1950," Dennis Cauchon; *USA Today*; April 12, 2010.

The United States was an economic basket case in the 1930s while it was in the Great Depression brought on in part by a contraction of the money supply, (spending cuts by government would also contract the money supply further) an outgrowth of conservative economics. That disaster wasn't solved in Roosevelt's first 100 days in office; it took nearly a decade. Therefore it was foolish for Reagan apologists to attack Clinton's failure to cure Reagan policies by the spring of 1993 or Obama's failure to correct Bush's disaster in the first few months of his administration. The Roosevelt/Truman cures started with increased government spending, higher taxes, full employment (finally obtained by World War II), then a splurge in demand following the war. (Note that the final step to prosperity is demand-side economics, not supply-side.)

Most important in the cured economy was a healthy middle class of consumers. Reagan/Bush policies (takeovers, lower pay, elimination of middle-class deductions, manufacturing plants moving to Mexico or Asia) led to a reduction in consumer ability. Capitalism needs consumers; supply will always chase profit and profit comes only from consumers. The GOP thought corporations would benefit if their products were built by foreign workers employed at near-starvation wages. While that looked good on some balance sheets, other businesses were hurt because they had fewer or poorer customers. When factory-worker customers lost their jobs and were no longer able to buy as they once did, merchants suffered as they did when GOP tax reforms eliminated many middle-class tax deductions, in essence raising taxes on consumers. The process of impoverishing consumers was the most-idiotic move Republican economists could conceive because it hurt those merchants who couldn't move to a foreign land.

Typical of the right's thinking was the GOP efforts in 1993 to introduce $36.6 billion in tax breaks for businesses, the wealthy and holders of individual retirement accounts that Republican politicians said would create 800,000 jobs, after they had blocked Clinton's $16.3 billion stimulus package of increased spending that he said would create hundreds of thousands of jobs. The right said its tax reductions would be offset by $45.7 billion in spending cuts, including reduced payments to retired federal workers. But, as already shown in several examples, less spending by the amounts demanded would have eliminated more jobs than the tax reductions could have created, even if they worked as promised. And the tax cuts wouldn't produce job growth if there were no consumers able to purchase the goods or services produced by the business getting the tax cuts. And numerous consumers wouldn't be there if the reduced spending eliminated their jobs.

George H. W. Bush had proposed similar tax cuts just before his 1988 election. His proposals never became law. The nation continues to be bombarded by the same lame right-wing argument: cut spending first. But cutting government spending first would reduce tax collections for government because of a slowdown in economic activity. Raising taxes on the consumer class would do the same thing.

Republican primary candidates for the presidency in 1995–96 all proposed alterations in the nation's taxing system. The following proposals were reported by *USA Today*:[45]

• Patrick Buchanan advocated a 17 percent flat tax on income over $25,000 on a family of four. He would allow mortgage-interest and charitable-contribution deductions. He would tax investments and dividends and would lower capital-gain taxes. He also proposed exemptions for the inheritance of businesses or family farms worth less than $5 million.

• Steve Forbes advocated a flat tax of 17 percent on earnings over $36,000 for a family of four, with no deductions for mortgages or charitable contributions. Forbes' tax would exempt income from interest, dividends and capital gains.

• Phil Gramm advocated a flat tax on incomes over $32,000 for that family of four but would allow deductions for mortgage-interest payments and charitable contributions and would tax interest, dividends and capital gains.

• Bob Dornan said the country should repeal all income taxes and institute a sales tax.

• Sen. Richard Lugar (R-Ind.) advocated a 17 percent sales tax on goods and services and the elimination of all income and corporate taxes. His plan would close the IRS and raise cigarette taxes.

• Morry Taylor wanted a tax of two percent on incomes up to $20,000; 10 percent on incomes of $20,000–$35,000; 17 percent on any earnings over $35,000 with no deductions.

• Alan Keyes advocated repeal of all income taxes and the institution of a national sales tax.

---

45 "Republican candidates' proposals"; *USA Today*; January 18, 1996.

• Bob Dole said he was studying flat taxes, and Lamar Alexander advocated a simpler tax system but said he hadn't seen a satisfactory flat-tax proposal. Only Alexander made any sense.

The problem with any type of sales tax or value-added tax is that both would subject that family of four earning $35,000 to the highest rate of taxation because all of its income beyond rent or mortgage and state and local taxes would be used on commodities subject to the tax. With the ever-popular 17 percent, about two-thirds to three-fourths of that $35,000 income would be taxed; a real tax rate of 11 to 13 percent.

A family with an income of $350,000 would pay a much lower rate when only a third to a half of its income went into taxable areas; much could go to stock-market speculation or Treasury bills. This family would pay a real tax rate of six to nine percent.

A family with an income of $3.5 million would benefit most from a sales or value-added tax if only 10 to 25 percent of its income was used on taxable commodities. In that case, the true tax rate would be from 1.7 to about four percent.

Many budget experts claim a 17 percent flat tax would not raise the funds needed to operate the government, more likely a rate of 21 to 23 percent or more would be needed. A 17 percent rate would raise 20 to 35 percent less tax funds than needed for a $3 trillion budget, resulting in an annual deficit between $400 billion to $1 trillion. This deficit would be closed by the superrich, who could use their untaxed millions to accumulate Treasury bills, bonds and notes—a Reaganesque raid on the Treasury all over again.

Middle incomes ($25,000 to $50,000) would not be overly damaged by a flat tax like those proposed, but multimillionaires, such as Forbes, would amass additional wealth even faster than under Reagan's 28 percent top tax rate. The privileged, not asked to help provide for the nation's general welfare proportionately to the benefits they receive from the nation's affluence, would accumulate more wealth at an accelerated rate and that money would need a place to go. The flat tax would allow interest and dividend income to be taxed at the corporate point of profit, but Treasury instruments would not have a source of profit before paying interest, so would be free of all taxation under Forbes's plan, and that is where one would expect Forbes and his wealthiest supporters to invest their vast fortunes.

Estimated taxes due in the middle of April, June, September and January provide money to government in uneven spurts; so even during times of balanced budgets, governments must resort to short-term borrowing to finance government operations and to pay salaries. Hundreds of millions of dollars repeatedly put into no-risk Treasury bills at four or five percent interest would be a far-more-attractive investment strategy than investing in areas with higher returns, but with risks. And, even if the government succeeded in balancing the budget any time soon, we might expect future Hypocright politicians to retry budget deficit mischief to benefit the privileged and themselves.

Removing deductions for charitable contributions was an odd proposal at the time a GOP Congress was talking about turning much of the federal welfare load over to private charities. Without deductions for donors, private charities would suffer huge losses in income.

After the Reagan administration persuaded Congress to enact its tax-reform law, replacing 14 rates with two—15 and 28 percent—and featuring fewer "loopholes," the economic miracle tax cutters and flat-tax proponents always promise never materialized. Instead, Bush shortly presided over the recession with its ballooning deficits that cost him his presidency.

One apologist for tax-rate mischief was Patrick Cox, who criticized Clinton's first budget plan and wrote in *USA Today* in 1993:

> "The heart of the problem with the notion that we can put a spigot in the rich is this: There are only two things the rich can do with their money: save it or spend it.

> "If they save it, it goes into banks, stocks or some other institution that lends savings to others. When government takes savings, the job base, wage growth and the entire economy suffer.

> "If the rich spend their money, it goes to carpenters, pool cleaners, jewelry store clerks, airline employees and everyone on the receiving end of that spending. When politicians take that money, the people who depended on it previously are out of luck."[46]

That spiel is nonsense.

When the nation had high tax rates, the wealthy had no problem paying carpenters, jewelry store clerks, airline employees, pool cleaners, or anyone else because such spending is done with early income. A Wall Street ex-

---

46 "New tax rates are wrong" an Opposing View column by Patrick Cox; *USA Today*; February 19, 1993.

ecutive with an income of $10 million—about 100 persons on Wall Street were paid that or more annually during the 1990s when Cox wrote his non-sense—doesn't pay pool cleaners with the last-gained million; such pay would come from the first few millions. And investing in Treasury instruments to drain wealth from the middle class doesn't provide funds for lending. Carpenters, jewelry store clerks, airline employees or others lose work because millions of jobs have been sent overseas and millions of other jobs have been eliminated in corporate downsizing and takeovers so those people who control wealth can have more for themselves while others have less.

USA Today reported in February 1996 that the prospering airlines were putting out help-wanted signs for pilots, customer-service agents and flight attendants after posting $1.8 billion in profits in 1995.[47] The hiring was because airline estimates called for much higher future profits. These profits were made after Clinton's 1994 fiscal year budget raised taxes on the rich. After Reagan's massive slashes of taxes on the rich—from 70 percent to 28 percent—the airlines suffered, at that time, their worst financial crisis in history until George W. Bush plied more tax breaks on the rich in the early 2000s. The lesson should be clear: accumulation of great wealth by a relatively small group doesn't create prosperity, and taxing money destined for Treasury bills or overseas villas doesn't hurt the economy. And the wealthy who own airline stock benefit from the well being of all other people, just as they benefited from a stock market that set record highs after Clinton's tax increases; highs that were long gone as the market registered a steady decline under Bush the Younger.

The California Experience should teach everyone that the economy, job base and wage growth are best served when everybody participates in the economy, not just the superrich, and Third World nations should be proof that the wealthy can't spend their fortunes in such manner to benefit an entire population. When politicians didn't take a little bit from everybody and spend it, those Californians who had devoted their lives to defense industries of the United States were the ones out of luck, and many paid for right-wing philosophy with their careers. If accumulation of wealth in the hands of a few was beneficial, Haiti would be the richest nation per capita in the Western Hemisphere, not the poorest.

---

47 "Prospering airlines hang help-wanted signs," Rhonda Richards; *USA Today*; February 1, 1996.

The super wealthy do serve useful purposes in society when their money is put into philanthropic endeavors such as building museums, concert halls, schools, providing scholarships and funding the arts. This spending provides civilizing and progressive aspects to society which otherwise would be provided by government. High tax rates and some accompanying loopholes often help the wealthy decide to provide these amenities, which are more important to society than are the wages paid to pool cleaners, and which Third World nations do not have but advanced nations do have.

High taxes on the wealthiest provide other advantages, other than directing money into needful areas with loopholes. A small group of persons is not allowed to use excess wealth to gain control of society and dominate or enslave the rest of the population and the low classes do not need to engage in revolution, insurrection or crime just to survive. To understand the folly of low or no taxes on the wealthy, we only have to look at the conditions in Haiti and many other Latin American nations where a small wealthy class historically controlled government to satisfy only its needs while suppressing everyone else. Those nations are the same ones whose excluded citizens are the illegal immigrants the American right constantly complains about. The history of Europe also offers examples where governments were used to restrict ownership of a nation's wealth and property only to royalty—those medieval nations were places where human life meant little and had some of the most-violent and most-miserable societies in history.

Whenever one group has been allowed to wield unregulated power, despicable things happen: pestilence, squalor, slavery, genocide, inquisitions and the crusades. Decent persons of all classes shouldn't want to re-create those conditions or those societies.

PRESENT PROBLEMS WITH THE SYSTEM

Too many people try to equate government income and spending with corporate or family income and spending. And most of what they advocate doesn't make sense. It is often proposed that the best way to prevent "wasteful" government spending is to conduct a tax revolt and reduce taxes. That's like saying that the best way to control wasteful family spending is to take a lower-paying job or a corporation should sell fewer products at a lower cost to curtail extravagant management spending on entertainment, takeovers, limousines or other executive goodies. Government incomes depend a large part on government spending because much of the money immediately comes back from "bureaucrats" as income taxes; the rest provides income for businesses and their employees, who also pay taxes.

The present taxing system is not the best the nation can do because it is too complicated, requires a too-large of an IRS and misses taxable income earned by those people who care more about their concerns than they do about the nation or fellow Americans.

The General Accounting Office reported that the gap between taxes owed and taxes paid between 1981 and 1992—the Reagan-Bush Republican administrations—grew by 67 percent. According to the GAO the lost revenue amounted to $127 billion in 1992, which individual taxpayers had to cover with their taxes. *USA Today* put the shortfall at $150 billion. In 1996, the IRS reported it had collected some of the delinquent taxes for 1992 but was still about $95 billion short of what was legally owed.[48] The IRS said 83 percent of taxpayers complied with the law and a 90 percent compliance was the goal for 2000. Small businesses and their owners who underreported income and over reported exemptions, deductions and credits were the biggest scofflaws. Others included physicians, accountants, street vendors, home repairmen or handymen, housekeepers and nannies.

Widespread fraud had reportedly become common with the advent of electronic return filing by individuals. One former IRS employee estimated that up to $5 billion were lost by the mid-1990s to criminals using names and Social Security numbers of people who were paid for such information if they had no income. At the same time, many wealthy—about 800 earning more than $200,000 yearly—were not paying income taxes because they could use mortgage deductions, medical expenses and casualty losses to offset their income. And nearly 500 with more than $200,000 in annual taxable incomes had an average income of almost $400,000 from tax-free municipal bonds.

Along with these fraud problems comes annual federal tax income lost to special breaks given in specified areas of the economy in the 1990s. According to the Office of Budget and Management they include:

- Employer pension contributions and their earnings, $51 billion;
- Employer Medical insurance contributions, $43 billion;
- Mortgage interest deductions, $43 billion;
- Nonbusiness state and local tax deductions, $24 billion;

---

48 "IRS audits less as tax gap grows"; May 19, 1994; and "IRS barely makes dent in $95 billion tax gap ," Anne Willette; May 10, 1996; *USA Today.*

- Deferral of home-sale capital gains, $14 billion;
- State and local property tax deductions, $13 billion;
- IRA pension contributions and earnings, $5.4 billion;
- Preferential treatment of capital gains, $3.6 billion;
- Interest exclusion on industrial-development bonds, $3.3 billion;
- Credit for child and dependent-care expenses, $3 billion.

Many of these tax breaks were given for good reason; they helped the general welfare of the nation, but some tax breaks are dubious. In the Pacific Northwest, nearly one-fourth of logs harvested in the region—mostly from private lands—were shipped to Pacific Rim nations with the help of about $100 million in federal tax breaks and subsidies. At the same time, thousands of lumber-mill workers were being idled because of a shortage of trees. Some of the logs were owned by the state of Washington, which justified selling unmilled logs overseas because income went to public schools. But, had the logs stayed in the state to be milled by Washington workers, their salaries would have also provided taxes to help fund schools. When the state halted log exports from public lands, one lumber mill came out of its bankruptcy of the early 1980s, resumed business in the 1990s, paid off its debts and hired 200 workers. And those 200 employees paid taxes and supported the local economy in Grays Harbor County.

Another problem, albeit not serious to the nation, is the inheritance tax that forces heirs to dispose of property to pay the tax. That was publicized in 1993 when heirs to Joe Robbie were forced to sell 34 percent of the professional football team the Miami Dolphins to pay the taxes then wound up selling out. Although inheritance runs counter to the Republican Party's mantra of "individual initiative," or "meritocracy" it, nonetheless, should remain viable. Taxes should not be so stiff that asset need to be sold to pay the tax bill, but that can be accomplished only after all other businesses pay their fair shares, which were estimated at that time to be evaded by between $127 billion and $150 billion yearly. Uncollected taxes were estimated to be $350 billion by 2008. And the inheritance tax can be easily avoided if the heirs were to buy shares in the estate (the Dolphins) before the principal owner died. Their inheritance then would include enough cash to meet any outstanding obligation. Chapter 12 will present a better option.

Tax breaks to close manufacturing plants in the United States and move them elsewhere need to go. In 1993, the American Broadcasting Company television news program Prime Time Live reported that $12.5 billion had been "wasted" under Section 936 of the United States Tax Code that encouraged American firm to close their mainland plants and open new plants in Puerto Rico. A 100 percent tax exemption for doing business in Puerto Rico cost the Treasury about $3 billion a year "and keeps going up every year," according to one tax expert. Because Puerto Rico is a United States territory, an improved economy there is important, but not at the expense of a weakened mainland economy.

A final problem is the method of controlling potential for inflation by the Federal Reserve Board. When there is a hint of inflationary pressure, the Fed hikes interest rates to dampen the economy. But that makes servicing the national debt more expensive because higher rates also affect government borrowing. As the economy slows, thousands or millions of workers lose their jobs and no longer pay income taxes while costing government billions for unemployment benefits. Higher rates do bring in more money from banks who borrow from the Fed, but that is shortly ended when the economy slows and banks borrow less. If borrowing slows enough, the Fed may eventually get less in interest payments than it received before hiking rates. Higher interest rates to slow the economy hurts the working middle class most because that is the class that loses jobs, has homes and automobiles financed on credit and often must rely on its credit cards until payday. If interest gets too onerous the wealthy, who can buy automobiles, yachts and other luxuries with cash, aren't harmed; the middle class that cannot pay cash is harmed.

A more-logical method of dealing with inflationary pressures is to use taxes as a calming mechanism. Taxes would bring more money into the Treasury before the economy slows, would not cost government more for its borrowing and could be directed to those areas of the economy that are most threatening. Interest-rate hikes affect the entire economy, controlling the areas threatening to be inflationary but throwing into recession areas that were not inflationary. Tax increases would affect only the area on which the increases were imposed; they would not damage an already-frail area.

We have to learn from the energy crises of the 1970s caused by oil embargoes when inflation ran wild and interest rates rose beyond 20 percent for everyone. Thousands of farmers, burdened by inflated energy costs and onerous interest rates, went bankrupt from that double blow. Higher excise taxes on those commodities fueling the inflation could have been used to combat that inflation while leaving agriculture's borrowing expenses un-touched. Many family farms might have been preserved had the government used taxes, not interest rates, to battle inflation. Taxes and interest pay-ments are the same thing: expenses.

Using taxes rather than interest rates to combat inflation also would lessen the need for homebuyers to gamble their futures with adjustable rate mortgages (ARM). Steady interest rates would return stability and certainty to the lives of home buyers while protecting lending institutions from being caught in a situation where they must pay savers or institutional lenders more for money than they could get on mortgages, a situation that helped fuel the S&L financial fiasco. (While this paragraph was written in the mid-1990s, it foresaw the damage adjustable rate mortgages would have later, specifically in George W. Bush's second recession. If a journalist/intelligence agent with a Bachelor of Business Administration degree, with honors, could anticipate the damage, why couldn't holders of PhDs from Harvard, Yale, Stanford and the Massachusetts Institute of Technology?)

Not all wealthy Americans put self-interests first when dealing with the debt. Many well-to-do Americans applauded Clinton's call for tax hikes because they saw the increase as "good for the country," and wouldn't hurt their stations in life. Most had accumulated enough under the Reagan eco-nomic policy that they were capable of absorbing higher taxes easily. Most of the complaining came from right-wing politicians and their talk-show puppets and political journals.

TAXING THAT WOULD WORK

So what is needed for America is an entirely new taxing system and that system would eliminate all income taxes on the salaries paid to both employees and executives. The Social Security/Medicare payroll tax would also be eliminated. Profit taxes will be reintroduced on America's busi-nesses and corporations to get them back to paying for the nation's general welfare close to their burden when America was the world's leader in all economic areas. Individuals will pay taxes on their profit-sharing income, as they do now for Social Security and Medicare, and those taxes will be designated for the same specific areas of the nation's spending.

A problem with the present system lies with foreign manufacturers doing business in America. Many of these firms practice what is called "transfer pricing," and that shifts taxes onto American firms and workers;

mostly onto workers. Transfer pricing involves a foreign firm operating a subsidiary firm overseas and that firm acts as the supplier for products or product parts used in the United States. The foreign company sells to the American plant a product—a $25 item for $250—that is resold in the American market for $200. On the books, that can be made to appear to be a loss. It is illegal, but hard to detect because of the volume of goods in international trade conduits, according to experts. Those same experts estimated that the United States Treasury lost as much as $33 billion in taxes annually in the mid-1990s.

This scam can be used by America-based multinational corporations that would establish parts-manufacturing plants in nations where they escape taxation, because those nations offer plantation economics and where ownership can be easily hidden and appear to be only an independent supplier. The American corporation, which manufactures doodadds, can make the doos in Asia and the dadds in Latin America. It can pay its foreign plants $100 for each part, ship the parts to plants in the United States, assemble them here, then sell finished doodadds for $250 each to wholesalers. With $50 charged for salaries and overhead, the company's books indicate a break-even transaction even though the true cost of doos and dadds might be $25 apiece, if manufactured in the United States by the American company. With honest bookkeeping, the real expense of manufacturing one doodadd was $100 ($25 for a doo, $25 for a dadd and $50 for labor) resulting in a $150 taxable profit.

Democratic Capitalism would help put an end to this practice. Any company assembling doodadds in the United States could pay no one at its plant, including its executives, more than the $25,000 yearly salary. It then must demonstrate a profit, after paying federal taxes, before anyone would rise above that minimum income. If a company insisted on playing games with its books to show a loss when a substantial profit should be shown, it would have a difficult time competing with American firms. Its underpaid employees and executives would soon leave the company for better profit sharing elsewhere. Morale would suffer, as would products, and honest American firms would benefit if dishonest firms marketed inferior products.

Capital-gains taxes have been a constant battle point between the political right and the political left with the right claiming a reduction in such taxes would usher in an economic boom. The left insists on taxing capital gains as close as possible to any other income, regardless of source. With Democratic Capitalism, such arguments might be defused. Industrial capital gains normally would be treated as ordinary business transactions and all taxes would be leveled at their source of profit, but other capital gains can be handled in a special manner.

One way to handle the tax on such things as stocks is to tie it to a sliding scale. Stocks owned less than one year would be taxed at the prevailing business-tax rate. That held from one to two years would be taxed at 90 percent of the prevailing rate; that held two to three years at 80 percent; three to four years at 70 percent on down until there is no tax on stocks held more than 10 years.

Dividend income received by individuals is to be subject of special treatment and is detailed in a later chapter.

In Democratic Capitalism businesses would be responsible for collecting most taxes paid in the country because they already have the bookkeeping mechanisms in place to serve that function. They would continue much as they do now except they would not pay exorbitant salaries to some employees while trying to keep other salaries as low as possible. Deductions would be allowed for all salaries and all expenses directly related to doing business. After all salaries and expenses have been paid and deducted, the business-profits tax would be applied and its rates would depend on how much is needed to fund that part of government operations dependent only on a business-profit tax. That should leave enough profits that most American workers may actually get a raise—if not in actual dollar amounts, at least in after-tax amounts since they are no longer responsible for taxes on income or payroll taxes.

Employees (labor and management) would not file income-tax returns and that may eliminate more than 100 million returns that should result in a smaller IRS. Employers would handle all reporting of profit sharing just as they now do for Social Security and Medicare taxes. This can be accomplished without additional payroll employees at any company. A for-profit employee would receive the $25,000 basic salary and profit sharing relative to the importance to the company just as present employees are paid varying amounts depending on position or seniority. Commissioned employees, such as stock brokers or real-estate sales, would continue to operate much as they do now except they would receive that minimum-wage salary from their sales, then the rest of their sales commission would be considered profit. Provisions would also be made for apprenticeships. An apprentice would receive the basic wage but would not be entitled to profit sharing until the end of an apprenticeship. Most apprenticeships should not last beyond one year and a veteran apprentice could not be terminated, except for cause, just to avoid inclusion in profit sharing.

Employed contractors (government and nonprofit concerns) will be handled the same as for-profit employees, but bookkeeping for them would be simpler: the first $25,000 of income is tax-free; the rest is taxed just as is profit sharing. This, also, would not require extra bookkeeping.

Independent contractors (carpenters, longshoremen, farm workers or anyone in a similar position) would be responsible for filing tax returns, as they now do, and would have business-related tax write-offs. The main difference from the present is that they would take the first $25,000 after deductions as salary, the rest would be handled as if it were profit sharing. But independent contractors would have to be licensed by the state in order to claim deductions or to be employed. Employers would have to furnish the state license number in order to deduct any payment to an independent contractor.

The self-employed would not have it as easy as the employees of for-profit and nonprofit organizations. The self-employed would have to continue filing returns as they do now in order to account for their business-related expenses. Athletes and entertainers need to pay for agents, managers, advisors or brokers. Artists and writers also need to deduct for agents or managers but also have expenses for artists' materials and models and work-related necessities, such as a writer's computer or an editor. When a self-employed person hires a full-time employee, a business is formed.

The crossover earner creates a special situation. Only the first $25,000 or any person's income shall be considered off limits to federal taxation, so income from outside activities, such as book royalties for a reporter or professor, would be reported on tax returns as if it were profit-sharing income, but there would be no need to file a return on employment income, the employer would do that. The two-job worker would treat all income from a second job as profit sharing unless both jobs were part-time. Then, the worker would earn up to $25,000 tax-free and the rest would be profit sharing. Two part-time jobs would make the employee similar to an independent contractor.

Retirees would have the same division of income as all the others: up to $25,000 coming from private pensions, Social Security or other sources such as rental income would be tax free.

Interest from bank accounts would be free of taxation because the small amounts received by millions of small savers does not justify the expense of bookkeeping and the banks would be taxed on profits, in essence, covering the taxes for savers.

Dividends from corporate earnings, whether they go to other businesses, pension plans, employed persons, retirees or the idle rich, could be handled in one of two ways. First, they could be handled the same as profit sharing for employees because dividends are profit sharing for the corporation's real owners, shareholders. Retirees would not have to include this income on their returns but would have to consider anything on their returns over $25,000 to be like profit sharing to be taxed. An ideal method is to eliminate all federal taxes on dividends and tax the profit of the corporations paying the dividends. But a special temporary tax could be levied to pay off the war debt and it could be paired with a tax on financial transactions such as stock and bond purchases. When there is no war debt, there will be no tax. Richard Nixon put his share of the Vietnam Conflict on the national credit card as did George W. Bush for his two wars while cutting taxes for the wealthy. Since the rich are not paying for those wars with either taxes or personal commitment they should fund them with these financial taxes. The lower middle class and the poor are paying for wars with the lives of their sons and daughters so should not have to also pay with their taxes. Because they also have little or no dividend income, the lives lost should be sufficient. And, if the wealthy paid for war with their dividend income and financial transactions there will be fewer wars of choice.

These profit-sharing taxes would go to fund the Human Services Budget (chapter 8), but all persons will share in taxation and benefits. That means taxes will no longer be cut off for high-income recipients as under the present payroll tax but will be applied to the full amount of income from profit sharing regardless of how high that is. A graduated system of taxation is also possible. If the right is serious at reduction of government, it might consider a top rate of 75 percent on any income over a million dollars a year with a "loophole" included for those high-income Americans who use the write-off to invest in matters that aid the "general welfare" of the nation, such as urban real-estate redevelopment. Not development that intrudes on the rural environment and creates urban sprawl, but the rejuvenation of abandoned and dilapidated inner-city areas. That private-sector activity would reduce the need for government involvement in housing, would provide consumers for merchants by providing employment for area residents which in turn could also lessen the need for welfare and might reduce homelessness or crime rates when real jobs are available. This is an area where tax laws can be written to address several problems and can realistically help reduce the size of government.

Another problem—one that troubled the Clinton and first Bush administrations when they tried to fill Cabinet positions or other jobs—will also be eliminated. Zoe Baird, Kimba Wood, Steven Breyer, Linda Chavez and many others were caught in a situation where they didn't pay Social Security taxes for people who worked for them in positions such as nannies, house cleaners, lawn mowers or handymen. With Democratic Capitalism no one would be required to pay for someone else because the employees would be licensed independent contractors responsible for their own taxes. Baby-sitters and lawn mowers wouldn't have incomes above $25,000 and neither would little girls operating lemonade stands. If all businesses and individuals paid their fair share, we wouldn't have to worry about, or be upset over, taxes on those who are barely surviving on meager incomes. Baird, Wood and Breyer are lawyers, indicating how complicated tax laws have become because lawyers should understand laws much easier than persons in all other professions.

With businesses, from the self-employed individual to the largest corporation, responsible for paying federal taxes the minimum income on salary and wages is a must. For a taxpayer to pay federal, state, city, property, sales or any other type of tax he/she must get the income from a business activity. Interest, dividends and bond yields for the idle rich are also generated by business. The minimum wage provides government with a method to assure profits are not hidden by false costs—i.e., Hollywood's creative accounting—because there must be profit for sharing if a business wants to keep capable employees, and the quality of the employees will determine the profitability of the company. This arrangement provides the structure needed to reduce the IRS because only one tax return will be needed from major corporations and their hundreds of thousands of employees.

The small-business owner who misrepresents the business income or profits would also be stealing from the company's employees. That would also be true of Hollywood producers or studio executives who use phony expenses to hide profits. If that practice continues, a producer or head of a major studio would be receiving $25,000 a year under Democratic Capitalism, and nothing more, and to avoid that they would make sure the books reflected a healthy bona fide profit. When employees detect that they are being short changed on profit sharing, they would have recourse for legal action and the Treasury might not suffer the uncollected taxes estimated earlier at between $127 billion and $150 billion a year during the Clinton administration and pegged late in the George W. Bush administration at $350 billion. And employees would have a harder time cheating because all taxes would be collected at the source of income or profit.

This new taxing system requires an entirely new budgetary system for the federal government, and that is detailed in chapter 8.

Chapter 6. Not Business as Usual

A New Commerce

There are many valid reasons to regulate commerce despite the protesting of the right about "overregulation" of business. Governments in democratic republics must work through the powers given to them in their constitutions, and the ability to regulate commerce gives governments the authority to outlaw many undesirable activities. It is only through this power that governments can hope to address the drug problem in the United States or to combat gambling and prostitution. Without the power to regulate commerce, government could not keep liquor and cigarettes away from juveniles nor could it punish for frauds, scams and briberies.

Government's ability to protect businesses from fake products not covered by copyright or patent laws rests on the power to regulate commerce. Protection under trademark laws would apply to the specific trademark, so power to regulate commerce must protect business from frauds perpetrated with distorted spellings of a valid trademark or trade name.

The power to regulate commerce must also be used to protect the nation and its citizens from mischief by corporations. Less regulation will not afford this protection, just as less regulation did not benefit the nation in the savings-and-loan debacle, or the financial meltdown of 2007-9, nor has the nation benefited by polluting industries and dangerous products. Regulation of commerce has led to a cleaner environment, safer products, advancements in technology, middle-class consumers, equal rights and a method for excluded Americans to become part of the included classes and to share in the nation's general welfare.

When many Americans were poisoned by tampered headache remedies in the 1970s and 1980s, government proposed that manufacturers package their products with tamper-proof containers. The political right howled that such a burden would be so costly it would force many drug producers out of business, and Americans would be losing their "freedom." But tamper-proof packaging has become standard for nearly all manufacturers and none of them has gone out of business for producing safer products, totalitarianism didn't overwhelm the republic and Americans are now more free, knowing full well the potato salad they brought home from the grocery store hasn't been poisoned by a maniac.

One has to wonder if conservatives have the faintest idea of what socialism is. The political right makes much noise about the dangers of "socialism," even branding president Barack Obama as a "socialist" for his efforts to use government as a tool to solve economic problems brought about by "free-market" ideology.

In Alaska, probably the most conservative state in the union, rights to natural resources under state land—most notably oil and gas reserves—are leased to private industry and the proceeds from those leases are distributed to all qualified citizens of the state each year since 1976 (those convicted or jailed for felonies or some misdemeanors are not qualified). Under this constitutionally-established program, called the Alaska Permanent Fund Dividend Program, Alaskans may receive checks for several hundred dollars in one year or a thousand or more dollars in another year. That is pure socialism, and there is no concerted effort by "socialism"-hating Alaskan politicians, past or present, to end the practice. Nor is there a public outcry by Alaska citizens about their freedoms being stolen because of this socialist program they seem to support whole heartedly.

While writing on Europe's economic problems recently, attorney and author Ellen Brown said:

Neither states in the US nor those in the euro zone can print their own money, but they CAN own banks, which can create bank credit on their books, just as all banks do. Over 95 percent of the money supply is now created by banks in the form of loans. The banks are not lending their own money or their depositors' money. They are just advancing credit and collecting interest on this advance. Governments could advance their own credit and keep the interest. This would represent a huge savings to the people. Interest has been shown to make up about half the cost of everything we buy.

Only one US state actually owns its own bank—North Dakota. As of last spring (2010), North Dakota was also the only US state sporting a budget surplus. It has the lowest unemployment rate in the country and the lowest default rate on loans. North Dakota has effectively escaped the credit crisis.

The Bank of North Dakota (BND) is a major profit generator for the state, returning a 26 percent dividend in 2008. The BND was set up as "North Dakota doing business as the Bank of North Dakota," making the assets of the state the assets of the bank. The BND also has a captive deposit base. By law, all of North Dakota's revenues are deposited in the BND. Municipal government and private deposits are also taken. Today, the BND has $4,000 in deposits per capita, and outstanding loans of roughly the same amount.[49]

In his latest book talk-radio host and writer Thom Hartmann wrote:

Because banks can be enormous profit centers, North Dakota started its own bank to inexpensively loan (sic) money to its farmers and small businesses; and when it does so (as it has all these years), all the profits from the interest paid go back into the state's coffers. This has a lot to do with why that state was among those least affected by the Bush financial crisis that began in 2008.

If every state did this, over time these state-run banks would provide strong competition to corporate banks, running many of them out of business or forcing them to operate more efficiently and to pay their CEOs less. State-run banks could also offer loans to citizens at a lower interest rate than the commercial banks, thus stimulating and stabilizing the states' local economies.[50]

North Dakota is also a very conservative state, but its bank is also socialism; proving once again that conservatives can live comfortably with socialism as long as it serves them well and is not the dreaded disease conservative politicians make it out to be. But they do decry socialism as evil if

49 "Austerity Fails in Euroland: Time for Some 'Deficit Easing'," Ellen Brown; Truthout.org; January 20, 2011.
50 *"Rebooting the American Dream,"* Thom Hartmann; Berrett-Koehler Publishers © 2010.

it benefits persons other than themselves. And, like Alaska, its politicians make no attempt to eliminate this socialism.

Regulation should do more to end corporate mischief such as "downsizing" or moving operations out of the United States to save a few dollars per product unit because those actions eliminate the very consumers that business needs to continue making profits and the nation needs to maintain its world leadership in commercial activity. Forcing middle-class workers to compete with wages of Plantation and Sweatshop Economies overseas will not maintain that leadership nor will lower taxes on business or less regulation. Those approaches have been tried and have failed.

Regulation of commerce also protects commercial ventures from unnecessary and costly litigation by providing a valid defense in lawsuits. Removing many regulations would open up business to even more litigation than they now face, which in turn will lead pro-business politicians to regulate society and the victims of corporate irresponsibility by restricting the ability to seek justice by ordinary working-class Americans.

Regulations are not created to harass, punish or damage business; those practices have been declared unconstitutional and any regulation not proven to be "necessary and proper" will get the same treatment in America's courts. Like all laws, regulations are created because there were evils to be confronted and business regulations are, in fact, only commercial law and order. Just as business will always expand to fill a need, regulations will be created or expanded to fill a need. To claim, as Hypocright politicians do, that deregulation would be beneficial to society is like saying removal of criminal laws would result in a more-peaceful society. The key to easing of the regulatory burden is for business executives to take responsibility for their actions and stop polluting, lying, cheating and endangering citizens.

Regulations also create jobs. Regulation of the automobile industry led to the creation of industries to manufacture seat belts, then air bags. Environmental regulations led industry to manufacture catalytic converters for motor vehicles and smokestack scrubbers for polluting manufacturing plants. American industry only had to take advantage of those regulations to add to their product lines. The Americans with Disabilities Act was reported by *USA Today* in 1992 to be an entrepreneur's dream.[51] The newspaper said, "More than 170,000 products and services have been introduced"

---

51   "Disabilities law inspires entrepreneurs," Rhonda Richards; *USA Today;* November 18, 1992.

before the act was in force six months. Firms that had to provide easy access for all persons found their businesses benefited from increased patronage and some firms were able to hire a few superior employees when all persons had access to their establishments. Misuse of the law by some persons who sued for discrimination for the slightest provocation should be expected because Americans have a talent for testing the limits of any new concept, but an equilibrium is eventually found. Environmental regulation led to the recycling industry that, in newsprint alone, will save much of America's natural resources for better use or for preservation for future generations to enjoy.

But deregulation is costly. Results of easing of regulations on the savings-and-loan industry have been well documented as have been the troubles experienced by the airline industry for several years. Airline troubles spilled into other areas as the quest for market share led to years of money-losing, labor problems and economic troubles for the airlines' suppliers, especially aircraft manufacturers. Shareholders of electric-utility stocks have suffered from an easing of regulations or lack of regulations. Since the mid-1980s many utility companies have eliminated dividend payments to the "owners" or slashed the payout after venturing into many nonutility areas to evade the types of regulation that have historically been imposed on their utility business. Utility executives usually attribute the dividend cuts to an evolving industry facing new competition created by easing of regulations.

Tucson Electric Power Company (Arizona) was managed nearly out of existence and a once-robust and profitable company had its stock nearly reduced to "penny" status after losing 95 percent of its value. It stopped paying a dividend in 1990 and only recently reinstituted a dividend that is a mere pittance of what it was. To pay off much of its debt the company issued new stock to debt holders, raising the amount of outstanding shares from about 25 million shares in 1991 to more than 160 million at the end of 1992, then conducted a one-for-five stock constriction, commonly called a "reverse split." Even as the company regains profitability, the original "owners" will never regain their original ownership status; that position will ever be diluted. Pinnacle West Capital Corporation (Arizona) eliminated its dividend in 1990—after buying a savings-and-loan business in the process of failing—and resumed a limited dividend in 1995 after turning the S&L's financial problems over to the federal government. Public Service Company of New Mexico also halted its dividend payment in 1990 and was even tardier than Pinnacle West in resuming a dividend. Portland General Electric Corporation (Oregon) slashed its dividend in 1990 after it ventured into unregulated nonutility businesses and only managed to raise the dividend slightly in 1996. It's management then proposed a merger with the Texas utility Enron that would result in a even smaller dividend payout to its "owners" before collapsing amid widespread corruption and crime. Pacificorp (Oregon), once regarded as one of America's best-managed utilities, reduced its dividend in 1993 after also venturing into many costly unregulated nonutility businesses.[52]

These same financial fates befell utility firms in other areas of the nation such as the Midwest, East Coast, South and New England. Some utilities, while not cutting or eliminating dividends, failed to protect shareholders' concerns by lagging far behind inflation. The Washington Water Power Company stopped increasing its dividend in 1983; the dividend of Public Service Company of Colorado (now part of Xcel Energy) was stationary between 1985 and 1995 while inflation continued to adversely affect many retirees depending on dividend incomes. While dividends were eliminated, reduced or stagnant, and thousands of workers were fired, compensation for executives continued to soar.

When regulations are not given the highest priorities, Americans sometime die. E. coli bacteria in hamburgers served by a fast-food chain resulted in the deaths of four children in Seattle early in 1993 following one in San Diego in late 1992. At the same time the American Broadcasting Company was reporting that there were 550 unfilled meat-inspection positions in the United States. *The Seattle Times* indicated that the underlying causes for the deaths and the shortage of inspectors were politics and economics. The paper said the food industry—historically a large contributor to political campaigns—often was the source of secretaries of agriculture as was the Congress, which receives the food industry's contributions. The paper said in 1993 that the argument about government's proper function in food inspection "was renewed with particular vigor six years ago when the USDA began pushing for a sharp reduction in the number of government inspectors in cattle slaughter plants. The reduction proposal ... was used for more than five years at five of the nation's largest slaughterhouses, including one

---

52   The author is well aware of the failings of these corporations in their rush to avoid regulations, having been a shareholder in all of them.

of the plants that supplied beef" to the restaurant chain where the children were poisoned. [53]

That push for fewer food inspectors was made during the end of Reagan's term when the political emphasis was more on corporate profitability than the individual's well being. Washington state news organizations also reported that the emphasis on profits over people contributed to undercooking the hamburger. Federal standards called for hamburger to be cooked with an internal temperature of 140 degrees, which would have destroyed most bacteria. But Washington state regulations called for 155 degrees, which would have destroyed all bacteria. Cooking tainted hamburger at the lower temperature to save a fraction of a cent was deadly and eventually cost the firm more to settle wrongful-death claims. Following the stricter regulations would have been better for all involved: children would not have died and the company would not have been sued because of those deaths.

Avoiding needful regulations is also expensive. After Hurricane Andrew caused more than $15 billion dollars in damage in Florida and Louisiana in 1992, officials blamed much of the devastation on shoddy construction of houses that fell well below requirements of building regulations. Andrew left many insurance companies bankrupt and others facing huge losses. To stay in business, insurance companies eventually raise premiums to offset the losses, and that leaves less spendable cash with policyholders to be spent in other businesses. So, businesses that had nothing to do with the construction industry wound up helping pay for construction mischief.

In Colorado, the Summitville Mine in the Rockies was proposed as a godsend to a sluggish Rio Grande County economy. Instead, the mine was abandoned after less than 10 years in operation with the parent company claiming millions of dollars in losses while declaring bankruptcy in the early 1990s. The federal government was then saddled with expenses of up to $70 million, according to *USA Today*, to clean up the environmental damage that had been caused. That damage, from mineral deposits seeping into the Alamosa River, included the killing the fish population over several miles of river and damage to farm and ranch irrigation equipment using water from the river. Critics cited a lack of realistic regulations for the damages.[54]

---

53 "Why inspections of meat fails," Terry McDermott; *The Seattle Times*; January 31, 1993.
54 "Failed Colorado mine a reform 'poster child'," Jana Mazanec; *USA Today*; June 11, 1993.

While such economic devastation was hitting everyone, Righty politicians were calling for dismantling the government regulations that would have prevented the deaths and financial disasters had those regulations been obeyed in the first place.

Equally irresponsible is the Righty pleas for "self-regulation." Self-regulation is as bad or worse than no regulation, and government displays that. Among the worst polluters in the United States has been the military that dumped hazardous waste—paint, solvents, fuel, metals, pesticides, bombs—whenever and wherever it wished. Much of that dumping polluted the ground water used by neighboring communities and will cost hundreds of millions of dollars to clean up.

This record of pollution should teach an important lesson: the institution charged to make and enforce regulations should never be the institution being regulated. There is little difference between a system in which government owns and operates commerce and a system in which commerce owns and operates government.

Right-wing propagandists, always arguing against all regulation in the extreme or self-regulation as a compromise, should live in those nuclear wastelands to experience the results of the absence of regulation or of self-regulation. Government's regulations should be strong enough that there are no more commercial evils and commercial concerns should be managed well enough that government need not become involved in commercial ventures except in those areas commercial firms can't make a profit.

This lesson should also be used to sidetrack a 1996 proposal by an advisory panel that recommended that excess cash in the Social Security system should be invested in stocks rather than in government bonds as a method to prevent insolvency in the system by the year 2030. (A solution to the Social Security financing problem will be presented in chapter 10.) Investing government money in the private sector would result in a conflict of interest by government; it might try to maximize stock value by minimizing protection for citizens and environment. That would make government a partner with the "Corporate Killers" who eliminated millions of American jobs in profitable companies in order to enrich themselves and who came under widespread criticism in the past few years for that practice.

Conservatives usually do not learn from mistakes. In a 1996 *USA Today* column Linda Chavez wrote the standard Righty mantra:

For years, conservatives have counseled that the answer to all economic problems is less government, fewer regulations and lower taxes. The idea is that freeing up more private investment and placing fewer controls on how that investment is spent will create more jobs.[55]

Conservative counsel is wrong.

The results of less government have been the elimination of millions of jobs by unnecessary corporate downsizing just to increase short term profits and boost stock prices, the California experience of lingering recession; high unemployment, state budget shortages, deteriorating education, rising crime and making minorities the scapegoats for society's problems. The conservative GOP, which continually kissed up to business since World War I, found some of its presidential candidates criticizing business in the 1996 presidential primaries because of the abuses the corporations perpetrated while government looked the other way. Fewer regulations include the savings and loan debacle, the 2007–9 financial meltdown and the just-mentioned pollution records of the United States military.

Business in the mid-1990s paid less than 20 percent of all income taxes collected by the federal government compared to the nearly 50 percent that business paid for all federal tax collections in the 1950s—the period of history conservatives love and which they cite as an economic model—so it seems lower taxes on business have been counterproductive. Income taxes account for less than half the tax haul of the national government, therefore business income taxes amount to about 10 percent of total taxes. Further reducing of taxes on business would involve a figure so insignificant it would do little to create the economic miracle conservatives always promise. High taxes on middle- and lower-income individual taxpayers—tax rates on the highest incomes are much lower than they were in the 1950s—persist because of the Reagan administration's raid on working-class wage earners to pay for conservatives' illogical economic theories. Chavez was part of that raider administration.

The call for reduction in commercial regulations will benefit only one section of society: that area composed of con men and scam artists. At the present time, commercial markets could use fewer scams and confidence games, and regulations target those areas. Proper regulations do not prey on honest businesses which can protect themselves from harmful regulations

---

55 "Progress, not greed, destroys jobs," Linda Chavez; *USA Today*; March 6, 1996.

with the Constitution's provision in Article I, Section 8, that all laws—regulations are laws—must be "necessary and proper," the First Amendment's right to petition government for a redress of grievances if regulations aren't necessary or proper, and Article III's provision that federal courts can hear all cases and controversies arising under United States Constitution, laws and treaties.

Liberals and moderates have long counseled that the answer to economic problems is that the economy will expand to benefit all persons when all persons are allowed to participate in the economy. That philosophy of full participation is behind the creation of civil-rights and affirmative-action laws that have lifted many persons from the excluded class and moved them into the productive middle class. The political right has long retarded the economy by excluding many people from the economy while cutting taxes for itself and its friends.

Wall Street, hardly a friend of liberal politics, fares much better under the Democratic administrations many investors claim to despise. Stock prices have historically risen more than 13 percent annually under Democratic presidents while averaging about six to seven percent under Republican presidents. The reason is clear; having as many people as possible participating in the economy with livable incomes enables corporations to do more business and improve their profit margins under Democrats. When those livable incomes are reduced (to pay interest on the Reagan-Bushes debt, shifting taxes off business and onto individuals or moving jobs overseas) corporations do not have the same strong customer base and profits shrink under Republicans. The GOP only offers tax reductions to business, if the business still pays taxes, while the Democratic Party offers customers who are able to afford the business's offerings and the business, which supports Republican politicians, usually fare better under Democratic politicians. That is proven in chapter 11.

EXPERTS HAVE THEIR SAY

Many corporate experts or economic and business specialists seem to agree that "the answer to all economic problems is" to concentrate on real growth, not on the failed gimmicks espoused by Chavez and others with the conservative mindset that constantly ignores proof.

Among those with a message to corporate America, that many managers might not want to hear but who ignore it at their peril, is Gerald Greenwald, chairman and CEO of United Airlines until retirement in 1999. Greenwald, who lived through corporate downsizing as chief financial officer at Chrysler Corporation, said in a 1996 interview with *USA Today*:

> "I now believe very deeply that the traditional form of downsizing leaves bad waves behind and hurts the bottom line of a company.

> "Simply stated, if you one day walk in and tell 1,000 people, 'sorry, but there will be 900 of you a month from now' the 900 who stay are no longer loyal to your company. They're loyal to themselves...

> "So, Lesson One, don't overexpand. Don't bet your people's jobs. If you want to bet your people's jobs, then, damn it bet your own. Put your name on saying you're going to be one of the hundred who leave if it comes to it, because you will have failed.

> "There are good reasons for downsizing, but most companies have time to do it with attrition."[56]

Dwight Gertz, of Boston's Mercer Management Consulting Inc., and co-author of the book *Grow to Be Great: Breaking the Downsizing Cycle*, wrote in the same newspaper in 1996:

> "Recent studies by the American Management Association reveal that two-thirds of downsizing companies have gone back for two or more rounds of large-scale layoffs. Because the smaller a company shrinks the less opportunity it has to shrink further, companies that get stuck in a downsizing cycle inevitably find that each wave of firings brings steadily diminishing returns.

> "Continual downsizing also devastates corporate morale.

> "The best managers and workers, tired of the turmoil, begin to jump ship, while the remaining employees, disheartened and distracted, become ever less productive. Ultimately, downsizers find that they've cut the muscle from their companies, not just the fat.

> "To stay healthy over the long run, companies need to grow. Growth strengthens morale and productivity, produces organizational momentum and earns the greatest rewards for the investors."[57]

Both men cited the steel company Nucor as the kind of corporation that does it right. Greenwald said the firm has never had a layoff in its 25–30-year history at that time, even though it's in a cyclical business, because

---

56   " 'Downsizing' leaves bad waves behind," Gerald Greenwald: *USA Today*; July 1, 1996.
57   "Growth, not downsizing, leads to greatness," Dwight Gertz; *USA Today*; February 7, 1966.

its management and workers have a working agreement that everyone has reduced income if there is reduced business. If there is only enough business for four days of work, everyone—including management—works four days and is paid for four days. Gertz said Nucor posted yearly sales increases of 19 percent in a no-growth industry by using a simplified production process of small teams of high-paid workers. Teamwork and sharing the wealth (and the poverty) by all persons involved in creating that wealth are features of Democratic Capitalism at its best.

The Wall Street Journal, usually an apologist for all things corporate, also decried the downsizing frenzy. In 1995, it wrote:

> A shrinking corporation becomes anorexic when it gets hooked on controlling expenses, closing plants, slashing inventories and eliminating jobs that it neglects the fact that a company should seek growth, not fade away.

> ... After nearly a decade of frantic cost-cutting, the downside of downsizing is beginning to take its toll: Decimated sales staffs turn in lousy numbers. 'Survivor syndrome' takes hold, and overburdened staffers just go through the motions of working. New-product ideas languish. Risk-taking dwindles because the culture of cost-cutting emphasizes the certainties of cutting costs over the uncertainties—and expense—of trying something new ...

> A recent American Management Association survey underscores the surprisingly mixed results of the decade of corporate budget-slashing. The study concludes that profits rose at only 51 percent of the companies that downsized between 1989 and 1994. Only 34 percent showed an increase in productivity. But employee morale slumped at 86 percent."[58]

The Journal said that many companies offered generous buyouts and the experienced and competent people the companies should have kept, took the money and left. One company lost the only engineer it had who could understand the design specifications of a compressor. The company needed his expertise, and scoured the area but could not find him.

Many corporations have also found that after massive budget-slashing the workplace became a meaner, less-cooperative environment, and that resulted in hurting the company's profitability and that spreads into the economy.

---

58 "Some firms cut costs too far, suffer 'corporate anorexia'," Bernard Wysocki: *The Wall Street Journal* reprinted in *The Denver Post*; July 9, 1995.

How we can expect Democratic Capitalism to benefit US businesses and employees?

Democratic Capitalism would eliminate unnecessary positions at a company because employees, not executives, would determine the proper amount of effort needed by employees to create the wealth. The practice of fear, intimidation and threats from above—Gestapo Management—could become a thing of the past because management would benefit from enlarging the business and adding employees instead of downsizing, and contentment of the workforce would be an essential contributor to profitability. Unions, where they still exist, would negotiate to end "featherbedding" because their members would benefit more from a small efficient workforce. The two forces (management working toward a bigger workforce and labor striving to maintain a smaller workforce) should result in an ideal workforce that may not be disrupted by greed of employer or of union.

Democratic Capitalism could lead to better labor relations, a commodity sorely needed in America's businesses. Employment is a contract between employer and employee and should usually be ended for cause—failure to produce a profit would be cause, so layoffs could occur at a profitless point. This would put an end to the practice of firing 50-year-old middle managers in a profitable company just to save their salaries at a time in life when they are unlikely to find jobs elsewhere. The corporation would not add a cent of profit by inhumane treatment of employees; increased profitability can only be achieved by earning it. More likely; as profitability declines, some employees will voluntarily leave for better positions elsewhere and remaining employees will fill any vacuum caused by a departure because picking up the slack means sharing of what profits are available. Management can concentrate on improving business activities, not on abusing, antagonizing or threatening the workforce.

Democratic Capitalism could lead to a reduction in unemployment if accompanied by fair legislative action. Conservatives, who constantly harp against government interference in private lives, began trying to reverse no-fault divorce laws and to outlaw same-sex marriages in many states in the mid-1990s because they claimed such things lead to breakdown of the family, causing conservatives to want more government regulation in order to preserve what they consider admirable. The same logic should apply to the workplace. Gainful employment may be just as important to family preservation than is an absence of divorce because financial hardships often lead to divorce. Therefore, government must put a halt to no-fault terminations of millions of employees by American businesses and make corporate downsizing a thing of the past except when the survival of the company is the main consideration. With such legislation, business would not be allowed to dump employees onto government when the economy slows. Everyone would stay employed at a lower income from profit sharing and government wouldn't be saddled with high expenses for unemployment compensation or retraining. There is no argument about government having power to regulate commerce, so it clearly could halt no-fault terminations, but it is still unclear the extent of government power to regulate marriage—except in Utah—other than matrimony's contractual aspects. Governments usually do not have laws outlawing a breach of contract, they do have laws providing compensation for the damaged parties.

Democratic Capitalism would instill in many employees the risk-taking bravado that is needed for entrepreneurship to flourish because all workers will learn to profit from their abilities and to rely on their wealth-creating skills rather from a predetermined income that would not change regardless of profitability of the workers' efforts. This enterprising spirit will lead to more small-business formations to provide employment opportunities for others. A new small business will benefit from Democratic Capitalism because it will not have to promise high salaries to potential employees; it will pay the minimum, just as established firms do, but it can offer a prospective employee the opportunity to grow and gain wealth as employees did with Microsoft's version of Democratic Capitalism in its early days of existence. Newly established companies will not be held back because of inability to provide healthcare benefits just as a potential entrepreneur will not be prevented from leaving a job, because of health concerns for self or for dependents, to take the risk of forming a business (See chapter 9).

Democratic Capitalism will preserve the value of the dollar for all consumers when it eliminates wage pressure as a cause of inflation.

Democratic Capitalism may also put an end to the corporate practice of halting payment of dividends to shareholders while CEOs continue to draw million-dollar salaries and multimillion-dollar bonuses while enjoying other luxuries and perks. The owners' profits will be dividends for shareholders, and if there are no profits for the owners there are no profits for the CEO or for the employees.

Democratic Capitalism also may put an end to many bitter labor disputes over wages that lead to destructive strikes. Management will treat employees as partners, not as enemies, because there is nothing for management to gain by hostile labor relations. Management can only lose through such tactics and labor cannot get through striking or worker discord more income than it has created.

Democratic Capitalism will combat the problem of bad, discourteous or antagonistic service many people encounter in various American business firms. As clerks and technicians learn that their income is directly tied to the amount of satisfaction the customer receives or perceives, rude behavior and lackadaisical performances may disappear. Much of the unfavorable service imposed on the public comes from employees being subjected to Gestapo Management and more Gestapo Management trying to combat the problem only makes matters worse. *USA Today* reported in April of 1996 that Delta Air Lines discovered that its job cuts hurt customer service, which eventually hurt company profitability. When employees have a financial incentive to provide polite and prompt service, they will provide such service without managerial tyranny.

Other benefits will arise from Democratic Capitalism and they are discussed in the last chapter, a wrap-up of what has been proposed so far.

Chapter 7. Where We Are

Our Problem

There is no secret about what is the top problem facing the United States. The top problem is not crime, although many fearful Americans believe it to be. The top problem is not foreign hostility, and probably never was, although anti-communism hysteria since World War II made it appear so, just as present-day "terror" is doing.

The top problem is not inadequate education, although many people decry what they call inferior education while proposing schemes to make education even poorer for the have-not classes and ignoring the thousands of teenage "geniuses" US public education turns out every year. The top problem facing the United States is the massive national debt that reached $5 trillion under Reagan-Bush in the mid-1990s, then exploded to more than $12 trillion under the younger George Bush. Our diverse problems—crime, education, the economy, quality jobs, healthcare coverage, drug abuse or others—cannot be adequately addressed until the national debt problem has been solved.

Neither the political right nor the political left downplays the importance of the debt and continued deficits. The only contentions between the two are how the nation got into this situation and how the nation is to get out of it. The political right blames taxes for the mess; but that is not true. The right also blames government spending on entitlement programs for the mess; but that is also not true. The debt, as shown in previous chapters, came about by dishonest politicians chasing fantasies, such as paying for the Vietnam Conflict with a figurative credit card begun when the majority of Americans and nearly all politicians loved that "anti-communism" crusade. And when America turned against the war, the politicians still refused to pay for it. That mistake was then followed by Ronald Reagan's "trickle-down" economic fairytale that created an artificial deficit that had to be covered by borrowing, usually borrowing from the very same financial institutions and people who had their taxes lowered by hundreds of thousands, if not millions, of dollars per year.

The partial closing down of the federal government in the fall and winter of 1995 should have been no surprise to anyone who has followed national politics since the war in Vietnam sent the nation on its path of fiscal irresponsibility. Neither should it be a surprise that most Americans felt that the Republican Congress should bear most of the blame for not reaching a budgetary agreement with the administration of Bill Clinton.

Clinton policies had reduced the annual budget deficit from the approximately $290 billion at the end of the Bush administration to a figure slightly more than half that amount by 1995. Conservatives had spent the greater part of a quarter of a century screaming about deficits but enacted policies when they held power that only produced ever-expanding deficits and mounting debt while preventing any measures that could solve the deficit problem if those solutions involved taxes. With their campaign slogan being pre-empted by Democratic successes, Hypocrights had to "get tougher" than Clinton about taming the deficit, even if it meant harming some social programs that make America desirable for most Americans, while not touching spending that further enriches the already-rich or provides welfare for corporations. To prove they were tougher on the debt, Republicans bought television time to broadcast commercials accusing the President of "opposing" a balanced budget after he refused to totally capitulate to their inflexible demands. That was dishonest.

Bush's $290 billion deficit in 1992 was accompanied by a $292 billion interest payment on the debt, which indicates there would have been a $2 billion surplus had the nation paid off its World War II debts, had it not embarked on new debt financing for war under Richard Nixon and had it resisted the Reagan Ponzi scheme. With no debt, the 1994 budget would have had a surplus of about $90 billion (more than $295 billion in interest payments on a $205 billion deficit). The 1995 budget had a theoretical surplus of $169 billion (a deficit of $164 billion and interest of $333 billion).

When Clinton turned government over to George Bush the Younger, the nation had a surplus in excess of $250 billion and estimates of a $5-trillion-plus surplus for years to come. Bush squandered that almost immediately.

But before that happened, the right caused the government to be partly shut down to satisfy Rep. Newt Gingrich's peeve about not getting a preferred seat on Air Force One during a trip with President Clinton.

If Hypocrights thought that closing the national government would demonstrate "freedom" for average Americans who finally had the much-dreaded federal bureaucracy "off our backs," they miscalculated and found that the American public doesn't hate the United States as much as Gingrich does. Americans complained that many services they relied on were no longer available, just as unavailable as was the pleasure of visiting national parks, monuments, museums or other American treasures. Americans lost jobs when their employers' businesses dwindled for various reasons. Businesses outside national parks had no tourist dollars to support their concerns. Private-sector businesses that contracted with government could not be reimbursed for their services. Some businesses could not obtain loans; others couldn't get licenses to conduct import-export business. Many people thrown off their jobs couldn't pay rents or automobile payments and their landlords or banks shared in suffering the losses. Persons who needed to travel overseas to tend to urgent matters couldn't get passports. And Americans didn't rejoice at this "freedom" from government because the federal government is not an enemy of its citizens nor is it as intrusive into private lives as Righties have maintained since the right first opposed the creation of the Constitution after trying to prevent America's independence from Great Britain.

At the time of the government closure, a right-wing spokesman labeled the President and Vice President "the budget-busting barons of bankruptcy," totally ignoring that it was the right that busted the budget with Reaganomics fairy tales, and some politicians who led the efforts to close government were the very people who helped enact Reagan's nonsense. Some of America's most-cynical observers concluded that the closure of government was an attempt to sabotage the economy leading up to the election so that the right could recapture the presidency.

The national financial problem of debt continues to be troublesome, but it is not by government taxing and spending on needful programs. Money from that spending quickly goes into the economy to help keep the economy moving. Government spending which goes to pay interest to those people who manipulated the system contributes to the problem, but so does that part of the private sector which views an American dollar as being more important than America.

US corporations, whose leaders are among those persons who complain about the size of government, have spent several years "downsizing" their work forces, which adds to the annual deficit in two ways. Downsizing deprives government of taxes it would have received from jobs had those jobs not been eliminated and costs to governments rise for many social programs. Persons who lost long-held jobs seldom resort to crime to survive, but their addition to the unused class forces some of those people at the bottom of the excluded class into crime to survive.

Downsizing removed almost 440,000 jobs from the United States in 1995, a decline from the peak of more than 615,000 jobs eliminated in 1993 and more than 500,000 jobs lost in 1994. Among job cuts announced in 1993 were 124,000 military positions; 100,000 federal civilian workers; 20,000 at General Motors; 28,000 at Boeing; 10,000 at Eastman Kodak; 13,000 at Woolworth; 8,000 at BellSouth; 7,500 at Digital Equipment; 5,000 at Travelers Corp.; 4,800 at Pratt & Whitney; 2,500 at Continental Airlines; 1,500 at Chevron, and many other smaller cuts. Prior to that Sears, Roebuck had announced 50,000 jobs to be eliminated while International Business Machines lopped off 25,000, United Technologies cut 10,500 jobs and 8,700 were gone at McDonnell Douglas.

Early in 1994, US corporations cutting jobs were GTE, with 17,000 jobs eliminated; Nynex, 16,800; Pacific Telesis, 10,000; Scott Paper, 8,300; Westinghouse, 6,000; Bristol-Myers, 5,000; Food Lion, 3,500; Eli Lilly, 2,600, and Gillette, 2,000. Later in the year, Sara Lee announced a reduction of 8,300 jobs to be followed by Digital Equipment's second round of cuts, this time 20,000 jobs to reduce the company to 65,000 employees from a 1990 level of almost 120,000. Other 1995 cuts were Fleet Financial, 5,000; US West Communications, 9,000; DuPont, 4,500; Raytheon, 4,400; and AT&T, 15,000. [59]

---

59 "Economists are different from you and me," Joe Urschel; *USA Today*; June, 23, 1994.

On the first working day of 1996, AT&T announced another 40,000 jobs to be eliminated and Apple Computer followed days later with plans to trim its 13,000-employee work force by 7.5-to-10 percent. Apple increased its layoff figure by 1,500 in the spring after a change of leadership. The American Broadcasting Company news program Nightline reported that 100,000 jobs were eliminated in January of 1996. Mergers have the same negative effect on the economy. After Wells Fargo Bank took over First Interstate Bancorp in January of 1996 it announced that it would close about 350 overlapping branches in California, and that would eliminate thousands of jobs. National layoffs were reported to be almost 170,000 in the first quarter of 1996—after Ford Motor Company announced 6,000 job losses—compared to less than 100,000 in the same period of 1995.[60]

In the four years from 1992, AT&T cut 123,000 jobs, according to *The New York Times*. IBM erased 122,000; General Motors, 99,400; Boeing, 61,000; Sears, 50,000; Digital Equipment, 29,800; Lockheed Martin 29,100; Bell-South, 21,200; McDonnell Douglas 21,000; Pacific Telesis, 19,000; Delta Air Lines, 18,800; GTE, 18,400; Nynex, 17,400; Eastman Kodak, 16,800, and Baxter International, 16,000.

Parade Magazine put the number of announced job layoffs between 1989 and the end of 1995 at three million and said the early 1996 figures were 74 percent higher than the figures for the same period in 1995. And all of that grew from Reaganomics. And in spite of it, Clinton's administration managed to add more than 22 million jobs to the economy (see chapter 11 for figures).

Job cuts from downsizing and mergers might help corporations cut expenses short term but those job cuts also removed hundreds of thousands of persons from the economy and reduced the amount of taxes those workers might have paid. If profits at the corporations improved, taxes on those profits could offset some of the taxes lost from idled workers, if corporations still paid taxes anywhere near their prewar levels. The layoffs increased costs for government for unemployment insurance, retraining and welfare, while pushing the excluded class further away from ever gaining employment that would help them escape exclusion.

Many of these job losses were through attrition or through early retirement that also costs government for Social Security payments, but keeps

---

60 "Layoffs increase during first three months of 1996," Del Jones; *USA Today*: April 9, 1996.

some people in the consumer class, although at a lower level. Some of the jobs may not have been lost as the economy improved and companies found they needed their employees. (After Boeing won a large contract in January 1996, it announced it would be hiring thousands of workers, although only a small percentage of the number terminated in previous years) Some of the jobs may reappear in the future, but many may be overseas where corporations can benefit with near-starvation wages. Some of the workers were absorbed in new companies or started their own business ventures.

But these hundreds of thousands of jobs will not be available for younger Americans joining the labor force.

After the layoffs, Wall Street investors perceived a more-profitable future and bid up the stock prices enabling corporate managers to exercise their stock options to make quick-and-easy financial windfalls. It's for this reason that Wall Street professionals are not best suited to determine what's best for the nation or what's best for any person who isn't an investor; they are too biased in perceiving only what's best for a company or for themselves. It was Wall Street insiders who wrote the regulations while in government service then went back to the private sector to exploit the economy with takeover fever conducted under their regulations. They cannibalized some firms by closing them to reduce competition or to sell the real estate for a quick profit and throwing thousands of people out of work. Such actions would lower taxes for government and increase the national and state debts, just for a quick profit increase, although the businesses were already profitable.

Other down sides to corporate layoffs were that unemployed workers put a downward tug on wages and salaries in other companies, which also retarded economic activity, and workers still employed had their morale and motivation damaged because of overwork or anxiety about their futures. This situation also points out an important fact that must be considered by politicians as they try to solve the budget mess: business goals and needs are not always compatible with national goals and needs. Business cuts "fat" and dumps the problem onto government. Government then needs money and must raise income; which it does with higher taxes, usually taxes on the consumers business needs to continue making a profit.

Special privileges for business, usually tax bribes or stagnant minimum wages, don't always benefit commerce when they lead to less consuming ability by the middle class that supports America's small businesses. As shown in previous chapters, middle-class Americans simply don't have the money to put into the economy because millions of high-paying jobs have gone to foreign nations, middle-class taxpayers have to pay for Reagan's transference of wealth to the upper class, the emphasis since World War II has been to take taxes off businesses and put the burden onto wage earners, and millions of jobs have been lost to corporate downsizing and mergers.

The problem of trickle-down economic problems was pointed out in *The Los Angeles Times* by David Kusnet in January of 1996 when he wrote, "you can't build prosperity on pink slips and pay freezes. Sluggish retail sales during the holiday season were only the latest sign of an economy dragged down by declining wages. New-home sales fell by 2.7% in October, despite declining mortgage rates. And auto sales dropped by 1 million from 1986 to 1994, despite a 10% growth in the adult population ... During the 1990s, workers' productivity has increased three times as fast as their real wages." He also said, "... it's a matter of common decency, as well as maintaining consumer demand, to let workers share in the wealth they create."[61] That's what Democratic Capitalism is all about.

SOLUTIONS, NONSOLUTIONS

As with any problem, there are no shortages of people or organizations proposing solutions. All proposals are needed because in some of them there may be the idea the nation needs. And more proposals are needed than that of simply cutting government spending or increasing taxes, although higher taxes on money intended for Treasury instruments would help a little. When the economy started to expand early in the Clinton tenure, one Wall Street disbeliever tried to downplay the success by intoning, "Yes, the economy is improving. But beyond beautiful speeches, what really has this administration had to do with it beyond some credit for deficit reduction?" But that's the entire idea. By reducing or eliminating the deficit, money that might have been invested in Treasury instruments would have to be directed into wealth-producing endeavors in the economy. A Wall Street insider should know that.

Horace Deets, executive director of the American Association of Retired Persons until 2001, opined in a 1992 column that:

---

61   David Kusnet; quoted in *USA Today'* s Opinionline from the *Los Angeles Times*; June 23, 1996.

"During the last 15 years, both defense expenditures and net interest payments on the federal debt have grown faster than entitlements in real terms as part of the federal budget. Include the savings-and-loan debacle, the revenue lost from tax cuts of the 1980s and skyrocketing healthcare costs, and you have the true causes of the budget deficit...

"AARP believes that one of the most effective ways to reduce the federal deficit is to control healthcare costs throughout society and ensure affordable, high-quality coverage for everyone. This is why our Association continues to make comprehensive healthcare reform a top priority."[62]

While Deets appears to have identified part of the problem and offered a partial solution, he failed to say how to control healthcare costs or how to ensure coverage for everyone.

Other so-called solutions included the typical right-wing stance. Scott A. Hodge of the Heritage Foundation dished out the standard conservative line in a *USA Today* opinion piece weeks later. He wrote that the only way to control the deficit and pare down the debt was through reduced spending on "wasteful programs" while trying to debunk the argument that higher taxes could be useful. Hodge wrote, "Not only will higher taxes hurt the economy, but it is doubtful that the money they raise will go toward deficit reduction." [63]

As already shown, higher taxes on money that otherwise would have gone into buying Treasury instruments did not hurt the economy, those taxes helped cut the deficit, and money spent on "wasteful programs" flowed into the economy to help keep it expanding. The Heritage Foundation said it would get rid of the deficit by making 120 budget cuts totaling $788 billion over five years and that would balance the budget by 1998.

But, as explained, cutting $788 billion out of the budget would take $788 billion out of the economy, and that would increase business failures and unemployment, would lower tax collections for all governments and increase costs for government programs such as unemployment insurance, Social Security, retraining and welfare. To handle these additional costs, government would have to raise taxes, exactly what the Heritage Foundation has always said it opposes.

---

62 "Curb the deficit by targeting *real* causes," Horace Deets; *AARP Bulletin*; September, 1992.

63 "Taxes not needed to cut deficit? Bunk!," Scott A. Hodge; *USA Today*; October 21, 1992.

Without using the ideas from the Heritage Foundation, Clinton had the budget showing a surplus in 1998 that lasted until 2001, when George Bush the Younger squandered it all.

One of the areas criticized by Hodge was the government paying $210 billion for overhead expenses (rent, utilities, travel, office expenses). But to reduce that spending would mean that real-estate corporations, utility firms, airlines and office-supply manufacturers and distributors would suffer a drain on their incomes. A more logical approach is to spur the economy first, then use the taxing authority to dampen inflationary pressure by draining excess money from the economy. That would reduce the deficit.

Americans, especially those at the Heritage Foundation and other Righties, should know that there is one important "wasteful program" in the federal budget and that is the payment of interest on the Reagan-double Bush debt that zipped past 20 percent of the budget in the second Bush's administration and was the second-highest budget expense—not counting entitlements programs of Social Security and Medicare—behind defense. This waste subtracted about $240 billion a year from the economy in 2008 to enrich the privileged few who then continue recycling their interest payments through the Treasury to attract more interest. That $240 billion figure is kept low by the paltry interest rates accompanying Bush the Younger's 2007–09 recession.

OTHER SOLUTIONS OFFERED:

Several solutions were cited in a USA Today column:

> *The Arizona Republic* said, "The only responsible way to reduce the debt is to pay it off, to resist new borrowing and slowly draw down the debt to manageable size." The newspaper didn't say how to accomplish that.

> In a *Philadelphia Inquirer* column, Edwin M. Yoder Jr. wrote, "The sane alternative is to stop piling up debt, and start paying it down." He, likewise, didn't say how.

> Debbie M. Price, a columnist for *The Fort Worth Star-Telegram* wrote that the nation should, "Cut spending first. Not later."[64]

A person only has to look at the California Experience to see that this approach does not work and is counterproductive.

Other positions were offered in a later Opinionline column.

---

64 "Tax hikes always roll down hill"; Opinionline; *USA Today*; February 25, 1993.

The *Chicago Tribune* said, "Deficit reduction requires raising taxes, slashing spending or both." Raising taxes works best when it targets money not intended to be used in the general economy and a reduction of spending works best when it's interest on the debt that's reduced.

Conservative Texas politician Rep. Dick Armey was quoted from *The Washington Times* in May of 1993 that, "The Clinton plan ... is the same old tax-and-spend approach we saw in the years of 'malaise' under Jimmy Carter. It is pure, Big Government liberalism and it will not work ... Unfortunately, this tax bill will grow the government and shrink the private sector."[65]

Armey was totally wrong. Clinton's plan cut the Reagan/Bush Republican deficit by nearly two-thirds and, by administration estimates, created more than 11 million jobs in Clinton's first term and reduced government bureaucracy by 200,000 in an expanding economy while being attacked by the Republican Congress. In his second term, Clinton added another 11 million jobs and produced four years (1998–2001) of surpluses.

The main thing that did not work in the Clinton administration was the deregulation zeal inherited from the Reagan/Bush regime. All that deregulation passed through a Republican Congress without a peep of warning from the GOP, most written by Republicans and slipped into must-sign bills as riders at the last minute, but some were also promoted by Clinton's Wall Street-linked advisors.

Carter's "malaise" left to Reagan the lowest ratio of debt to gross domestic product (32.58 percent according to the *Statistical Abstract of the United States*) since before the Great Depression and the lowest rate of poverty in the history of the nation (11.4 percent) in 1978 before being beaten in 2000 by Clinton who posted an 11.3 percent rate. Carter also had a record of job creation much greater than the record of Reagan/Bush. The theories of the far right, espoused by Armey, created the debt problem under Nixon, made matters worse with Reagan and would be devastating to the nation if ever they were tried again. They were tried again; by Bush the Younger and the result was a $12-trillion debt when he left office that won't be controlled for years, as it grows larger regardless of who must try to control it. Armey also has emerged as a leading proponent and sponsor of the "Tea Party movement, a right-wing rebellion protesting the very conditions Armey helped create and defend.

---

65   "Spread pain: Tax and cut"; Opinionline; *USA Today*: May 6, 1993

About the Clinton tax bill of 1993, another former Reagan aide wrote in *USA Today* that, "Taxes cannot be the solution to the deficit problem." That aide, Annelise Anderson of the Hoover Institution at Stanford University, claimed that, "The federal deficit is less important than federal spending; spending determines how much the government must take from the economy, whether in taxes or borrowing. Taxes always hurt the economy, and government borrowing makes less available for the private sector."[66]

Most of that is hogwash.

Government spending does not reduce money in the economy, it puts money into the economy; the same money that was taken from the economy in taxes. Taxing and spending is a valid way to move money out of nonproductive areas and into productive areas. i.e. stock-market speculation is nonproductive when it only transfers money from one person to another without an increase in value. Treasury bonds are nonproductive when interest paid goes for more Treasury instruments or stock-market speculation without passing through the economy.

But stock-market investing is productive when it funds creation of new industry or provides dividend income for retirement. Government spending likewise is productive when it results in jobs (taxpayers), construction-company contracts, sales for materials bought from merchants and better facilities for trade such as expanded ports for increased foreign trade. The key to economic benefit is how and where money is spent, not who spends it or how much is spent.

Taxing and spending are not the problem. To understand why the United States got into its financial mess we only have to look at the Republican presidential advisors, the same advisors who helped Reagan preside over the biggest peacetime borrowing binge in history—until Bush the Younger came along.

In 1992, columnist George Will pinned the nation's financial woes on the growth of entitlements and problems with worker productivity and savings.[67] Growth in entitlements is not the problem; growth of interest payments on the right's debt is a problem. Productivity shall continue to suffer as long as corporations conduct downsizing wars on their work forces or exclude employees from sharing in increased profits. More savings

---

66 "It's federal spending, sweetheart!," Annelise Anderson; *USA Today*; February 17, 1993.
67 "Make savings the only deductible," George Will: *Seattle Post-Intelligencer*; October 4, 1992.

are unrealistic when wages and salaries for most Americans are stagnant as prices rise, when many new jobs pay only at subsistence levels so a few executives can have more, when American factories close only to reopen in foreign lands, when taxes are continually shifted off business and onto individual taxpayers and when tax receipts must be used to pay interest on the folly of Reagan and the Bushes. After advisors, politicians and journalists offered silly, false or unworkable economic advice, some intelligent heavyweights offered their proposals.

Peter G. Peterson, industrial leader and Commerce secretary under Richard Nixon, proposed various suggestions in his book *Facing Up: How to Rescue the Economy from Crushing Debt & Restore the American Dream*. His proposals:

• Raise $532 billion with a five percent national sales tax. (That would remove $532 billion in spending money from the economy if money raised in taxes is not spent by government. And if it is spent, it doesn't help reduce the deficit.)

• Raise $166 billion with a 50-cent gasoline tax over five years. (That would make $166 billion less available to be spent elsewhere in the economy.)

• Create an "affluence test" for all recipients to "save" $249 billion. (This would be valuable, although not consistent with the equality principles of the nation. High-income retirees drawing Social Security benefits who use the extra income to buy Treasury instruments harm the economy.)

• Cut defense spending to "save" $230 billion and trim domestic spending 10 percent to "save" $118 billion. (See the California Experience.)

• Raise the Social Security age to 68 from 65 by the year 2006 to "save" $52 billion. (Probably Peterson's best suggestion but it must be accompanied by other moves, such as an end to corporate downsizing and mergers that eliminate hundreds of thousands of jobs and an end to moving American jobs overseas so corporations can benefit from near-starvation wages.) Limit the tax exclusion for employer-paid health care to boost tax revenues by $118 billion. (That idea might cut corporate profits, but corporations in the 1990s, when Peterson wrote his book, enjoyed record-high profits.)

• Increase premiums paid by Medicare recipients and increase deductibles for $99 billion in additional government revenue. (That would leave $99 billion less for spending in local small businesses.)

• Raise "sin taxes" on alcohol and tobacco to gain $76 billion more in revenues. (This also takes spendable cash out of the economy but would lower medical costs for persons who might quit abusing both products because of the added taxes.)

• Limit mortgage interest to boost $22 billion.[68] (That also reduces spendable cash by $22 billion.)

Peterson's later advices require the middle class to shoulder the burden most of all, very little from the aristocracy, with such things as slashes in Social Security and Medicare. He is famous for touting means testing to receive Social Security benefits, which would affect well-to-do Americans but not the ultra-wealthy. Peterson never suggests means testing for pensions of former members of Congress or political appointees, such as himself, who are mostly multimillionaires. Peterson is a billionaire (he was ranked 149th on the "Forbes 400 Richest Americans" in 2008 with a net worth of $2.8 billion). And he doesn't call for those who spent decades under Reaganomics loading up on Treasury instruments to help solve our problems.

Reformed politicians Paul Tsongas and Warren Rudman zoomed in on entitlement spending (Social Security, Medicare, farm support) going to the nation's well-to-do elite. They were right in their contention that people receiving more than $40,000 a year (that would be $50,000-plus today) could give up some of their income from government according to income levels. Tsongas wrote in *USA Today* that, "We make $81 billion in annual payments to individuals and families, mostly retirees, whose annual incomes are over $50,000. Clearly, we can no longer afford to do this."[69] But, also, no mention of the Reaganites and their raid on the Treasury.

During his run for the presidency in 1992, Texas billionaire H. Ross Perot advocated a plan that included:[70]

• Cut federal-government spending by $315 billion. ($315 billion less in the economy. Also, see the California Experience.)

---

68 "The Plan," Peter Peterson; *USA Today*; November 8, 1993
69 "How to cut deficit to zero," Paul Tongas and Warren Rudman; *USA Today*; September 20, 1993
70 H. Ross Perot presented his views in a television commercial that ran during the 1992 campaign for the presidency.

• A $49 billion increase in business taxes such as business-lunch write-offs and foreign-firm avoidance of taxes. (This would be a $49 billion decrease in business profits, but as shown above, that's not devastating because of record-high business profits at that time.)

• Other tax increases of $293 billion. (That $293 billion comes out of the economy.) But it would be a good idea if it targeted money that doesn't circulate in the economy, such as the continual flowing into and out of the Treasury that does nothing except add to the debt

• Entitlement reform, such as taxes on Social Security payments for the most-affluent and a decrease in healthcare spending. (Some of this is workable.)

• Tax decreases of $62 billion in the form of addition write-offs for such things as investments, research and development, worker training and startup investments.

Perot claimed this would "save" $754 billion, but as already shown, a reduction in government spending doesn't save money on a dollar-for-dollar basis. Nor would tax increases add to the Treasury on a dollar-for-dollar basis. Perot said we cannot do nothing. He was right. But we can't do what he suggested economically. Some nonbudgetary proposals by Perot had merit, such as election reforms, five-year wait for ex-politicians to become lobbyist and never lobbying for foreign governments, a simplified tax system, adequate TV time for all office seekers, and an adjustment of congressional retirement plans to reflect pensions ordinary Americans have.

Perot, who rightfully blasted trickle-down economics that created our problems, said we have 19th-century capitalism while our competitors have modern-day capitalism (co-operation of government and business working together for future benefits) but we really need 21st-century capitalism that features a supportive relationship between government and business. This observation was much more valuable than his proposals for tax cuts, spending increases, spending cuts and tax increases.

Just before the 1992 elections, Washington Post columnist David S. Broder addressed the problem in a column in which he wrote, "We can't ignore the problem because it is literally eating up our future. We can't gimmick our way out of it."[71]

---

71 "Gimmicks won't end our deficit woes," David S. Broder: *Washington Post* columnist, in *The Seattle Times*; October 4, 1992.

That is true. Raising taxes is a gimmick just as is cutting taxes. Cutting spending is a gimmick just as is increasing spending. But the most foolish of all gimmicks would be to go back to the "no taxes" refrain that started the deficit problem during the Vietnam Conflict or to go back to the trickle-down folly that exacerbated it. And revival of trickle down was the driving theme behind the 104th Congress under the leadership of then-Sen. Bob Dole and Rep. Newt Gingrich, who also made much noise indicating a desire to return to an America Righties think existed before the advent of the New Deal programs of President Franklin D. Roosevelt.

To address the conservative-created deficit/debt fiasco of the United States, President Barack Obama, early in his administration, appointed a commission of political insiders to come up with solutions to the problem. True to form, these insiders proposed the standard solutions: lower Social Security and Medicare payments while raising the eligibility retirement age for both. Added to the recommendations released late in 2010 were some spending reductions and/or tax increases in areas that would impact the working middle class the most.

Matters where the recommendations gave little or no concern:

- Income disparity in which the top one percent get nearly 25 percent of the nation's income;
- Unearned salary and bonuses for top corporate executives;
- Lagging wages for workers;
- Job creation;
- Outsourcing of jobs;
- Secret campaign contributions and spending by special interests;
- Fairness in taxation;
- Tax avoidance by huge campaign contributors;
- Government pensions and healthcare for millionaires;
- Allowing banks and corporations to run wild;
- Business corruption and/or scams;
- Those who have spent three decades loading up on Treasury instruments with money saved from tax cuts for the aristocracy;
- Reaganomics; the heart of all our financial problems.

Until the nation starts to address these issues, all "solutions" will be temporary.

Now we come to a real solution: Democratic Capitalism and how it would affect government taxes and budgets, healthcare and retirement, commerce and foreign aid.

And we must use Democratic Capitalism because the standard proposals all have problems, have been tried and have failed. The usual Republican response to cut spending only deprives the economy of money and that slows economic expansion or progress, which reduces tax intake. The common Democratic action to raise taxes does similar things as GOP spending cuts, it takes money from the economy and slows economic expansion, but when it puts that money back into the economy the result is often what it might have been had the taxes not been collected. Its only redeeming feature is that the new taxes can be used to spur economic growth by spending in some other area. But that doesn't necessarily reduce the budget deficit or shrink the debt. The solution to the nation's budgetary problem will require absolute co-operation among government, commerce and the citizenry, not the constant bickering that has marked the process recently. That co-operation is a must because it was co-operation of government and business, with the endorsement of the voting public, that caused the problem. But indications are that many creators of the problem wanted no part of the solution.

When Clinton's first economic package called for an increase from 34 percent to 35 percent on business profits above $10 million, many executives threatened to fire wholesale numbers of employees to compensate for the increased tax payments. Many of those businesses benefited greatly from the manipulation of the tax-and-spend budget process in the 1980s by accepting lower tax rates that provided an enlarged profit and allowed some business leaders to load up on Treasury bonds, bills and notes without hiring a single new employee. Under Clinton's plan, a small company with a $20-million pretax profit would see its net profit fall from $13.2 million to $13 million, hardly a reason to fire dozens, if not hundreds, of employees. Nor did budget proposals from the Republican Congress in 1995–96 call on business to assist in the deficit problem; most proposals mainly targeted programs that benefit citizens.

Democratic Capitalism offers the best way out of the nation's budget mess and could solve some other pressing problems in the process. Democratic Capitalism basically calls for all persons in a business to share fairly in the wealth they create. It does not allow for the top person, who controls the wealth, to take an unfair proportion for him/herself while leaving only bare essentials for those at the bottom who create the wealth—that's Plantation Economics.

How Democratic Capitalism Would Work:

Because business leaders love to claim that minimum wages are just fine for employees and higher minimums are detrimental to business, all persons employed in for-profit concerns shall receive minimum wages—the best figure is no more $12 per hour. That will guarantee every employee from janitor to chief executive officer a yearly income of $24,000 on 2,000 hours of work. An extra $1,000 can be added for December. Overtime will be paid in time off, not with more money, to assure the system is not abused. After deductions for legitimate expenses, the business will pay its taxes—on profits, not on income—and all profits after taxes shall be divided by the employees (75 percent) and owners (25 percent); a division that is fairly close to most present divisions of income.

Each employee shall have a designated number of profit-sharing shares according to relative his/her value to the company. The division shall provide one share for the lowest-compensated employee up to 25 shares for the highest compensated. But the 1:25 ratio would only apply to the largest concerns; smaller concerns would start at a 1:1 ratio and increase according to how many persons are employed in the company until reaching the top ratio.

An alternative method would cap the employer-to-employee profit ratio at 10:1 and the initial base wage also at the 10:1 figure, rather than the 1:1.

In an economic recovery, businesses seldom hire additional people to handle additional activity. Present employees are expected to handle increased productivity without increased compensation except for possible overtime. Only after the recovery has been sustained will new employees be added. With this minimum-wage/profit-sharing arrangement employees will be fairly compensated for their added productivity. Eventually that will result in a working arrangement where the workload is fair for everyone because workers will determine the point fairness starts and exploitation begins.

There has been much controversy in recent years about executive pay programs that often seem to have little relationship to a company's success. Government, which must look out for the interest of all people, and large shareholders have taken the lead in trying to rectify the situation but there is little each can do. Government has tried to use tax codes to control unjustified executive pay such as not allowing a deduction for excessive pay unless pay is tied to performance. But a little extra tax is not a strong enough deterrent on a multibillion-dollar corporation. Shareholders can complain and try to use their voting privileges to make needed changes, but management usually controls the majority of votes and controls the entire board of directors that determines pay, which is why management often can overcompensate itself.

Democratic Capitalism can solve problems when other schemes cannot. In Democratic Capitalism, business expenses and payroll come first, but political campaign donations by business will not be considered a business expense and cannot be written off. A business owner is free to make any political donation he or she wants but only from profit-sharing income and with no tax deduction possible. A company with an owner and one employee would have an equal split of profits after the owner takes the owner's 25 percent share. On a $10,000 monthly profit, the owner would take the $2,500 owners' share. Each would have their $2,000 monthly salary and the two would split the $7,500 employees' share of profits. The owner would have an income of $8,000 a month and the employee would make $5,500. No matter how low or how high the company's profit, the owner will always have a higher income.

Companies that don't create enough profit to provide profit sharing wouldn't be taxed by the federal government, and neither would the owner or employee. Presently, the payroll tax extracts much-needed cash from both owner and employee and that would end, making more money available to circulate in the economy.

As the company grows, the owner as the highest-compensated employee will be able to command a larger number of profit-sharing shares. With 10 employees, a ratio could be 2:1 with stages between the top and bottom (i.e., 1.1 shares, 1.2 shares, 1.3 shares). With the 2–to–1 arrangement the lowest-compensated employee in the example above would still get $5,500. The owner employed in the business, would greatly increase his or her income, and that would be incentive to increase the number of employees, which would only be possible with increased income. Productivity increases will be beneficial to the entire nation.

At 25 employees, the owners' profit-sharing advantage could be 3:1; at 50 employees, 4:1; at 100 employees, 5:1; at 250 employees, 6:1; at 500 employees, 7:1; at 750 employees, 8:1; at 1000 employees, 9:1; at 1550 employees, 10:1; on up until any firm with more than 100,000 employees would allow the top executive to have a 25:1 ratio. The CEO would have $250,000 in profit sharing annually if a clerk had $10,000. This ascending scale will provide business leaders with incentives to increase the size of their firms, not to fire employees just to "save" a dollar. These figures are only proposals; they can be adjusted whenever a better ratio might work.

In this arrangement, it is incumbent on all employees to take an active part in creating as much profit as they can because they all benefit from profitability and there would be no limit on how much anybody could earn. The highest compensated—the CEO—will want more employees, not fewer, and the lowest-compensated employees will want more profit. Labor unions will be concerned about not having more jobs than are needed—featherbedding—because too many employees would reduce the income for veteran union members. This should lead to an acceptable equilibrium because the CEO won't hire too many people just to get more profit sharing since over employment would dilute each share's value. Nor would an employer benefit by using part-time employees just to escape an obligation to provide benefits. Each employee, full-time or part-time, would get the same rate of pay and would receive profit sharing, although a person working 20 hours a week would get half a share for each full share provided to full-time employees.

Matters such as bonuses for executives would also be handled fairly. Much anger permeated society in 2010 when Wall Street firms offered billions of dollars in bonuses to executives after those firms were given billions of dollars in "bailout" funds from the federal government because the same executives drove the firms into financial ruin and the nation into the worst recession since the Great Depression. Under Democratic Capitalism bonuses would come from real profits, not paper scams. And those bonuses, with no government say on the size would, have to come from the profit-sharing funds of the corporation's employees or the owners (stockholders) and would have to be approved by those groups in supervised voting. Corrupt boards of directors would have no say. If a CEO is valuable to the corporation, a bonus could be approved to keep that executive, but an incompetent executive would not get approval. Executive-termination packages—called "golden parachutes"—would also have to be approved in like manner. A totally incompetent manager might get something to leave, and again, corrupt boards of directors wouldn't be involved. This rewards competent, valuable executives but not incompetent executives. Such bonuses and golden parachutes would be taxed as if they were employee profit-sharing income.

It should be clear that Democratic Capitalism is biased in favor of the entrepreneur, who stays on to manage his/her creation, and it is fair to employees who help create a company's wealth. It is less generous to professional managers who cannot profit merely by controlling the wealth; they must improve wealth-creating activities through their leadership in order to gain higher incomes. By benefiting the entrepreneur/manager the most, a firm's creator has the income to reinvest in the company to make it grow. Professional managers at corporations also hold numerous shares in the corporations they manage, so they would increase their income by paying dividends to all shareholders. In that way they would be rewarding themselves for their successes, not merely for control.

Computer software giant Microsoft has been credited by many industry analysts with creating more employee millionaires than any company in the history of commerce—*The Seattle Times* reported in the 1990s 3,000 millionaires in a work force of less the 20,000 persons; and most employees haven't been on the job long enough to become wealthy. Microsoft created millionaires with a form of Democratic Capitalism; compensating employees with low or moderate salaries and with stock options and merit bonuses. As Microsoft stock continued to rise in price and split into additional shares, many employees became wealthy. Some then retired early—in their 30s and 40s—and turned their attention to enterprises that have benefited the greater Seattle, Washington, community.

Startup companies that may be pinched for profits can emulate Microsoft and pay employees with stock for any amount over the minimum wage. Employees, who have relied for years on profit sharing for a major portion of their income, are the type of employee a startup company would want and who would be more receptive to an opportunity to grow with the company than would employees who have had all income generated from a set low or moderate salary. Established corporations should not pay their employees in new stock because that would diminish the value of stock now held by the company's owners, but established firms can profit by sharing with employees the wealth those employees created.

This form of Democratic Capitalism would work fine with for-profit businesses but it must be modified to fit nonprofit concerns or special types of employees.

The second type of employee would be contract employees, who would be employed by nonprofit concerns such as government, foundations or churches. They would be compensated with a contracted amount, exactly as now.

Independent contractors would be those people who toil for profit-making concerns, but not as permanent employees. They would work for many firms or individuals in such fields as carpentry, lawn care or gardening, or as longshoremen, farm workers, house cleaners or painters. They would be paid as contract employees with a set amount for their work just as they are now paid.

The fourth type of employee would be the self-employed. This field would include such people as entertainers, athletes, writers, artists or free lancers in several other fields. They may work for one firm or one individual, several firms or several individuals or only for self. Noncorporate farmers would also be included. They would differ from independent contractors in that they have added expenses for agents, publicists, managers or brokers, who also would be self-employed or corporate employees.

The fifth type of employee would be crossovers, such as a newspaper reporter employed full time who has income from magazine articles or books, and persons who must work two jobs in order to make ends meet.

Retirees would be similar to independent contractors because their income may come from several sources.

How each group would be subjected to taxation is covered in detail in another chapter.

Democratic Capitalism would benefit the nation in several ways. Democratic Capitalism, if accompanied by realistic healthcare reform, will enhance the enterprising spirit of Americans and should lead to more business formation based on ability to create rather than on desperation. That business formation could begin to provide the type of jobs needed so that members of the excluded class can begin to move into the included class. Inclusion would start to solve social problems like welfare dependency and

crime, which could lead to true smaller government, not smaller government created by a refusal to assist the lower classes.

Democratic Capitalism would ease inflationary pressures in the United
States, because there would be no affect on wages and salaries dictated by
unemployment statistics. A low unemployment rate would not create upward pressure on salaries, which often leads to inflation, and there would
be no need to increase unemployment to remove inflationary pressures.
Inflation wouldn't be affected if unemployment were at one percent or 10
percent. The nation would benefit from only low unemployment figures.

Democratic Capitalism would make the dollar a stable commodity and
will stabilize foreign currencies of nations that join in practicing Democratic Capitalism. When two or more nations with Democratic Capitalism
engage in trade, the relative stability and value of currencies would allow
totally free trade—as New York now enjoys with Pennsylvania—without
advanced nations being victimized by nations practicing Plantation Economics; the main reason companies now leave America to exploit foreign
labor.

Democratic Capitalism should lead to a reduction in unemployment and
the costs to government that entails because companies would be able to
avoid some financial problems that lead to layoffs and management would
benefit more from employing workers than from forcing employees into
unemployment.

Democratic Capitalism could solve the problem of too little savings in
the United States without any outside force or entity trying to compel more
savings. Because management and labor alike would be assured of only a
basic income, both would soon learn the importance of saving and investing
during times of prosperity for times when incomes lag. Savings then could
be used for economic growth.

Democratic Capitalism would reduce the need for regulations over corporate acquisitions and takeovers. A company could use only owners' profits to acquire another company because using workers' money would be the
same as theft from those employees. In those occurrences where employees'
profit is used, workers must give their approval and those workers must
benefit from the takeover. That benefit may require promotions for all employees who received less profit because of the cost of a takeover. That facet
could prevent takeovers that are harmful to competition without imposing
heavy-handed government interference.

Democratic Capitalism would provide a mechanism to monitor the necessity of price increases in the economy. When gasoline prices rise each spring, many critics claim the oil companies are gouging the consumers at the beginning of the traditional warm-weather driving season. Oil executives and business apologists said the 1996 rise in prices was due to a colder-than-usual winter in which crude oil had to be used for heating fuel rather than being refined into gasoline for automobile consumption. In other years, price increases are blamed on oil spills, turmoil in oil-producing countries, hurricanes in the Gulf of Mexico, inadequate refinery capacity or many other reasons. In the 1996 "crisis" executives said prices for crude oil had risen from $17 a barrel to $24 (a 41% increase) during the spring. The left called for "investigations" to find out the cause for the price increases, while the right used the situation to reissue another call to cut the taxes that were being used to combat the debt that was increased by the right's shenanigans. With turmoil in the Mideast in early 2011, prices again skyrocketed with the price of a barrel of oil well above $100 and the same political stances emerged. As in the past, where the American public adjusted, it will adjust again.

With Democratic Capitalism, the amount of income derived by oil-industry workers would indicate if there was gouging or if price increases were justified. If personal income in the industry took a gigantic leap upward, there would be evidence the industry was gouging the public only to take advantage of the increased driving during the warmer months. If personal incomes remained stable, we would have evidence that any price increase is justified.

Democratic Capitalism might also lead to a much-smaller Internal Revenue Service, but smaller because a large IRS would no longer be necessary rather than an IRS made smaller so special interests could be more capable of escaping their obligations after tax laws are tinkered with to benefit the privileged class.

Later chapters will demonstrate the workings of these principles.

And Democratic Capitalism might save major-league baseball from itself. Professional baseball has always practiced a form of Plantation Economics peculiar to an industry composed of millionaire employees and multimillionaire employers. In baseball, income is heavily dependent on the television-market size of each team rather than on the ability to generate attendance and the teams of the major markets keep for themselves all the income. Even though a smaller-market team, such as the Seattle Mariners, often has higher attendance than the biggest-market team, the New York Yankees, the Yankees are financial winners because of the television contract in the large market while the Mariners had been money losers because of a small market. (It's also surprising that Seattle was considered a small-market team when the population within a day's drive is about 15 million persons while the Colorado Rockies were considered a large-market team when the population within the same distance to Denver, Colorado, without entering another team's market area, is about half the Seattle-area market.) When new ownership made the Mariners a profitable enterprise, with a new publicly financed stadium, its status was upgraded to nearly large market.

When two teams play, only the home team profits, and that is Plantation Economics because the visitors no longer get a share of the game's receipts. This unequal distribution of money forces a small-market team to demand financial concessions from its home city or it threatens to leave for another city which would agree to those concessions. Wherever the team plays, the host city is forced to provide a playing stadium. The stadium is often operated by the city or county as a "loss leader" because a major-league franchise creates peripheral economic activity on game days.

When a proposal to build a $250 million stadium in Milwaukee, Wisconsin, was defeated in 1996, major-league baseball issued a warning that without the stadium the Milwaukee Brewers would be encouraged to relocate. Baseball is merely taking advantage of an opportunity that state and city governments brought on themselves by historically offering tax lures and other freebies to entice corporations to expand into their areas or to close an old plant elsewhere and put a new plant where tax bribes are offered.

This maneuver has always been easier for politicians than expanding the state's economy to create the same number of jobs a moved plant would provide.

The Democratic Capitalism solution for major-league baseball, which claimed a $376 million loss in 1994 and a $325 million loss in 1995, is to evenly divide all after-expenses revenue between the two teams because each team is responsible for generating half of the income. It doesn't matter in which stadium a game is played or which team has the television contract, a game between the Yankees and the Kansas City Royals depends equally on both teams in the same game. The Yankees' large television contract would generate no money if the Royals and their small television contract were not present. So, all money—even the TV money of a visiting team—should be divided 50-50 because it was earned 50-50. Baseball is unlikely to solve its problems because owners and players both profit from the present chaos. Cities and states are helpless because other cities and states will take any team that can't profit from the original city or state.

Baseball's losses are generally attributed to the multimillion-dollar salaries paid to superstars and journeymen alike. Baseball needs to use the Democratic Capitalist approach of paying all players the minimum amount, then dividing profits in accordance to which players are most valuable to the team. The superstars would get the majority of the money and the rookies would get the same minimum they now receive. If a player becomes indispensable to the team, his larger share of the profits should not be resented by his teammates because they would recognize his value. If he is not worth the amount paid, his teammates would make sure management knew of the overcompensation. Many professional sports suffer from the multimillion-dollar free-agent superstar who signs a multiyear contract then proceeds to perform below expectations because he no longer has motivation to excel. Democratic Capitalism is designed to maintain consistent incentive for all because good performance would generate income while underperformance would reduce income. With owners being assured of 25 percent of the team's profit, they could afford to finance stadiums for themselves or to pay enough rent that government-provided facilities are no longer money losers. Owners could no longer claim that the team is losing money and needs to be subsidized by taxpayers or it would move; every major-league team would generate a profit.

Chapter 8. Better Budgeting

Budget Baloney, Not Pork

The main obstacle to enacting a federal budget in 1995–96, even though both Republican and Democrats agreed on a seven-year plan using economic figures from the same source, was the insistence by many right-wing Republicans that the nation return to a new version of Reaganesque "trickle-down" shenanigans. That insistence was similar to the millions of Russians who want to return to Stalinism, even though it was the main cause of present Russian social ills, as Reaganomics is the root cause of many of America's problems.

It was dishonest to repackage "trickle-down" economic theories that called for tax reductions for the well-to-do on the argument that about $350 billion in tax cuts would move down through the economy to create jobs for the working class, and that growth would provide more taxes needed to reduce the deficit, which would solve the national debt. Never mind that this argument was Reagan's contention for his trickle-down plot which greatly increased the debt just as earlier trickle-down schemes helped accelerate the decline of the Great Depression and George W. Bush's trickle down of this century exacerbated the problem. Even Clinton's call for about $80 billion in trickle down was risky as was George W. Bush's "Troubled Asset Relief Program" scheme to rescue huge banks and Obama's tax reductions and part of his bailout in his first budget, a retooling of Bush's plans.

It was also dishonest for Republicans to proclaim that their budget proposal would eliminate the deficit. The Congressional Budget Office certified that the GOP figures would indicate balanced books, but Republican figures didn't reveal that the GOP budget called for borrowing hundreds of billions of dollars through 2002, the year the budget was to be balanced. That borrowing was to come from Social Security funds that are considered surplus after paying required benefits. Clinton's budget plans also called for the same borrowing. This type of borrowing is another way of shifting the tax burden onto the working middle class while leaving the well-to-do Americans less taxed because no payroll taxes were levied on high incomes. Social Security over taxation is also part of the Reagan legacy, coming from the 1983 "reform" of the retirement system by the administration, the Republican Senate and the conservative House on the argument that Social Security had to be "saved" from bankruptcy.

Also dishonest was the claim that less government spending amounted to "savings" and spending by government was "waste" from "pork-barrel" spending. The California Experience showed that a dollar unspent does not mean a dollar saved. Most money spent by government, no matter how silly or unnecessary, causes economic activity that creates jobs and that means profits for businesses, income for workers and taxes for government, and none of that is "waste."

All the whining over "pork-barrel" spending wears a little thin when analyzing commercial activities. "Pork," according to the political right, applies to spending which would provide many construction workers with a year or two of work at modest wages, plus income and profit for their employers. After Clinton's 1993 stimulus package of $16.9 billion died in a Republican filibuster, Texas billionaire H. Ross Perot, on NBC's Today show, criticized the plan that called for building some swimming pools for inner-city residents, saying it would have cost $89,000 just to create one job for one year. But, that's a too-simplistic look at a stimulus plan.

If government spends money to build a swimming pool, the money is spread around in the economy. Most will go to businesses that furnish the materials and to wages of the construction firm's workers. Some will go for the firm's overhead and profit and what is spent with suppliers or to rent equipment. If private industry spends money to build a similar swimming pool, the same economic principles would apply—only a fraction of the total spending would go to create one job. A contract of $890,000 to

build swimming pools would create 10 jobs, by Perot's calculations.
With $25,000 for salaries, $250,000 would pay those 10 workers for one year. Another $250,000 may go to the construction company for executive salaries, business expenses and overhead, equipment rental, taxes and profit. That leaves $390,000 for building materials, which is income for the supplier firms. That income provides taxes paid from salaries and from business profits. An $890,000 contract issued by a private firm to provide executive comfort would do much the same except it would decrease tax intake to government because the initial $890,000 would be a business expense and that would be tax deductible. So eliminating "pork-barrel" projects to balance the budget is just another way of attacking the working class while leaving unaffected the tax bribes that go to some special corporations to entice them to do many things they ought to do just to conduct business.

The criticism didn't factor in the possibility that these swimming pools could be in use for 50 years up to a full century, providing jobs—and tax revenues—the entire time in addition to the recreation uses for the local population.

In the spring of 1995, the Republican Congress unveiled its proposals for federal spending which it said would "balance" the budget by the year 2002 by reducing expenditures by $1.4 trillion and would help pay for the proposed tax cuts.

The resolution's proposals with some of its biggest problems:

• Medicare spending would be pegged at a level below the projected paces of inflation and enrollment to save $280 billion. (If Medicare spending lagged projected needs, the shortage would have to be made up somewhere else, which would mean less money available to be spent in local small businesses. Savings are questionable.)

• Medicaid spending would save $187 billion by being set at a rate of increase also unlikely to accommodate future costs and enrollment. (Same problem as with Medicare, therefore there may be no savings.)

• Welfare programs would be turned over to the states with block-grant funding from the federal government. Under the Constitution's Fourteenth Amendment, state laws must apply to all persons equally, and illegal immigrants, as persons, would be eligible for state welfare programs.

- No new public housing would be built and federal employees would contribute more to their retirement plans. (This also reduces spending in the economy.)
- Defense spending would rise $92 billion for weapons and military pay and the GOP projected that some savings would be realized by reducing the number of civilians in defense work. (Increases in unemployment will never contribute to savings for government, as repeatedly shown in this book.)
- Aid to Russia would be reduced. (That would be shortsighted, for such spending is our best bet for maintaining good relations and is thus the best defensive spending this nation could ever do.)
- Farm price support would be cut, as would agriculture research and some state co-operative programs to save $20 billion.

The House said it could save even more by eliminating hundreds of programs and some agencies, such as departments of Commerce, Education and Energy. Also targeted were the Legal Services Corp., Clinton's Goals 2000 education reform—two programs that assist the lower classes—and funds for the Corporation for Public Broadcasting. (As often shown often in this book, less spending doesn't translate into savings.)

But many economic experts questioned whether the Republican plan would work. Balancing the budget was an admirable goal, they acknowledged, but slashing some government spending could be counterproductive. One economic analyst said, "Our grandchildren might be closer to being out of debt from a balanced budget, but they will be poorly educated and driving on pot-hole-driven roads."

Others warned about reducing public investment in technology, because foreign nations could move ahead of the United States leaving America with reduced export trade and a further loss of high-wage jobs. Creation of new industry for employment of millions of Americans may disappear. Experts cited the American-dominated computer industry as an example of success of government-funded public investment. *The Chicago Tribune*[72] cited nearly 400 economists saying in an open letter to Congress that America must increase education and training and that the inner cities must be rebuilt, bridges repaired, airports expanded, technology generated and poor children kept healthy. Some of the GOP-proposed spending cuts might

---

72 "Experts fear budget-cutters will hurt standard of life," William Neikirk: *The Chicago Tribune* printed in *The Seattle Times*; May 21, 1995.

jeopardize these areas, but wouldn't save the money promised because future tax income would be lowered.

Whenever the issue of the budget comes up, everyone with a list of programs or items to be cut and will offer what they deem to be workable solutions. The favorite target of the right is always social spending; the target of the left is the Pentagon.

In the early months of 1993, both *The New York Times* and *USA Today* offered articles explaining why military spending could be slashed to facilitate "savings."[73] We only have to re-examine the California Experience to see that simply spending less on the military doesn't equate to savings, just as less spending on social programs won't solve any problems. Agriculture-support spending is also frequently cited as an area of "savings." But farm subsidies for family farms are beneficial because those farms spend money for seed grain, fuel and farm equipment while maintaining these types of small businesses as going concerns. Payments to Beverly Hills "farmers"—those who speculate in agricultural land only for subsidies—goes into Treasury instruments or stock-market speculation.

Americans should not be conned into thinking that merely spending less by government will be economically beneficial or that more spending by corporations or individuals contains a magical quality that will solve all problems. Unbiased observations point to evidence that some types of government spending can be more beneficial than either corporate or individual spending. Nor should Americans be conned into thinking that political pontificating for prudent spending and for a balanced budget will result in either. The American Broadcasting Company's "Prime Time Live" reported in June of 1993 that in the last days of the first Bush administration, Cabinet members or department heads were paid or recommended for more than $650 million in bonuses before the administration relinquished power. The Republican National Committee then bought a full-page ad in *USA Today* March 23, 1993, to denounce the Clinton budget proposal and to offer an alternative plan. The ad said Clinton was wrong because:

> Tax increases have never reduced the deficit." [Not true; the GOP/ conservative deficit was greatly reduced after the tax increases by four years of surpluses, 1998–2001.]

---

73 "Saving found at Pentagon," Jerome Weiner and Kosta Tsipis; *The New York Times* printed in *The Seattle Post-Intelligencer*; March 7, 1993 and "There's room to cut defense budget safely"; *USA Today* editorial; February 9, 1993.

President Clinton's tax increase will slow economic growth and cost jobs." [Proved false as the nation embarked on an economic recovery on lower interest rates which resulted in the Dow Jones Industrial Average surging from 3,241.95 the day Clinton was inaugurated to 10,678.28 the day Clinton left office as unemployment rates dipped even while corporate America was eliminating millions of jobs through downsizing, mergers and moving plants to foreign nations.]

President Clinton's new spending increases the deficit." [That didn't happen as the deficit began an immediate decrease after the budget plan passed without a single Republican supporting it. Under Clinton the deficit of $290 billion left by Bush was reduced to about $255 billion the first year and then to about $200 billion the second year. A new budget was submitted—again massively opposed by Republicans—and the deficits were cut even more moving down to $164 billion and then down to $107 billion, at which point the GOP jumped on the bandwagon and submitted a proposal to balance the budget by 20002. But Clinton beat them to it and balanced the budget years before the deadline without Republican assistance.]

The GOP ad concluded, "We don't have a $300 billion deficit because we tax too little; it's because we spend too much."[74]

Americans must learn that it was not "spending too much" on needful social programs that caused that "$300 billion deficit," it was the Reaganite raid on the Treasury that resulted in "spending too much" on interest payments to Reaganites. For all its rhetoric about the national deficit, the Republican Party has done nil to solve the problem it was instrumental in causing and its "solution" of cutting federal spending has been tried and has failed, as the California Experience has shown beyond any doubt, just as tax cuts for the wealthy to create economic miracles have been dismal failures.

Now for Something Entirely Different

Because Republican plans never work and usually make matters worse, it's time to give up on trying to get the same old tired formulas to produce new miraculous results. To get new results, the nation must embark on new formulas in a new direction.

That new direction calls for four or five budgets, not one, and no government spending could be considered "off budget." Also to be a must, is

---

74 "An Important Economic Decision Is About To Be Made And There Is A Clear Choice"; an advertisement in *USA Today* by the Republican National Committee; March 23, 1993.

that one budget could not "borrow" from another, as the general budget has done from the Social Security program since 1984, and each budget must be funded by only its lawfully designated sources. Short-term borrowing by the Treasury would still be authorized to pay salaries and bills until tax revenues arrive. But borrowing must be restricted to one specific budget and that budget would be responsible for paying its debt.

Budget No. 1 would be the National Defense Budget. It would include such things as the departments of Defense, Homeland Security, Veterans Affairs, the National Aeronautics and Space Administration, Federal Emergency Management Agency and Office of Personnel Management. It would also be responsible for the national debt. This budget would be funded entirely by profit taxes on corporations. The total cost will come down by hundreds of billions of dollars because it contained programs that will be moved to the third budget.

Budget No. 2 would be the General Government Budget. It would include all activities not covered in the other budgets. It would be funded entirely by profit taxes from noncorporations that engage in interstate commerce, such as franchises. It, too, includes some costs to be shifted to the third budget.

Budget No. 3 would be the Human Services Budget. It would include the Department of Health and Human Services and bureaus and programs from the other two budgets. It would be funded only by taxes on the profit-sharing income of American workers, retirees, and those amounts exceeding the basic tax-free income of others. It will have two areas of concern; Social Security and a new-and-expanded health system for the nation. The cost of this budget will grow greatly when such things as "universal healthcare for everyone" is added, taking all healthcare costs off America's business community and shifting the cost to the consumers through this budget. That program will be detailed in Chapter 9.

This Human Services Budget will lower the costs of the first two budgets because all healthcare expenses for federal employees, including members of Congress, will be shifted to this budget. Members of Congress will then have to live under the same programs they think are fine for the American public; they can no longer provide superior benefits for themselves while leaving ordinary Americans fretful about the future if hit by devastating illnesses or injuries.

A fourth budget would be for transportation. It would be funded by gasoline taxes and such incomes as airport or docking fees and taxes on anything related to transportation. It would handle all facets of transportation, removing them from the first two budgets.

A fifth budget would be temporary and would pay for the wars the past administration so dearly wanted. It would be funded by a tax on all dividend payments from corporations and a tax on stock and bond transactions, and when the war costs are paid, all dividends could be tax free; this provision would only be resurrected for future war funding. It would reflect the dictum of James Madison who said: "Each generation should be made to bear the burden of its own wars, instead of carrying them on, at the expense of other generations."

By reducing the debt by this five-budget proposal, several hundred billions in interest costs can be saved and used to create wealth for the nation instead of draining wealth to enrich those who loaded up on Treasury-debt instruments over the past three decades. And the nation could begin to retire the debt held by foreign nations that drains billions of dollars in interest payments annually from the United States economy. Funding for these needful programs can be achieved without the wholesale firings of federal workers that the right wants to conduct. Funding can be done without devastating important areas of the economy, as the California Experience shows will happen with only reliance of reducing government spending.

Keep Congress Busy

With four or five budgets to consider, maybe Congress would be busy enough that it wouldn't have time for harassment such as the White House travel-office affair in which independent auditors found financial irregularities serious enough to warrant some discipline of the seven-man staff. Congress took up considerable time over many years using the Whitewater real-estate venture and the travel-office matter in an attempt to "Nixonize" President Clinton and his wife, but may find themselves targets for "Nixonization" in the future.

It was strange that the Republicans in Congress were "shocked" that Hillary Rodham Clinton supposedly "sacked" seven veteran government employees in the White House travel office to "turn the operations over to her friends" at the same time Congress was trying to force the nation to accept GOP plans to sack hundreds of thousands of veteran government employees and "privatize" many government functions.

One Republican candidate in the presidential primary campaign of 1996 promised to fire "one third" of federal employees if he were elected. The seven "sacked" travel-office bureaucrats ended up on other government jobs or retired with government pensions many Republicans often denounce as lucrative; unlike the hundreds of veteran nonpolitical government employees the GOP fired soon after taking control of Congress in 1994. Many congressional Republicans then boasted in their 1996 re-election campaigns that they had reduced congressional staffs by a third (i.e., fired 33 percent of employees for no reason other than political and none of the fired employees had ever been accused of any wrongdoing). That mass firing hasn't resulted in any benefit to the nation, as the present financial situation shows.

At the time of the travel-office hysteria, an oceanic-research ship ported in Seattle was decommissioned because of budget cuts, its crew was fired and its mission was put up for bid by private concerns. Some of the deposed crewmen wound up unemployed or toiling at whatever part-time labor they could find. A Russian ship, with a Russian crew, was awarded the research contract worth more than $1.5 million. Those Russians didn't pay United States taxes on their income.

With up to five budgets to consider, Congress then could go back to the Founding Fathers' original intent that congressional hearings be used to gather information to assist Congress in its legitimate function of legislating to benefit the nation and should never again be used for harassment as done in the travel-office affair and during the McCarthy era of the 1950s.

CHAPTER 9. HEALTH OF THE NATION

REFORM A GOOD BEGINNING

Republicans in the 104th Congress ballyhooed their Contract with America pledge to make laws imposed on the American people also applicable to Congress. That was an easy promise. The GOP Congress never made an attempt and its leaders never mentioned any intention to make laws benefiting members of Congress applicable to the people. The two congressional benefits withheld from the people involve one of the most-generous pension plans in America and top-of-the-line healthcare benefits. Not much can be done about the pensions other than paring down benefits for politicians so they resemble what the middle class has; but Congress most certainly will never to do that. But healthcare can be altered so politicians have the same coverage as other Americans. And, if politicians do not want health coverage for all Americans, they shouldn't have any for themselves.

The 2010 healthcare reform bill passed by Congress was a beginning to clean up a problem after a century of failures, but it was only the beginning. Much more needs to be done.

Typical of Hypocright positions were counter arguments concerning Medicare spending. When President Bill Clinton attempted healthcare reform in 1993 Republicans argued that reducing projected future spending on Medicare and on Medicaid in the seven years ending in 2002 would "reform" the system and "save" the programs. But when President Barack

Obama proposed reductions in Medicare spending in 2010, Republicans rushed in to claim reduced spending would imperil retired Americans and the GOP would "save" the system by opposing all Medicare spending cuts.

To proclaim that a three, five or seven percent increase in future spending would "save" Medicare when no one is capable of knowing how much future spending would be needed is dishonest. With medical-care inflation and increases in enrollment, the system would most certainly need increases in spending. Should medical-care costs deflate and Americans become healthier needing less medical treatment, less funding would be required.

If Medicare spending does not keep pace with cost increases and enrollment growth, the program would experience a cut in services; regardless of politicians' protestations to the contrary. A two percent annual increase in enrollment and an eight percent yearly inflation rate for medical care (the lowest annual figures during the first half of the 1990s) over seven years result in a need for nearly doubling of the funding just to maintain par on services. But, when members of the populous Baby Boom generation begin retiring en masse this century, enrollment growth will be much more than the historic annual two percent. The eight percent increase rate for health-care was historically low, annual inflation usually ran into double digits.

But right-wing politicians constantly distort this situation by excluding pertinent information. Rep. Steve Stockman, R-Tex., in a 1996 radio ad paid by House funds asked his constituents to participate in an hour radio town hall show in which, "I will be discussing the fact that Medicare spending is actually increasing from $4,800 per person this year to $7,100 per person by the year 2002."

That increase is a $2,300 rise and is 48 percent of $4,800. What Stockman didn't say is that, using real historic figures on inflation and enrollment growth, Medicare would need a 97 percent increase in funding over seven years, not the 48 percent that he cited in his ad and which most conservative members of the Republican Congress demanded. If medical inflation were miraculously eliminated and the only increase present was the two percent enrollment growth, a 15 percent rise in funding over seven years would provide the same services. If medical inflation is controlled original funding would exceed the cost and enrollment growth, the program would then be overfunded and could be adjusted downward in the future. Simply making less government money available would do nothing to control medical inflation or to address waste and fraud in the system; the waste and fraud Righties complain about but do nothing to fight. Requiring a higher copayment and deductibles from retirees or forcing their adult offspring to pay more for the retirees' care to compensate for shortages in funding only leaves less money to be spent with local small businesses. In the early 1990s, conservative politicians in Washington state pushed through a voter-approved referendum that limited state government spending increases to a formula based on inflation and population growth. But, when it came to Medicare's future, conservative Washington politicians in Congress refused to use the same formula.

In his 2010 State of the Union speech, President Obama said that if anyone had a better idea about reforming healthcare in America than the proposal before Congress at that time he would like to hear about it. Such a better idea is proposed in the following paragraphs.

That better system needed to "save" Medicare and Medicaid involves an entirely new system of providing healthcare coverage in the United States, merely tinkering with government spending or leaving it up to the states or to the "private sector" won't do. Tinkering with finances by merely providing less money doesn't result in "savings" or "reforms" and the private sector is primarily concerned with profit, not with healthcare. And the estimated 45,000 needless deaths that occur annually in the United States because Americans can't afford the healthcare all other industrial nation can afford at lower costs, should be considered homicide by government; by a government that refuses to do what other nations easily do.

The 100 percent GOP opposition in Congress to attempts in Obama's administration at reforming the system came almost exclusively from the same people who thought Reaganomics was a great idea and who were wholeheartedly behind George W. Bush's destruction of America. They harped that Obama should just scrap his efforts, "start over again and do it right." They never say what "right" is and in the 20-year reigns of Ronald Reagan and the two George Bushes they never attempted to do the right thing about the healthcare system in America. When Clinton attempted reform, their hissy fits resulted in destruction of his efforts and they never offered any better ideas. They should not be listened to on this matter.

Whatever the outcome of Obama's campaign for healthcare reform and what he is able to extract out of Congress over the next few years; one thing is certain: it won't be enough, because it is only tinkering. Tinkering would only be a temporary fix that should be enhanced by something better.

What is better follows.

Taxes on individual profits pay for Social Security and health insurance for all, and nothing else. This is a replacement for the present payroll tax and personal income tax. When we can match other advanced countries with universal health coverage spending only 10 percent of GDP on health, we will free up hundreds of billions of dollars to circulate in the economy. That will create growth. And we don't need to reduce spending to 10 percent; 15 percent would be much better, 13 percent even better.

One of the lamest ideas in President Obama's proposal and included in the healthcare reform bill he signed is the requirement that Americans be forced by government to buy health insurance from a private-sector insurance company or that employers be required to offer health coverage. That does little to cover all persons, because the main reason nearly 50 million Americans didn't have coverage is the prohibitive costs. Proposals to offer cash assistance to those who couldn't afford health insurance only brought out irrational fears about increasing the deficit by politicians who spent much of three decades adding debt on debt on debt under Reagan-Bush-onomics. And our businesses are less able to compete in the global market because healthcare costs are too cumbersome.

Because most corporations pay little or no federal taxes, the cost of health insurance and Social Security taxes are major drains on their profits since they don't benefit from the deductions that would be beneficial if they did pay taxes. Democratic Capitalism would remove those costs making the corporations more profitable, which, in turn, would make the employees and shareholders more profitable. Then, individuals would pay for their healthcare and Social Security and still have a higher income.

Requiring individuals to buy health insurance may be unconstitutional because government doesn't have a specific constitutional authority to dictate that to any American. Government can regulate interstate commerce to require most businesses to provide coverage and to tax and spend to provide the coverage as "general welfare," and that's the only methods government can use for universal healthcare. It can't dictate Americans to spend their money to provide for personal welfare. But government can require anyone who uses a government hospital to have valid insurance.

Many of the political left defend this mandate by citing government requirement for automobile insurance and George Washington signing into law the Militia Act of 1792 that required most "free able-bodied white male citizen" between ages of 18 and 45, purchase a firearm and accessories. The law stated, "That every citizen, so enrolled (in a militia) and notified, shall, within six months thereafter, provide himself with a good musket or fire-lock, a sufficient bayonet and belt, two spare flints, and a knapsack, a pouch, with a box therein, to contain not less than twenty four cartridges, suited to the bore of his musket or firelock, each cartridge to contain a proper quan-tity of powder and ball."

But automobile insurance is only required when the vehicle is used on public property and the requirement that militia members in early America buy firearms is justified by Article I, Section 8, power of Congress to provide for "organizing, arming and disciplining the Militias." (The requirement that only certain individuals be required to be armed should have put to rest the argument that the Founders intended the right to keep and bear arms to be an individual right. But it didn't.)

Whether the courts find the mandate unconstitutional or perfectly legal won't obscure the fact that it isn't the most-effective financial system possible.

The only solid solution is a universal sharing of the costs, and that was never discussed other than some people proposing Medicare for all or the "public option" that progressives liked so much. Better, but not ideal.

A dual-payer system could very well be more workable than a single-payer system. The United States, after all, has a dual system in place with the national part called Medicare and the state function known as Medic-aid; what the nation doesn't have is universal coverage.

We divide healthcare into two parts: states would pay the premiums for all residents in health maintenance organizations (HMOs) or clinics that would practice preventive medicine, diagnostic services and outpatient care. These local entities would be able to alert their clients by e-mail to needful things—such as flu vaccinations—quickly and efficiently. Those facilities would be private-sector HMOs and clinics.

It will become apparent to health providers in any given area that under Democratic Capitalism they would be well suited to band together to form nonprofit clinics or co-ops to perform the same functions as the HMO cor-porations, thereby letting the market control costs by providing competi-tion to for-profit HMOs.

For the first time in their lives most Americans will have complete free-dom to choose the physicians and facilities they want to provide healthcare.

Under the present system, an employer will choose the provider whether it is an HMO or an insurance company and employees have only that source for use. This has left the nation with a situation in which an employer, either on its own or under pressure from an insurance company, would fire a worker when he or she begins to show signs of an illness that would impact the cost of the insurance policy. How the 2010 reform law would affect that is still unknown. Many individuals and companies have bought affordable insurance coverage only to find out when they go to use the insurance the whole coverage was a scam.

The United States Constitution says in the Fourteenth Amendment that a state cannot "deny to any person within its jurisdiction" equal protection of its laws, which would mean states would have to include all "persons" living in the state in their programs and that would assuredly pertain to immigrants, legal and illegal, at the very time the right is complaining about immigration. But since these immigrants are the primary laborers harvesting our food it would be wise to see that they were free of contagious diseases. They would not necessarily be eligible for the federal program since the federal government doesn't have an equal-rights clause in the Constitution. And the system doesn't need to be "saved" or "protected" from too much money available for health care. Money doesn't threaten the system; it is threatened by inflation and a greater increase in participants when Baby Boomer Americans begin to retire.

When all Americans are enrolled in the dual-payer system, millions of new jobs will be created at the state level. The new jobs would be private-sector jobs.

The second part would be a federal insurance program to cover hospitalization, recuperative treatment and rehabilitation of illness and injury. Everything else would remain under private insurance jurisdiction. Enrollment in a state system provides automatic participation in the federal system.

State governments require automobile owners to purchase medical liability as part of their basic insurance required to operate vehicles on public property. With universal coverage as outlined in this chapter, such coverage would be unnecessary, saving consumers hundreds of millions of dollars a year which they could spend elsewhere in the economy fueling growth. And homeowners' insurance policies would not need a medical clause, saving American hundreds of millions more in costs.

And if insurance companies suffer some financial setbacks, so be it; that would be minor compared to the hardships they have inflicted on Americans for far too many years. If people in the health-insurance industry lose their jobs, they can always find work in the areas that factory workers relied on when their jobs were "outsourced," but that doesn't seem likely as shown above.

Insurance companies have destroyed the healthcare system. Insurance companies are the ones that refused to pay for lifesaving medication. It's insurance companies that refused payment for new but effective procedures, calling them "experimental." It is insurance companies that refused to pay for preventive treatment that would forestall many of the problems insurance companies also refuse to pay for when they occur. It's insurance companies that denied coverage to any person not in perfect health. It's insurance companies that dropped policy holders when they become ill after years of paying premiums while healthy.

It's insurance companies that placed a ceiling on coverage and then required copayments so high that few can afford insurance at all, forcing thousands into bankruptcy each year. It's insurance companies that denied or delayed paying for treatment until a patient dies, only then agreeing to pay for what was no longer needed. Insurance companies pay their chief executives millions annually to inflict such conditions on the public. And insurance companies send hundreds of millions of dollars, better used for healthcare, to politicians to maintain that corrupt system. How the 2010 reform act will alleviate those issues is also unknown.

In his *New York Times* column, economist Paul Krugman issued his take on insurance company practices, writing: "Yet private markets for health insurance, left to their own devices, work very badly: insurers deny as many claims as possible, and they also try to avoid covering people who are likely to need care. Horror stories are legion: the insurance company that refused to pay for urgently needed cancer surgery because of questions about the patient's acne treatment; the healthy young woman was denied coverage because she briefly saw a psychologist after breaking up with her boyfriend."[75]

When we eliminate the income and payroll taxes—eliminating the payroll tax on the approximately 145 million jobs in America (Bureau of Labor Statistics for third quarter 2008) would free about $555 billion dollars (figuring 15.3 percent deduction on $25,000 annual income to equal

---

75 "Health Care Realities," Paul Krugman; *The New York Times*; July 30, 2009.

$3,825 per job)—that states can tap into to enroll all their residents in basic preventive-care program in which some insurance companies can partici-pate by opening HMO clinics that would reclaim some of the threatened insurance jobs, leaving hospitalization and recuperative expenses with the federal program. The federal program can work through private insurance companies rather than create another government agency, if the cost is not too high; but there would have to be a cap on administrative costs which reduce the 17 percent of the nation's wealth we now pay for healthcare to 16 percent, then down to 15 percent and so forth without sacrificing quality. But savings would be much greater if the payer were nonprofit, like Medi-care. The only idea more ridiculous than mandates was to leave the situa-tion as it was.

The political right is adamant against insuring everybody, claiming any government involvement is "socialized medicine," which in their minds equals re-distribution of wealth, a free hand-out: a cardinal sin.

Losing 2008 GOP presidential candidate Sen. John McCain has received or been eligible for government-provided healthcare from government-owned clinics and hospitals and government-employed physicians and nurses his entire lifetime. He was born in a naval hospital under the care of government physicians and nurses in a government facility. He grew up the son of a Navy admiral, which entitled him to government healthcare then went to the US Naval Academy where his healthcare was also govern-ment provided. He received government healthcare the entire time he was on active duty with the Navy. From the second he left the Navy, he has been eligible for healthcare from the Department of Veterans Affairs. All of that is socialized medicine. McCain has gladly accepted for himself that "social-ized medicine" while telling the rest of us that a universal healthcare system that is not socialized, but government funded, is bad for the rest of America. Even during the time he was a prisoner of war in North Vietnam, McCain received government healthcare from a North Vietnam government, and while the quality may have been poor it was better than what close to 50 million Americans get under present conditions.

The treatment a wounded GI receives on the battlefield comes from a government-trained-and-employed medic using government-provided medicines and equipment. That is socialized medicine. When the wounded is evacuated to a field hospital, the treatment received from government-employed physicians, surgeons and nurses in a government-owned facility is socialized medicine. All military forts, bases or ships at sea practice socialized medicine in their hospitals, clinics or sick bays. The work of Walter Reed Army Medical Center in Washington, DC, is socialized medicine as it is at the Bethesda Naval Hospital, Bethesda, Maryland, military hospitals across the nation, and as is the Veterans Affairs program. But we never hear politicians who claim that a government-funded system for all is socialized medicine—when it is not—clamoring to rid the military of its socialized medicine, even though Walter Reed was seriously neglected in the George W. Bush administration when tax cuts for the American aristocracy were deemed more important than medical treatment for the nation's protectors.

Death by medical mistake is a major problem in this nation with estimates running as high as 100,000 people dying needlessly each year, far more than any other form of mistakes or accidents. The dual-payer system can address that problem. First off, it has the necessary second opinion built in. After the preventative-care physician diagnoses a malady, the patient will be referred to a hospital for treatment, where a second diagnosis is elementary. HMO mistakes will rarely lead to the death of a patient, for HMOs will have specific duties, none of which is treatment for serious illness or injury. Hospitals will be more efficient by restricting their duties to those things they do the best.

HMOs and clinics, that make their profits by the number of clients they have, will soon learn which hospitals do the best jobs in keeping patients alive and clients of the HMOs and clinics. So they will refer their clients to the more-successful hospitals, creating the competition conservatives often claim will cure many economic ills. And that can be accomplished without heavy-handed government intrusion or mandates. There would be no copay that drives Americans into bankruptcy for serious illnesses. There will be no ceiling at which point insurance will pay no more. And there will be no cancellation of policies when the policy is actually used.

There is no rush of politicians in the White House or Congress or in state and local government so repelled by their government-funded health-care that they refuse it and run to pay out of their own pockets, as they want us to do. Using government for their taxpayer-funded healthcare insurance is fine for them, just not fine for taxpayers. There was one Democratic representative in the House who wouldn't enroll in Congress' plan unless all Americans were insured. But since his salary to serve in Congress approaches $200,000 a year he could easily afford to pay for a private policy.

That's much harder for an ordinary American whose income may be but a tenth of that.

Under this dual-payer system Medicaid can be eliminated as can Medicare's monthly premiums and stiff copays and deductibles as can other programs insuring Americans by government, especially that covering all members of Congress and their families and that covering the entire government civilian workforce including state and local governments. States struggling under the financial strains of the latest GOP-induced recession could get much needed relief if most medical costs for their public employees were taken out of state budgets. And by eliminating the payroll tax at the federal level, much needed money is freed up for states to keep providing needed services to their residents.

The Veterans Affairs health program, which those using that system prior to the George W. Bush administration raved about for its superb quality of care, is the only true "socialized medicine" in the United States—outside the military or prisons—and can be reduced by restricting it to veterans on pension or still afflicted by combat or service-related injuries. Elimination of these redundant programs would save hundreds of billions of dollars. Hospital emergency rooms would no longer be required to treat the uninsured for free because everyone would be insured.

Opponents of universal health coverage claim, "We can't afford it." But paying more than 17 percent of the nation's wealth for healthcare to cover only 85 percent of the population is ludicrous when other advanced nations less wealthy than the United States spend 10 percent—some less—of their wealth to cover 100 percent of their population and obtain results just as good or better than in the United States. Ordinary Americans already pay for the healthcare in the nation through their labor with money they earned going to insurance companies or being diverted or deferred while also paying most of the bill for all social activities as special interests and corporations contribute little.

In 2009, an article in *The Independent*[76] of the United Kingdom (Great Britain) broke down the comparisons of the two countries. It reported spending in the United States per person at $7,290 (16 percent of GDP, which just a year later reached 17.3 percent); $2,992 in the United Kingdom (8.4 percent of GDP), with life expectancy at 78 years in the US, 80 years in the

---

76   "The Brutal Truth About America's Healthcare," Guy Adams; *The Independent UK*; August 15, 2009.

UK; infant mortality in the US at 6.7 deaths per 1,000 births, 4.8 in the UK. The UK had more physicians than the US, 2.5 per 1,000, compared to 2.4 in the US. The only area the US led was in number of nurses, 10.6 per 1,000 Americans versus 10 per 1.000 people in the UK. The newspaper said public financing of health care was slightly above 80 percent in the UK and slightly below 50 percent in the US. It attributed the figures to the World Health Organization, the same organization that in 2005 rated the United States health system as 37th best in the world, the United Kingdom 18th, well below the top two, France and Italy. And top-ranked France spent only 11.2 percent of its GDP on healthcare while second-place Italy spent 8.9 percent.

We can't afford not to reform the system and do it much better than the initial successes by the Obama administration.

Paying for healthcare under Democratic Capitalism is not a problem. That 17-plus percent of the nation's wealth we now spend on a wasteful system would easily fund universal care with billions left over for other economic uses. In a $15 trillion economy, we send about $2.6 trillion for America's 300 million-plus residents. With private-sector healthcare funding about 55 percent of the total we're considering almost $1.5 trillion in the private-sector market. That market presently operates under administrative costs around 30 percent making private-sector care much more expensive than public-sector care. Reducing administrative costs to five percent—about twice as high as the VA and Medicare systems spend—would free up about $400 billion dollars a year that would more than pay to insure the presently uninsured and provide much better coverage for the underinsured. That five percent administration costs might not be hard to do in companies such as Aetna in which the CEO pays himself more than $24 million annually year after year (more in one month than millions of Americans will earn in a lifetime). Other CEOs continually take $10 million or more. A $1 million income should suit them just fine.

That $400 billion represents about $8,000 for every person in the uninsured 50 million ($32,000 for a family of four) which is almost $700 per person more than what the Independent reported the United States to be spending. If one wants to downplay the problem by claiming only 45 million Americans are uninsured, the waste and fraud in the system would be $8,900 per person. And politicians who claim that government spending is fraught with waste and fraud—but do nothing about it when in power—seem not to be concerned with waste and fraud in the private sector.

Under the health plan covering Congress, that $8,000-per-person would cover an entire family (members of Congress pay a small co-premium out-of-pocket for their coverage) with no co-premium required, proving there is already enough money in the system to pay for universal healthcare without a dime of extra taxes needed. *The Oregonian* newspaper (Portland, Oregon) reported that a typical senator (it cited Ron Wyden , D-OR) had the choice of 23 different plans to choose from in 2009 in the program that covers all federal employees. [77]

The breakdown of Wyden's policy was:
- Cost: $1,120.47 a month
- Wyden's share: $356.59 a month (up $42.12 from 2008)
- Annual deductible: $300 per member or $600 per family
- Routine physical: $20 for doctor, screening tests fully covered
- Well-baby care for the twins: fully covered.

That cost was for the more-generous of two standard family plans offered by Blue Cross–Blue Shield. The annual cost of the Wyden's coverage that covered his family of four was $13,445, well below that $32,000 above that could be available with reform. All 23 of these plans were from private-sector for-profit insurance companies. The newspaper added that another bonus available to all member of Congress was a program available for "about $500 a year for access to Congress' medical clinic, which handles colds, first aid and other minor matters." And that $42.12 increase in Wyden's share of premium costs represents almost 12 percent rise, showing healthcare inflation runs unabated while the political right (some Democrats included) refuses to join efforts to combat it.

Paying for healthcare under present proposals is more problematic. The proposals of this dual-payer system concentrate on funding the healthcare system, most of the provisions in the 2010 reform bill could remain intact.

Under the healthcare reform plan proposed in this chapter, members of Congress and their families can be enrolled in an HMO that is exclusively for only them. And those who hate healthcare for everyone can be left out.

If United States spending on healthcare approached the 10 percent average of other industrial nations, total spending would be $1.5 trillion, leaving more than a trillion dollars available to be used in other areas of the economy.

77　"Just how good a health plan does Congress have?," Charles Pope; *The Oregonian*; August 3, 2009.

The people who have the most trouble figuring out how to pay for healthcare in America are the very same people in Congress who had no problem paying for a totally unnecessary war against Iraq and who can find all the money necessary to buy military equipment the Pentagon says it doesn't want and which is unneeded, but would be produced or based in the state or district of a powerful politician. They can find money anywhere to pay for pet projects through "earmarks," such as the infamous "Bridge to Nowhere" in Alaska and tens of thousands of other projects, some valid and beneficial, others not. And they had enough money available that they could present massive tax cuts to members of the aristocracy that already had more than enough to maintain their luxurious lifestyles and who used the tax saving to continue recycling money through the US Treasury to add to their wealth without ever contributing to economic growth.

And it is questionable if conservative politicians really care about deficits and the national debt or are merely insulting our intelligences, because they refused to consider measures to address the deficit-debt problem, such as repealing or allowing the Bush tax cuts for the aristocracy to expire when they first began exploding the deficit and piling up massive debt. Nor have they ever considered repealing massive tax cuts on corporations that allowed the Enron fraud to eventually destroy that company.

For some reason, conservatives and some moderates of both Republican and Democratic ilk can't see the logic of reform. Americans need to determine which is better for the nation: an insurance-company chief executive who paid himself tens of millions of dollars annually to preside over withholding of healthcare payments for decades or using those millions for several hundred healthcare professionals actually delivering healthcare?

CHAPTER 10. SOCIAL SECURITY

'CRISIS' CAN BE AVOIDED

One of the problems facing Social Security and its prospects for the future is the healthcare mess in the United States in which more than 200 million persons receive healthcare insurance through employment of self or of a business. Because of this illogical method of providing healthcare coverage—perhaps the world's worst system—millions of Americans are forced off their jobs in late middle age so that the corporate employer can hold down benefit expenses. That tactic forces millions of Americans into the Social Security system to draw retirement benefits much sooner than they might have wished and which costs the federal government billions of dollars paid out to recipients.

Most people are concerned with the future of Social Security, not the present condition because the system had until the Bush financial crisis done just fine, producing more than enough revenue to meet today's needs. Excess amounts of money collected by the Social Security System is used to purchase Treasury debt instruments, another legacy of Ronald Reagan's economic failures. Reagan got massive increases from Congress in 1983 on the payroll tax which funds Social Security and Medicare in order to "save" the system. When that generated huge surpluses—contrary to right-wing arguments that tax increases always hurt the economy—Reagan and Congress created the Deficit Reduction Act of 1984 to mandate all Social Security/Medicare surpluses from the payroll tax be used to purchase Treasury instruments, which allowed the payroll-tax collection to be used in other areas and to mask the severity of the Reagan deficits.

When George W. Bush proposed to "privatize" Social Security in his second term, he claimed that the system would be better off investing in the stock market than in the Treasury instruments he called "just pieces of paper," but which he used through his administration to fund much of the government. But the stock market took a major dive the rest of Bush's time in office, which would have devastated many near-retirees hopes just as it devastated many IRAs and 401K retirement funds. His plan also had serious constitutional issues.

In the 1920s, the most-conservative Supreme Court in history rightfully ruled that money once collected by taxation is the legal property of the government, not the taxpayer. In a related second case, the court ruled that money withdrawn from the Treasury under law—as the Constitution clearly specifies in Article I, Section 9—can be done only by Congress because only Congress can make federal law. It's clear that Bush's proposals that would allow individuals to determine where their tax dollars could be spent would violate our Constitution. And for the taxpayer to have any say about where tax money was to be invested, would be saying the money was still owned by the taxpayer and would run counter to the first Supreme Court ruling.

Whenever efforts have been made through the past century and into this one to reform our healthcare mess, demigods of all stripes help derail this much-needed effort by telling voters who have health insurance through employment that reform would force them to "subsidize" undeserving "others" who have no health coverage, Voters buy that argument without thought and the outrage gives antigovernment voices in Congress enough bravado to kill all efforts.

But it is those people with health insurance through employment being subsidized, often subsidized by those who have no insurance.

Insurance obtained through employment is paid for by money the employee created for his/her company. But that money, which is real income for employees, isn't credited to employees, it is diverted to a third party, an insurance firm or health maintenance organization (HMO). If that insurance is worth $10,000 for a family, the employee who thinks he/she is getting "free" medical coverage doesn't pay income taxes on what is clearly "income" so would avoid $1,000 to $2,800 annually in taxes, depending on tax bracket. The company that issued the insurance would write off the cost on its taxes, if it still paid taxes, and would also get a tax break.

Those taxes the employee doesn't pay, nor does the employer, have to be made up by some other sources. Those other sources would include tax-payers without health insurance or nations that buy our debt instruments, mainly under Republican administrations. And those debt instruments draw interest, also paid in part by people with no health insurance, and will eventually have to be paid off, obviously by Americans as yet unborn.

Since surplus payroll taxes for Social Security are presently funneled into the general budget, those excess funds help cover the tax shortfall from those who do not pay taxes on their employer-provided healthcare. And those working poor who have no healthcare themselves are paying payroll taxes on the first dollar earned on their jobs, which "subsidizes" those with health insurance.

This hits some people much harder than others. A single mother who makes a living cleaning houses of the affluent, who could be escaping all fed-eral taxes, would pay the full 15.3 percent payroll tax for both Social Secu-rity and Medicare but could not afford private health insurance for herself or her children. That portion of her payroll taxes considered surplus is then sent to the Treasury where it would help cover the taxes unpaid by others with work-based health insurance.

In this way, that single house-cleaning mother, workers with low in-comes, Americans unborn and foreign nations whose citizens labor away in sweatshops are subsidizing Americans with fine healthcare coverage, which would include the multimillion-dollar-a-year executive and overpaid mem-bers of Congress. Those same Americans falsely think that under health-insurance reform law they would be subsidizing "unworthy" others, such as the house-cleaning single mother who has been subsidizing them for years. That single mother and others like her have been scammed under this law of the land for decades after Reagan, a Republican Senate and conservative House passed the 1984 Deficit Reduction Act. And when that single mother uses her paltry income to provide food, shelter, clothing and education for her children, she is providing the income that businesses use to purchase health insurance for their employees and well-to-do executives, being hit twice for subsidies for more-fortunate Americans.

The same condition exists for mortgage payments. A multimillionaire can save tens of thousands of dollars annually by deducting interest cost of the mortgage on a country palace or mid-city penthouse and those unpaid taxes have to come from others, such as that house-cleaning single mother. That single mother can't afford a home of her own so has to rent a cheap apartment in which her rent pays the property tax of the apartment owner, who then deducts property taxes from his taxes. So the single mother subsidizes the apartment owner, in two ways, just as she subsidizes many multimillionaires. And the greedy think both situations are just fine.

While income used by the company for health insurance is diverted income, taxes for Social Security is deferred income, that is, it is earned by the employee who doesn't get it credited to him/her but is deferred through a third party, the US Treasury, to be paid upon retirement years later. It also should be clear that the half of payroll taxes supposedly paid by an employer isn't really paid by the employer because it is money that should rightfully be income to those who created it. It just isn't credited to the earners. And that deferred income isn't taxed, but some may be taxed after retirement if total retirement income is high enough.

Despite the evidence that the fortunate have been subsidized by the less-fortunate for nearly three decades, there is considerable nonsense coming from the privileged who whine about being victimized. Consider the world-famous "unfairness" explosion by CNBC reporter Rick Santelli, who recently ranted on national television: "How many of you people want to pay for your neighbors' mortgage that has an extra bathroom and can't pay their bills?"

Many man-on-the-street interviews with Americans nationwide show the same ignorance and contempt for rescuing the home-mortgage industry because "I don't want to pay for someone else's mistakes," the same argument long used to oppose universal healthcare for all Americans; until the present healthcare situation got out of control.

Let's consider the income Santelli likely has. He is in an industry that has paid Katie Couric tens of millions of dollars just for being adorable—thousands of other journalists could do as well as she on TV but few, if any, are as scrumptious—so its likely that Santelli is overpaid and might have an annual income of six figures, maybe the high six figures or even seven figures. With that kind of income, it is likely that he has a "palace" with a mortgage that is also possibly in the high six figures or into seven figures, of which the majority, early in the mortgage, was interest payments which he could deduct from his taxable income, saving himself thousands of dollars from taxation.

There is also the matter of health insurance that Santelli likely gets from employment. The money paid to insurance companies is money "earned" by the employee but is not treated as "earnings" of the employee, thus is untaxed. It is "diverted income. Again, Santelli gets a free ride around taxation on the thousands of dollars going toward his health insurance. Then his employer can write off the expense of insuring all its employees, again escaping taxation that could have been levied on CNBC.

In fact, all deductions, for anything, are items that escape taxation from the federal government. And home buyers who use standard deductions because their incomes and mortgages are too low to benefit from tax write-offs are helping to subsidize the well-to-do who can benefit from huge write-offs.

All these escapes from taxation have to be made up by someone else. For nearly three decades, that came from the excess payroll taxes paid by workers who may not have health insurance or homes for themselves. At present, what Santelli and his ilk don't pay is covered by borrowing from China, the Middle East or other sources and interest must be paid on that borrowing. That interest is paid by US taxpayers. Those taxpayers are indirectly subsidizing Santelli and other whiners who have major routes around taxation. Eventually that borrowing has to be paid back by someone, sometime. This leaves us with the conclusion that Santelli (and others such as he) are and have been subsidized by house-cleaning single mothers and Americans as yet unborn

People who have hated Social Security since its inception in 1935 continually howl that there is a "crisis" in the system because it may not be able to meet its lawful obligations sometime in the future. Estimates often say Social Security, if left untouched, would be able to afford only 80 percent of requirements three or four decades from now. But those estimates are considered valid if the economy grows at an average of less than two percent annually when it historically increases by 3.5 percent. The most-strident critics of Social Security seemed to ignore for three decades the financial crisis being created by their very actions on taxes, spending and the economy. The general budget is in crisis because of tax cuts and deregulation; the Social Security budget is not.

Proponents of Social Security say the system would be just fine as far into the future as can be anticipated if the economy grew at its historical rate and minor tweaking is done to the taxes with little or no tweaking to benefits. Since the economy grows at different paces—or contracts under far-right Republicans—it is of no value trying to determine when Social Security faces the "crisis" it supposedly has faced for three-quarters of a century but has never had to encounter.

When Social Security began, there were a reported 16 workers for every one recipient. When George Bush was trying to "privatize" the system there were 3.3 workers per one recipient. Estimates are two workers for one recipient by 2030, which appears onerous to those who have no imagination to come up with solutions.

It is important to keep Social security strong regardless of its cost. It often supplies less than half what is needed for a decent retirement and the political right keeps harming those areas of the economy, which supply the other half. As shown in a past chapter, deregulation of industry, primarily the utility sector, did irreparable harm to many companies. Electric utilities which, have historically been productive sites for secure dividend income, were severely damaged, so they slashed or omitted dividends, if not destroying the company such as Enron. Enron took over a healthy utility, Portland General Electric in the late 1990s and paid with stock—phony paper that would eventually become worthless—going out of existence only few years after the takeover and paying much lower dividends before dying. Enron sold Portland General Electric just before going bust, taking that company from its original shareholders to raise needed cash the executives used trying to rescue Enron or taking for themselves, leaving the original Portland GE owners with nothing. That could be the result for everyone should the right ever succeed in a new "privatizing" Social Security scheme.

And with the economy tanking, as it did in 2007, interest rates on savings accounts, certificates of deposit, or mutual-fund money-market accounts, dried up to practically nothing, leaving retirees relying on such income in dire straits. Sadly, many of those retirees continued to vote into office the same right-wing fanatics who caused the problem, directing their anger toward those trying to rescue the economy and fed by right-wing demagoguery.

Democratic Capitalism solves much of the problem; as productivity increases, so will profit of all, and that will increase tax collections just as it would increase spendable funds that would keep Social Security and healthcare solvent forever. And if Democratic Capitalism improves labor-management relations, as it should, people will not be so inclined to take early retirement and go onto Social Security.

Social Security will no longer be handled only by wages but by all income regardless of method of creation.

If rich feel altruistic they need not take Social Security but the United States should not impose a means test for well-off recipients and still pretend to care for all. All Americans with an income would share equally in funding Social Security and healthcare, so all should receive equal benefits and the ratio of active workers to retirees will be no problem.

Chapter 11. Learning from Success

Bold Action Needed

This book started with the premise that to overcome some of the major problems that have been spawned and enhanced over the past three decades and were given birth by the Reagan Revolution that at times seemed to be a reaction to the independence movement of the 1770s and a return to an aristocracy, but was an attempt to return to the classic economics under which Reagan was educated and which brought us depressions in the 1830-40s, 1870s, 1890s and the big one in the 1930s. That meant abandoning the new economics of the New Deal that solved the greatest depression and had prevented any new depressions ever since. Now the nation needs a bold new direction and an inventive spirit. We haven't gotten either; we have had to just nibble around the edges of our problems and leave intact the very conditions that put the nation on the edge of destruction.

Americans haven't always been so timid in facing their problems and have used inventive methods to eliminate problems, create new directions and make the nation better. The nation was begun under radical means to improve society as it was the first nation in history to definitely state that mankind was capable of ruling itself. Prior to the rising of American self-rule, governments had always been formed by a small segment of society taking power and ruling only for that small segment, isolating or suppressing the majority. Ever since Adam left Eden man has suffered under kings and queens; caesars, kaisers and tsars; under emperors, emirs, sheiks, and shoguns; under despots or all sorts. Trying to recapture an arrangement with the Reagan Revolution where only the elite rule was a bad idea. Americans can again do better, but we haven't.

With the United States economy once again coming out of an economic mess that arose under a Republican administration we ought to look at recent economic history and ask ourselves why we continually elect know-nothings to the presidency and to Congress.

The common wisdom in most circles of American life is that Republicans in power are better for the economy than are Democrats. It is said over and over that regulation-loving, high-taxing big-government Democrats usually harm or retard economic prosperity in the nation while less-government, low-tax, deregulation Republicans benefit the economy and bring prosperity to all.

Ben Stein, conservative actor, economist and speech writer in the administration of Richard Nixon, admitted on a TV talk show late in the George W. Bush administration that the nation at that time was already in the Great Recession but added that it would not become a depression and we will never again see another depression. That would seem to be a backhanded admission that the economic reforms instituted by regulation-loving, high-taxing, big-government Franklin Delano Roosevelt in the 1930s are working as planned and that regulatory reforms work, the very reforms Stein's intellectual brethren on the right have been dismantling since Ronald Reagan was first elected. We should also understand that an important segment of the economy is able to damage the entire economy if allowed to do as it pleases, as has been shown by the petroleum and financial industries.

This chapter looks at the historical economic performances of both left (Democratic administrations) and right (Republican regimes) in much of the 20th Century by using statistics and facts, not opinion or propaganda. What we find may be surprising.

What is not surprising is that 2008 Republican presidential candidate John McCain campaigned on the same old same old GOP mantra about how to handle the economy with more tax cuts and more deregulation while the Democratic hopefuls in the primaries were relatively silent about the

Donkey's economic history, as was Barack Obama in the general-election campaign. Al Gore wouldn't touch the subject in 2000 and John Kerry was equally as silent on the matter in 2004. Gore's stance was most egregious because as Vice President he was part of an administration that produced one of the greatest economic advances in history and mentioned it naught.

The 2005 Economic Report of the President, with data dating back to 1960, revealed some truths the Republicans probably wish weren't made public. Such as:

"Big government" federal spending has increased about $35 billion an-nually under Democrats but $60 billion under Republicans. Spending will rise each year because of inflation and population growth but that doesn't justify the difference between the parties.

In a column in the *Los Angeles Times* after the report was released, then editorial-page editor Michael Kinsley wrote:

> Now look at federal revenues (a.k.a. taxes). You can't take it away from them: Republicans do cut taxes. Or rather, tax revenues go up under both parties, but only about half as fast under Republicans. This is true no matter when you start counting, or whether you give a president's policies that extra year to take effect. It's the only test of Republican economics that the Republicans win.
>
> That is, they win if you consider lower federal revenues to be a vic-tory. Sometimes Republicans say that cutting taxes will raise gov-ernment revenues by stimulating the economy. And sometimes they say that lower revenues are good because they will lead (by some mysterious process) to lower spending.
>
> The numbers in the Economic Report undermine both theories. Spending goes up faster under Republican presidents than under Democratic ones. And the economy grows faster under Democrats than Republicans. What grows faster under Republicans is debt.
>
> The national debt has gone up more than $200 billion a year under Republican presidents and less than $100 billion a year under Demo-crats. If you start counting in 1981 or attribute responsibility with a year's delay, the numbers change, but the bottom line doesn't: Democrats do Republican economics better than Republicans do.[78]

Since 1960 until the release of the report, the federal deficit averaged $131 billion a year under the GOP and $30 billion for Democrats. In an av-

---

78 "More GOP Than the GOP," Michael Kinsley; *The Los Angeles Times*; April 3, 2005.

erage Republican year the deficit increased by $36 billion. In an average Democratic year it shrank by $25 billion.

Both the deficit and debt had been distorted somewhat by the George W. Bush administration because it paid for its Iraq and Afghanistan wars by off-budget borrowing and spending of hundreds of billions of dollars annually to mask the totals of both. It also handed off a deficit of more than $1.3 trillion to Barack Obama.

The gross domestic product from 1960 to 2005 (taking inflation into account) increased an average of $165 billion a year in 2000 dollars under Republican administrations and $212 billion a year under Democrats. On the average yearly rise in per capita income, Democrats score about 30 percent higher.

On inflation Democrats average 3.13 percent versus 3.89 percent for Republicans. Unemployment averaged 5.33 percent under Democrats versus 6.38 percent for the GOP and fell in the average Democratic year, rose in the average Republican year.

Figures from the White House Office of Management and Budget (OMB), U.S. Department of Labor (DOL), and White House Council of Economic Advisors shows the following facts (printed in *The Milwaukee Journal Sentinel* in late 2007 by Robert Weiner and John Larmet).[79]

Democratic Versus Republican Presidents

Economic Indicators

In six major criteria: GDP growth, per capita income growth, job creation, unemployment reduction, inflation reduction, and federal deficit reduction, for the ten post-World War II presidencies until Bush, there is a record by which we can track the reality of Democratic versus Republican economic success.

Democrats

• Lyndon B. Johnson's "Great Society" created robust economic expansion, first in both GDP and personal income growth. He also reduced unemployment from 5.3 percent to 3.4 percent. Economic growth remained robust through most of LBJ's presidency.

• John F. Kennedy campaigned on the idea of getting America moving again, and he did. Under Kennedy, America entered its largest sus-

79 "Presidential Economics: Myths, Facts," Robert Weiner and John Larmet; *The Milwaukee Journal Sentinel*; August 15, 2007.

tained expansion since WWII. GDP and personal income growth were second only to Johnson, all with minimal inflation. Contrary to Republican attempts to say Kennedy's tax cuts are like Bush's, Kennedy's were targeted at middle and lower incomes.

• The economy added 10 million jobs under Jimmy Carter despite high inflation; Carter ranks first in job creation next to Clinton during just four years in office. Carter also reduced government spending as a percentage of GDP.

• Harry Truman's second term saw the fastest GDP growth and the sharpest reduction in unemployment of any president surveyed (of course, FDR's post Hoover-depression New Deal jobs are first).

Republicans

• Ronald Reagan focused on reducing the cost of capital through cutting tax bracket highs for the rich and reducing the size and scope of government. But, instead of lowering spending, Reagan shifted money to the military (i.e. Star Wars) and the deficit tripled with the tax cuts and military spending—as under Bush II.

• Under Gerald Ford, the deficit soared and the unemployment rate grew from 5.3 - 8.3% in just 2 years. His "WIN" (Whip Inflation Now) buttons were no match for economic inactivity.

• It was under Richard Nixon that inflation started to spiral out of control, from 4.4% to 8.6%, and the deficit shot up from $2.8 billion to $73.7 billion.

• The Eisenhower years were characterized by slow growth (2.27% annualized GDP growth) and relatively high unemployment (7.7% at end of term).

• George H. W. Bush had the poorest record for both GDP and income growth. During his single term, the deficit ballooned (from $152 billion to $255 billion) more than under every president but his son and Ford.

REALITY ON RECESSIONS

Now, the ugly truth about recessions. Since World War II, every Republican president has governed over a recession (Dwight Eisenhower had three; Richard Nixon had two, one he shared with Gerald Ford and George W. Bush had two, his second the worst of the bunch) while Harry Truman and Jimmy Carter are the only Democratic Presidents with a recession, and

Carter's was the shortest (6 months), the mildest and caused more by the 1979 oil crisis following the Iran Revolution than by policy. Truman's recession was created when segments of the economy shut down to enable the changeover from wartime production to peacetime production. The recession count for the Dem team (Harry Truman, John F. Kennedy, Lyndon Johnson, Jimmy Carter and Bill Clinton) two. For the GOP team (Dwight Eisenhower, Richard Nixon, Gerald Ford, Ronald Reagan, George Bush the Daddy and George Bush the Younger) nine. And all this after the GOP gave us the Great Depression of the 1930s following recessions (during the Roaring Twenties for the wealthy) in 1923-24 for 14 months and 1926-27 for 13 months.

Our recessions (according to Geoffrey H. Moore, director emeritus of the Center for International Business Cycle Research at Columbia University in New York City using data from the National Bureau of Economic Research) have been (comments by the author):[80]

• November 1948–October 1949; 11 months; Truman, and mostly due to post-World War II readjustments from wartime production to peacetime production.

• July 1953–May 54; 10 months; Eisenhower.

• August 1957–April 1958; 8 months; Eisenhower.

• April 1960–February 1961; 10 months; Eisenhower. Ike's last recession ran into the first months of Kennedy's administration but JFK got the nation righted quickly.

• December 1969–November 1970; 11 months; Nixon.

• November 1973–March 1975; 16 months; Nixon and Ford. The recession began under Nixon but Ford prolonged it by cutting government spending, thereby starving the economy and preventing recovery.

• January 1980–June 1980; 6 months; Carter.

• July 1981–November 1982; 16 months; Reagan, and marked by an unemployment rate of 10.8 percent, the highest since 1940 when the nation was not yet out of the Great Depression.

• July 1990–March 1991; 8 months; Bush the Daddy.

• March 2001–September 2001; 6 months; Bush the Younger. The recession had achieved the six-month mark of economic contraction that establish an official recession by Sept. 1, before the terrorist attacks in New York and Arlington, Virginia, so we credit Bush with a six-month

---

80   "The Three Ds of Recession: A Brief History," Geoffrey H. Moore; *econlib.org.*

recession and not the economic problems that followed the attacks even though Bush's recession could have dragged on much longer.

The second Bush recession has been pegged at beginning in the fall of 2007 but didn't reach its destructive force until late in 2008 and wasn't declared as ended—or at least the slide had been halted—until late 2009.

Some of these recessions might have been cut short or prevented had government concentrated on rebuilding and repairing the nation's infrastructure, buying US-made automobiles, computers, software, office furniture and other American production rather than tax cuts for the wealthy or handing out rebates that were not spent in the economy. Republicans claim individual spending would end a recession but government spending is only waste. After the terrorist attacks of 2001, Bush pleaded for everyone to head to the malls and spend, spend, spend. Then he offered rebates to spend as if that would be a magical cure while claiming government spending the same money would be a disaster even though government buying could be directed at the weakest parts of the economy.

Republicans nearly always argue for lower government spending in recessionary circumstances, reducing even further the amount of money to circulate in the economy. That is why Republican administrations invariably have recessions that hurt the very people who elect them to office while Democrats do not.

In a capitalist society, the economy is based on one factor: spending. It is not based on barter or trading, nor is it based on hunting and gathering. It is not based on cooperative agriculture or any other nonmonetary system, such as the Haight-Ashbury communal living of the 1960s-70s in San Francisco.

In the United States, the spending that sustains the economy is from three sources; consumers, industry and government, with consumers accounting for approximately 70 percent of the spending, industry and government splitting the rest. When one facet of spending is reduced, such as consumer, the economy slows and heads for problems. Lower consumer spending will lead to lower industrial spending since there is little incentive for industry to spend on production when there is less demand for what is produced. This slashed spending leads to recessions unless government increases spending to replace those reductions and keep the system balanced, and when consumer and industrial spending increase to healthy levels, government spending can, and should, be eased. With consumer spending the primary engine of a healthy economy it borders on insanity for American government and businesses to base economic policies on suppressing wages and salaries of working-class consumers who are the most-important key to the success of businesses and the economy. But suppressing salaries and wages is exactly what this nation has been doing for the past three decades and only recently came out of the worst economic downturn since the Great Depression. That severe recession is not mere coincidence.

During most of the 20th century the Dow Jones Industrial Average increased by an average of about 10 percent annually, but under Democratic administrations the average has been in the 13-14 percent range while only 6–7 percent under Republicans. And those figures don't include the spectacular rise in the Dow under Clinton or the reduction under his successor, George W. Bush.

Clinton was inaugurated on January 20, 1993, the day the Dow closed at 3,242, and left office on January 20, 2001, when the Dow finished the day at 10,678 (that 7,436 point rise is a 230 percent increase, or more than 300 percent of the starting point).

When Bush left office in January 2009, the Dow was at 7,949; a loss of more than 25 percent. But the carryover effect from Bush's leadership has to be considered, and that saw the Dow Industrials at 6,547 (a 39 percent loss by Bush) in early March of 2009.

Exactly a year after succeeding Bush, Obama had the Industrials back up to 10,725 (an increase of 63.82 percent from its low point) when the economic downturn was halted but an upturn had not begun anywhere except on Wall Street.

In all fairness to the GOP, we must remember that the main reason it trails so dramatically in Dow Jones advances and other economic indicators is because Republican administrations must spend an inordinate amount of time laboring under a recession that they created or allowed to occur in the first place. Democrats fare better because they usually inherit economies so poor the only way to go is up.

About here, an invitation should go out to Republicans, conservatives and libertarians to prove that they are better stewards of the economy than are Democrats using facts and statistics to prove their claims, but it seems the facts and figures have been used up showing which political philosophy

and political party are the best on economic matters: that would be progressives and the Democratic Party.

With the data showing a decided advantage for Democratic administrations in all economic aspects, we have one last facet to examine: that of job
creation. It is important to remember that the population growth of the
country, and subsequently the increased numbers in the work-eligible age
group, the nation would produce about a one percent annual creation of
jobs regardless of government action.

JOB CREATION TELLS MUCH

So we look at nonfarm job growth by the millions from the number of
jobs at the beginning of an administration to the number at the end of that
administration.[81]

President	Term	Job Growth	Annual %
Roosevelt	1933–45	25.700m–41.903m	5.3%
Roosevelt/Truman	1945–49	41.903m–44.675m	1.7%
Truman	1949–53	44.675m–50.145m	3.1%
Eisenhower	1953–61	50.145m–53.683m	0.9%
Kennedy/Johnson	1961–65	53.683m–59.583m	2.7%
Johnson	1965–69	59.583m–69.438m	4.1%
Nixon	1969–73	69.438m–75.620m	2.2%
Nixon/Ford	1973–77	75.620m–80.692m	1.7%
Carter	1977–80	80.692m–91.031m	3.2%
Reagan	1980–89	91.031m–107.133m	2.2%
Bush, G. H.W.	1989–93	107.133m–109.725m	0.6%
Clinton	1993–01	109.725m–132.469m	2.6%
Bush, G. W.	2001–09	132.469m–134.333m	0.17%

We see that the leaders in job creation were the administrations of
Roosevelt, Johnson, Carter, Truman, Kennedy/Johnson and Clinton. All
Democrats. Nixon and Reagan were the most-successful Republicans but
finished below all Democrats except the Roosevelt/Truman combo that was
hampered when the economy experienced a major slowdown in 1948 as it

81 "Jobs created during U.S. presidential terms"; Wikipedia, the free encyclopedia,
using estimates collected by the Bureau of Labor Statistics.

switched from wartime production to peacetime production. During the 1980-1990 decade of Reagan-Bush "small government" the civilian federal payroll increased from 3,121,783 government workers (United States population of 227 million) to 3,508,463 (386,630 new bureaucrats with a national population of 250 million) but fell to about 2.8 million (about a 700,000 decrease) midway through Clinton's second term, according *The World Almanac*. Population at the end of Clinton's administration was 282 million. That means job growth in the private sector under Reagan would be well under the 16 million total jobs credited to him while Clinton's private-sector jobs would be closer to 24 million, well above the 23-plus million officially credited to him. The federal payroll has stayed below three million ever since on a population placed at 308 million by the 2010 census. Those figures should indicate the Reagan–Bush "small government" reputation is a fallacy.

We must take into consideration the carryover from one administration to another when examining successes or failures in job growth. An example is that the slight job growth under George W. Bush would actually be less than depicted because the loss of millions of jobs in the first year of the Obama administration should be credited to Bush because they were a result of his recession. So, it's likely that Bush was the first president since Hoover who lost millions of jobs. And it is impossible to determine the exact date when the Bush influence ended and an Obama influence began. Obama's job growth, if he has any, will be diluted because of the losses he inherited from Bush. Johnson left to Nixon an economy that had averaged 4.5 percent growth over his time in office and was robust enough to produce a budget surplus in 1969, so much of Nixon's job-growth statistics likely were inherited from Johnson. On the other hand, Carter handed Reagan a growing-but-weak economy and Reagan turned over the same type of sluggish economy to George H. W. Bush, who turned over the same lackluster economy to Clinton and Clinton gave George W. Bush a struggling economy slowing down after years of robust growth, so their job statistics likely evened out between what was inherited and what was passed on to successors. And what job growth there was under the Reagan administration could be logically credited to trillions of borrowed dollars.

The 23 million new jobs under Clinton translated into four years of budget surpluses that he turned over to Bush. But the 1.8 million new jobs under Bush—far less than the 11 million to 12 million that would be created just by population growth—coupled with the millions lost in the months after he left office produced a deficit of $1.3 trillion. With the lack of realistic job growth and the lost jobs, it is possible the nation has as much as 20 million jobs that are nonexistent and that means 20 million Americans not paying taxes, a sizable portion of that Bush deficit.

It should be obvious that there is a direct correlation between poverty in the United States and job growth. When more people are lifted out of poverty through increases in the minimum wage or government spending they have the means to join that 70 percent of the economy that is based on consumer spending. Businesses will then spend more to meet the increased demand and will hire more employees, which further reduces poverty, creates jobs and boosts the economy. The Kennedy-Johnson team cut poverty nearly in half and increased jobs by about 16 million. Jimmy Carter lowered poverty to 11.4 percent and created more than 10 million jobs in one term even with a mild recession. Clinton lowered the poverty rate to the lowest in history at 11.3 percent and created nearly 23 million jobs. Republicans raised poverty levels and trailed all Democrats in job creation; the job creation under Eisenhower and both George Bushes falling below what normally would be achieved just by population growth.

When poverty is lowered and job creation is robust, good things happen. Johnson left a budget surplus to Nixon, who squandered it. Carter left a slight deficit to Reagan as the economy was slowly recovering from recession, but Reagan exacerbated that deficit. And Clinton left four years of budget surpluses to Bush the Unfit, and he destroyed all that good.

Economic data from various sources and covering a variety of concerns clearly show that the right-wing Republican Party that supposedly represents the interests of business is actually harmful to business and to the economy. Also shown is that it doesn't matter whether a Democratic leader is a flaming liberal like FDR, or a temperate centrist such as Clinton or Carter; Democrats do better on the economy and for capitalism on all fronts than do Republicans, whether hard-core conservatives such as Reagan or moderates like Nixon.

Republicans have recently discovered the "American taxpayers" and claimed to be fighting for them to oppose Obama's economic agenda and its deficit spending that apparently halted the Bush recession in a matter of months. They appear to be a bit tardy in that discovery after piling $12 trillion of debt onto American taxpayers during the regimes of Ronald Reagan, George H. W. Bush the Daddy and George W. Bush the Younger. During those 20 years of right-wing accumulation of debt it was "the taxpayers be damned" because "Reagan proved that deficits don't matter."

This leaves us with an important question and that is: "Why are Democrats so reluctant, or afraid, to address this history with the American public?"

NEW DEAL'S "FAILURES"

One major deception the right tries to peddle to the American public is that the New Deal under Franklin Delano Roosevelt "failed." The New Deal was designed to correct the disaster brought about by conservative reign over an economy throughout the 1920s and which was predecessor to the Reaganomics that began our latest economic problems and its nation-threatening debt.

Republicans in Congress stood firm on their opposition to the so-called "economic stimulus" legislation of the Obama administration, promoted as a weak version of the New Deal program of Franklin Delano Roosevelt that has been credited with getting the United States out of the Great Depression of the 1930s. All the Republicans had to offer for our latest "depression" was the same as conservatives offered President Herbert Hoover as the economic calamity exploded in 1929 and which he followed throughout his administration. That is, cut taxes and reduce government spending—except for some "trickle down" schemes—to balance the budget and let the "invisible hand" of free enterprise work its magic.

That, they say, is the way out of a depression or recession and they insult our collective intelligence to claim the New Deal was a failure. Let reality determine if the New Deal failed or if their approach is correct. Let's look at some facts concerning the New Deal's "failure" and the "success" of the "invisible hand." Facts show that the New Deal was a rousing success despite what conservatives say about it.

Conservatives tell us it was World War II that finally solved the Great Depression not the New Deal. So we stop examining data before the United States entered the war to see if there is any validity to their claims. The dates used are for fiscal years that ended in the summer, not calendar years.

GROSS DOMESTIC PRODUCT UNDER HOOVER'S
CONSERVATIVE "INVISIBLE HAND" APPROACH

YEAR	GDP
1929	$104 billion.
1930	$91.1 billion
1931	$76.3 billion
1932	$58.5 billion
1932	$56.0 billion

GROSS DOMESTIC PRODUCT UNDER THE NEW DEAL APPROACH

1934	$65.0 billion
1935	$72.5 billion
1936	$82.7 billion
1937	$90.8 billion
1938	$85.2 billion *
1939	$91.1 billion
1940	$100.6 billion
1941	$125.8 billion

* *The reversal of progress occurred when Roosevelt ceased what was working and tried conservative calls to end deficit spending and balance the budget in 1937.*

The data clearly show the reduction in GDP under the conservative "invisible hand" approach and the growth under the New Deal approach. The growth from a $56 billion GDP Hoover left FDR to the $125.8 billion before the US entered the war is a 124.6 percent increase, or 15.58 percent annual growth rate when four percent growth is considered robust. If we remove the two wasted years when FDR listened to conservatives and tried to balance the budget while reducing government spending, the growth rate for the six positive years was 20.77 percent. That, conservatives claim, is "failure".

UNEMPLOYMENT UNDER HOOVER'S
CONSERVATIVE "INVISIBLE HAND" LEADERSHIP

Year	Percentage of Americans Out of Work
1929	3.2%
1930	8.7%
1931	15.9%
1932	23.6%
1933	24.9%

Unemployment under the New Deal programs:

1934	21.7%
1935	20.1%
1936	16.9%
1937	14.3%
1938	19.0% *
1939	17.2%
1940	14.6%
1941	9.9%

* *The reversal of progress occurred when Roosevelt ceased what was working and tried conservative calls to end deficit spending and balance the budget in 1937.*

It should be noted that the Works Progress Administration (WPA) and Civilian Conservation Corps (CCC) were implemented early in FDR's administration and had an immediate effect on unemployment statistics of 1933 when the WPA and CCC hired massive numbers of unemployed in the spring that preventing unemployment from skyrocketing well past 25 percent, maybe approaching 30 percent. But Social Security and minimum wages had no effect until late in the 1930s. Social Security was created in 1935 but didn't pay out significant retirement money until much later. A minimum-wage law was passed in 1935 but declared unconstitutional by a right-wing Supreme Court. It was brought back in 1938 and began having an economic effect in 1939.

The data show that the GDP took two years to recover from the conservative mantra to cut spending in 1937 until it reached 1937 levels in 1939 while it took three years for unemployment figures to approach their 1937 levels in 1940. That ought to be strong evidence that employment in the

private sector is the last statistic to improve in a recovering economy. Unemployment in 1934 did not have this lag time because FDR hired heavily in
late 1933 to man the government make-work programs of WPA and CCC.
This lag time was borne out in our latest recovery from a conservative economic disaster when the downturn was halted in late 2009 but employment
growth didn't show sign of recovery until mid-2010.

Figures for both Gross Domestic Product and unemployment should reflect the impact FDR's actions had on the Great Depression.

Now we deal with the response the economy had to spending; examining consumer spending, industrial spending (on physical matters such as
plants, machinery, materials, inventory, and not salary, wages and bonuses)
and government spending. As above we will consider mostly data that occurred before World War II which conservatives falsely claim was the reason the Great Depression ended.

CONSUMER SPENDING UNDER HOOVER'S CONSERVATIVE APPROACH

Year	Consumer Spending	GDP
1929	$79.0 billion	$104 b
1930	$71.0 billion	$91.1 b
1931	$61.3 billion	$76.3 b
1932	$49.3 billion	$58.5 b
1933	$46.4 billion	$56.0 b

CONSUMER SPENDING UNDER THE NEW DEAL APPROACH

1934	$51.9 billion	$65.0 b
1935	$56.3 billion	$72.5 b
1936	$62.6 billion	$82.7 b
1937	$67.3 billion	$90.8 b
1938	$64.6 billion	$85.2 b*
1939	$67.6 billion	$91.1 b
1940	$71.9 billion	$100.6 b
1941	$81.9 billion	$125.8 b

* The reversal of progress occurred when Roosevelt ceased doing what was working and tried conservative
calls to end deficit spending and balance the budget in 1937.

INDUSTRIAL SPENDING UNDER HOOVER'S CONSERVATIVE APPROACH

Year	Industrial Spending	GDP
1929	$16.2 billion	$104 b
1930	$10.3 billion	$91.1 b
1931	$5.5 billion	$76.3 b
1932	$900 million	$58.5 b
1933	$1.4 billion	$56.0 b **

INDUSTRIAL SPENDING UNDER THE NEW DEAL APPROACH

1934	$2.9 billion	$65.0 b
1935	$6.3 billion	$72.5 b
1936	$8.4 billion	$82.7 b
1937	11.7 billion	$90.8 b
1938	$6.7 billion	$85.2 b *
1939	$9.3 billion	$91.1 b
1940	$13.2 billion	$100.6 b
1941	$18.1 billion	$125.8 b

* The reversal of progress occurred when Roosevelt ceased what was working and tried conservative calls to end deficit spending and balance the budget in 1937.

** Industrial spending increased late in fiscal year 1933 to satisfy demand after implementation of the Emergency Works Progress Act that created the Civilian Conservation Corps and the Works Progress Administration that purchased materials from the private sector while consumer spending didn't pick up until 1934. This also prevented unemployment from being much higher than the 24.9 percent that was the official statistic.

GOVERNMENT SPENDING UNDER HOOVER'S CONSERVATIVE APPROACH

Year	Government Spending	GDP
1929	$8.5 billion	$104 b
1930	$9.2 billion	$91.1 b **
1931	$9.2 billion	$76.3b
1932	$8.1 billion	$58.5 b
1933	$8.8 billion	$56.0 b *

*Government spending in 1933 increased because of FDR's Emergency Works Progress Program began operations late in the year, as stated above.

** The 1930 spending had been determined in the budget that was enacted prior to the Wall Street crash and its increase was not in response to the Great Depression.

GOVERNMENT SPENDING UNDER THE NEW DEAL APPROACH

Year	Government Spending	GDP
1934	$9.8 billion	$65.0 b
1935	$10.0 billion	$72.5 b
1936	$11.8 billion	$82.7 b
1937	$11.7 billion	$90.8 b
1938	$12.8 billion	$85.2 b *
1939	$13.3 billion	$91.1 b
1940	$14.1 billion	$100.6 b
1941	$24.6 billion	$125.8 b ***

* The lower 1938 GDP occurred after Roosevelt ceased what was working and tried conservative calls to end deficit spending and balance the budget in 1937. It had a definite effect on consumer and industrial spending, as the data show. But there is an absolute correlation of spending to GDP: as government spending increases, so does industrial and consumer spending and that raises the GDP.

*** The 1941 figures are slightly skewed because of a quick increase in government spending to assist our European allies who were already fighting World War II.

In the quest to balance the budget, Hoover had a slight surplus in 1929 (before the stock market crash) of $1.2 billion and $300 million in 1930 but ran deficits the rest of the way. Roosevelt ran deficits the entire time, but except for 1936 and 1941 (early in the war in Europe) the deficits were similar to those of Hoover but Hoover wasn't producing growth in the Gross Domestic Product. In 1931, Hoover's approach produced a deficit of 2.75 percent of a $76.2-billion-and-falling GDP while a similar GDP of $72.5-billon-and-rising economy under FDR had a 3.59 percent deficit in 1935.

As shown, government spending by Roosevelt was not out of line with the spending by Hoover as a percentage of GDP. Hoover spent 13.85 percent of GDP in 1932 while FDR was constantly in the 13-14 percent range, except for 1935 when he exceeded 17 percent. But FDR was producing economic growth while Hoover saw only contraction. That economic growth under FDR came because his increased spending went to the working classes, who then spent their income in American businesses, benefitting all. Hoover's reaction to the crisis was for "trickle down" schemes that benefitted only the American aristocracy.

Raw economic data comes from a publication from the University of Houston, hardly a hotbed of radicalism, while commentary is the author's analysis.[82]

As is clear to see, spending by both consumers and industry steadily declined throughout the Hoover years and pulled the GDP down with it. Government spending remained relatively steady, except in 1932 when Hoover adhered to the conservative ideology of reducing government spending as a cure-all only to see the GDP continue to plunge and the Great Depression worsen. The same fate befell Roosevelt after he reduced government spending in 1937. But as government spending under the New Deal increased, so did industrial spending and consumer spending, even though government spending by FDR was not outrageous compared to spending by Hoover. And the outcome of heavier government spending to stimulate the economy does not appear to be "wasteful" as conservatives always claim government expenditures to be. The government spending that comes closest to "wasteful" is that going for lavish salaries and pensions for elected and appointed government officials who create our economic problems.

It is also noteworthy that Hoover's last full year in office (1932) government spending was 13.85 percent of GDP while FDR's last full year before assisting our allies in the war in Europe (1940) government spending was 14.02 percent of GDP, a difference hardly worth mentioning. But the 1932 deficit under Hoover was 2.56 percent of GDP while the deficit in 1940 was 1.39 percent of GDP, reflecting that heavier government spending was more efficient because it had created a greater GDP. Hoover's spending grew as a percentage of GDP because the GDP was contracting, while FDR's spending percentage was reduced slightly from the 15.08 percent of GDP in 1934 to the 14.02 percent in 1940, but otherwise remained constant because the GDP was growing.

In defense of Hoover; he was not the cause of the Great Depression as many like to claim. He had been in office less than seven months when the stock market collapsed and no one could be so incompetent to cause such a calamity in such a short period of time. It was, as Kinsley cited in his column, that a "president's policies" need "that extra year to take effect" that exonerates Hoover. The Great Depression belongs to Calvin Coolidge and his tax cutting, abandonment of Teddy Roosevelt's trust busting and wild

---

82 "Digital History: Unit IX, The Prosperity and the Depression Decades," educator Tom Ladenburg; University of Houston; ©2008.

speculation in housing and the stock market promoted by the banking sys-tem at the heart of the problems. Hoover's sin was that he didn't have a clue about how to handle the situation. Tax cutting, abandonment of trust bust-ing (deregulation) and wild speculation in housing promoted by the bank-ing system were also primary factors in the recent Great Recession

Most economists acknowledge that as consumer spending decreases it brings down industrial spending, creating a recession. When that hap-pens, it is imperative that government spending increase to fill the vacuum decreased consumer and industrial spending created, but when industrial and consumer spending increase enough to sustain a vibrant and growing economy government spending should be restrained. That was what hap-pened under the New Deal, government spending moved into the vacuum and spurred economic improvements which increased consumer and indus-trial spending and nearly brought us out of the Great Depression before the United States entered World War II, even though government spending couldn't be slowed or restrained because of the war. Had FDR not tried to balance the budget with less spending in 1937, the nation might have been well out of the depression before the United States entered World War II.

Conservatives' hatred of Roosevelt doesn't appear to be over his rescu-ing of the capitalism they adore; saving the democracy they give lip service to; or preventing revolution by a communism they detest; it is that his suc-cess proved all their theories and ideologies to be nonsense and he used gov-ernment to serve the needs of people not of the aristocracy.

Right-wingers, who are constantly rewriting history trying to exoner-ate themselves of responsibility for all problems, claim FDR "prolonged" the Great Depression. The only way that can be given serious consideration is to cite his reduced spending in 1937—at conservative insistence—trying to balance the budget and lost at least two years in the recovery; three years in job creation. Many astute economists (those who are not right-wing ideo-logues) say FDR didn't spend enough fast enough and that may have delayed the recovery. That's probably not what conservatives mean by "prolonged." And conservatives ought to be required to provide all the facts and statistics available that would prove when the Great Depression would have ended had the New Deal not been implemented.

Much has been written in recent years about "Reagan Democrats"; those undereducated, ill-informed workers of America clinging to issues that don't involve them. They obsess about such things as gay rights, same-sex marriages, abortion, prayers in public school and guns, and vote against their own best economic interests by electing politicians whose policies send their jobs overseas, destroy their unions and middle-class wages, dumb down education for their children and destroy the environment in which they live.

But we also have the problem of corporations paying their leaders tens of millions of dollars annually in salary, bonuses and stock options to lead the businesses, but who use their wealth, influence and positions to help put into power politicians who promise tax cuts or elimination of regulations, even though those policies actually harm the economy and negatively impact the performances of corporations while driving down the prices of the stocks that form much of the executives' wealth. It seems the "best and brightest" in business are no more capable of seeing what's best for America than are the undereducated and ill-informed masses.

CHAPTER 12. THE END

Among the Department of Commerce's missions is to produce the annual *Statistical Abstract of the United States*, which it has done so since shortly after the Civil War. Commerce also had published the *Historical Statistics of the United States*, compiling data from Colonial times until 1970.

Virtually everything the political right champions about taxes and commerce is shown to be a fraud by Commerce's two studies, which use information from the Bureau of the Census. Critics of right-wing politics might detect a correlation between what Commerce studies reveal and the desire of the right side of the Republican Party to eliminate Commerce and restrict Census to only head counting.

Among those things shown in the statistical studies are:

• Movement of taxes off business and onto wage earners;

• Movement of taxes off the wealthy and onto the working middle class;

• Major declines in American poverty rates under presidents John Kennedy and Lyndon Johnson and the lowest rate of poverty in the history of the republic under Bill Clinton (11.3 percent) to beat the previous low of 11.4 percent under Jimmy Carter;

• Major increases in poverty rates under presidents Ronald Reagan and both George H. W. Bush and George W. Bush;

• Steady decline of national debt as a percentage of the gross domestic product during administrations of Harry Truman, Dwight Eisenhower, Kennedy, Johnson, Jimmy Carter and the last six years of the Clinton administration and the first term of Richard Nixon before beginning to fluctuate;

• Lowest percentage of debt to GDP came under Carter and,

• Steady increase in debt to GDP under Reagan and the Bushes.

We find people who don't know squat about the economics of the nation they have put on the "eve of destruction"—as stated in a 1960s protest folk song—who charge headlong into the same old policies that created the problem in the first place. One such know-nothing is ex-President George W. Bush who in his 2008 State of the Union Address, repeated his call to make permanent the temporary tax cuts for the American aristocracy that made far worse the economic problems Reagan started. Congress extended the tax cuts for two years under an agreement with President Barack Obama. In his final press conference before leaving office Bush claimed it was only his bad luck that the then-present economic debacle just happened to occur on his watch, when in fact it was mostly created on his watch by him and congressional lapdogs with tax cuts for the aristocracy (themselves included), deregulation and turning the regulatory agencies over to minions of the special interests who worked to protect the industries from regulation when they should have been regulating.

It's time for the American public to understand that right-wing economics don't work, and the national mainstream media must stop pretending that the recently ended economic disaster "just happened" and start reporting the cause as conservative policies and actions. It should also be time for progressives in the Democratic Party to start saying just that, if they ever get up enough bravery to address the issue and begin labeling the disaster what it was, the "Reagan-double-Bush Voodoo Disaster." Comedienne Wanda Sykes called it the "Trickle Down Depression" which is an apt description for the disaster. And it's time to try something new, just as Franklin Delano Roosevelt tried something new amid the Great Depression after right-wing economics began the mess and right-wing politicians did little about it as it grew progressively worse.

Right-wingers have the idea that government exists only to keep the have-it-all elites atop the social pyramid while the have-nots are "kept in their place" at the bottom, and power must be used only to protect the privileged and never used to benefit the marginalized or excluded. They use government to help the top, who live like kings at the banquet table while the rest of us exist like dung beetles to scrounge up what the elites have dropped. That righties don't support the society they sponge from. Where Reagan and the Bushes have shaped government policy to enrich themselves, family or friends, the Roosevelts and Kennedys have a clean record on that score. Plus, Roosevelt and Kennedy children served their country militarily in World War II—some died. No Reagan or Bush children served in Grenada, Lebanon, Iraq or Afghanistan.

Government spending in a "stimulus" package may have helped halt the sagging economy from going down further but it won't sustain a vibrant and lasting economy. America needs to try something new—the Honest Deal of Democratic Capitalism—to save this once-great nation before in becomes permanently mired in hopelessness as we evolve into a country of Alice Tinkers and Baldricks,[83] but without the charm of either.

How the Honest Deal's Democratic Capitalism would address the budget crisis created by the political right was addressed throughout this book. We now look at several issues that could be solved or eased by Democratic Capitalism without heavy-handed government.

BASIC STRUCTURE OF DEMOCRATIC CAPITALISM

Eliminate both the income tax and payroll tax—they have been so distorted by special-interest exemptions that they are no longer useful or fair—and institute a profits tax. No profits, no taxation. That means, no profits, no executive enrichment. Every employed person gets a base income—free of taxes to meet housing and sustenance requirements—and profit sharing from their employment. When employees create profit, they should share in the distribution of that profit.

Taxes on employee profits pay for Social Security and health insurance for all. When we can match other advanced countries with universal health coverage spending somewhere near 10 percent of GDP on health, we will

---

83   Alice Tinker and Baldrick were characters in two excellent British television sitcoms. The delightful Miss Tinker in "The Vicar of Dibley" and the childlike Baldrick in Rowan Atkinson's "Blackadder." Both put a major "duh" into dunce.

free up hundreds of billions of dollars to circulate in the economy. That will create growth.

Tax corporate profits and profits of businesses engaged in interstate commerce to pay for government operations, including national defense and homeland security. If they dislike such a situation, they may stop doing those things that make government spending grow; such as polluting, which requires billions of tax dollars for cleanup, or unnecessary defense spending that only goes to the district of an influential politician. That the majority of corporations pay little or no federal taxes only underscores that they are the classic freeloaders in a nation that has made their profits possible.

In a January 2008, article, *The New York Times* reported: "Falling domestic profits. The government's estimate of corporate profits declined during the third quarter of 2007 to 1.621 trillion dollars, from 1.642 trillion during the second quarter. In the hard-hit financial sector profits fell from 521.4 billion dollars to 488.9 billion. Domestic non-financial profits fell from 806.4 billion dollars to 792 billion."[84] Late in 2010, it was estimated that corporations were holding nearly $2 trillion in idle dollars in their treasuries while the federal Bureau of Economic Analysis reported annualized profits of $1.68 trillion for the year.

Those corporate profits indicate that there is more than enough wealth for this country to provide for its government by just taxing a portion of corporate profits. There is enough to balance the budget almost immediately and enough to start paying down the conservative debt, which could be done with a surplus averaging $1 billion a year in only 12,000 to 13,000 years (as of 2010).

If the corporations yield enough revenue for government operations, profit of local small businesses, mom-and-pop enterprises and family farms would not be taxed by the federal government other than the profits tax on employment. This would strengthen local small business that the corporate takeover of America is threatening to destroy.

Keep the gasoline tax and taxes or fees from all sources of transportation to create and maintain the interstate highway system, railways, airport, ports; but all revenues collected must be kept and budgeted for only those purposes.

Make executive profit compensation dependent on the number of American employees at the business. As a company increases its workforce,

---

84   "United States: corporate profit outlook"; *The New York Times*; January 7, 2008.

the executive share of profits would increase. If a CEO needed one or two or more employees in order to increase the CEO compensation, those few employees would be hired, but leadership would not be inclined to over hire which would diminish the CEO's total income. During periods of economic slowdowns, corporations would not be inclined to fire large segments of their workforces because firing workers would not alter the percentage of income going for salaries and profits. The result will be ideal balance with management wanting more workers and employees wanting fewer in order to have greater profit income. And, if executive income were dependent entirely of economic success of the company, and not on a manipulated stock price, there should be no more speculation that created the financial mess just recently halted and enriched top-level executives as they drove their corporations to bankruptcy or so near bankruptcy they needed taxpayer bailouts.

Salary and profit compensation for the top executives could be capped at no more than 25 times that of the lowest-paid employee. This would not impose a straightjacket on executive pay, the amount of CEO income would rise or fall with the success or failure of leadership. There should be no restrictions on bonuses for executives other than the proceeds would have to come from either the employees' profits or the shareholders' profits and must be approved by vote by members of those two groups. When executives treat employees and shareholders right, they may get bonuses. Mistreatment would most likely mean no bonuses.

Business leaders should learn that in times of robust economic activity it would be wise to set aside a small amount of employee and shareholder profits to be distributed during economic slowdowns to offset lower employee profits and to prevent dividend reductions. If done throughout the business world, there may never be another recession, but if there were one it would be mild.

HEALTHCARE AND SOCIAL SECURITY

There are two things wrong with the recently enacted healthcare reform law: 1) Congress eliminated a government option, Medicare buy-in and a single-payer system, proposing instead to work through existing insurance companies that are at the heart of the healthcare problem in this nation and; 2) the effort brought out hundreds of millions of dollars from many sectors of the health industry—as happened to the Clinton plan in 1993—to water down and make meaningless much of the plan while further enriching insurance and pharmaceutical companies.

It is important to have two sources of healthcare financing in a universal system rather than one. The proposals to mandate everyone buy insurance won't contain costs. A single-payer system by the federal government will likely be cumbersome, although less expensive than the present system. If states enroll and finance all residents in Health Maintenance Organizations (HMOs) or physician-owned clinics whose duties are preventive medicine, diagnostics and minor outpatient care, there is an incentive to keep everyone as healthy as possible, and out of hospitalization care, which would result in lower taxes to pay for the federal system. And, the fewer Americans hospitalized because of treatment by a program for preventative medicine or maladies the lower malpractice insurance premiums should be for all medical practitioners.

The federal part of universal coverage would concentrate on hospitalization, cures, recuperation and rehabilitation, which would eliminate many programs now in existence. And the stiff Medicare premiums now levied on retirees' Social Security income can be eliminated. All other medical treatment not covered by state and federal programs, such as elective procedures, would remain in the private sector where individuals are free to seek out and buy private policies as they wish. And, the federal program can offer rebates to state HMOs and clinics for success in keeping their clients healthy and out of hospitalization.

When states enroll all residents in HMOs and clinics and meet the cost because Democratic Capitalism frees up billions of dollars for state taxes on individuals to pay for basic coverage, the present Medicaid program can be eliminated. And the double-payer system allows corporations such as Blue Cross-Blue Shield the opportunity to shift into HMO business, lessening the chances they will spend premium money best spent on health treatments to lobby against reform.

Many proponents of a single-payer system assail the "greed" of HMOs while ignoring the "greed" of insurance giants where one CEO paid himself—according to *The Providence Journal*, citing *Forbes* magazine's 2005 list of highest-paid executives [85]—about $125 million in one year while the industry was denying payment for medical treatment for thousands of policyholders. He took $2.4 million in one week; more than most Americans

---

85 "CEO Pay is Still on Steroids," Holly Skar; *Providence Journal*; May 10, 2005.

would earn in a lifetime. Single-payer proponents also forget that even in a single-payer system most Americans would still get their health care from HMOs because that system only transfers the obligation to pay medical bills from an insurance company to government; it does nothing about the quality of care offered. The dual-payer system can reform HMOs.

An added bonus of the dual-payer plan is that HMOs in small towns don't need to be staffed by licensed physicians—even though that is preferred—but by physician's assistants who are already capable of overseeing preventive health care like physical exams, diets, exercising, diagnostics and minor outpatient care. They also would have instant contact with a physician in a larger town and could transfer patients to hospitals for further diagnosis and treatment, assuring that even small out-of-the-way towns will have some form of health oversight where today they have none.

There are also financial matters to consider, such as the disparity between divergent economies as in the expensive and affluent New York City and the modest Opp, Alabama. Why should the Alabamans be taxed for premiums at the same rate as the New Yorkers when the New Yorkers will get much more expensive care than the Alabamans? Let New Yorkers pay for New York care while Alabamans pay for Alabama care. This is one area where leaving something to the states makes considerable sense and is handled better by a dual-payer system than by a single-payer arrangement.

Taking the cost of healthcare off our businesses and corporations will give them some financial leeway in competing with foreign corporations that do not have to pay for healthcare. Removing the payroll tax from the corporations and businesses will give even more leeway to confront foreign competition.

Social Security need no longer be funded with payroll taxes that hit the lowest-paid Americans the hardest. The political right has long favored a "flat tax" on income, but since Democratic Capitalism eliminates an income tax we will have to give a flat tax to fund Social Security by taxing all profit income and eliminating the ceiling, presently capped at slightly above $100,000, for the highest-paid earners. And since the first-earned dollars are not taxed, we free up billions for other economic purposes. With even those retired contributing to Social Security as if they were employed everyone contributes to the system that will benefit everyone and there will never be a "Social Security crisis" because it wouldn't matter what ratio of employed-to-retired there is.

The result is that those individuals who use healthcare and Social Security retirement, or other social programs pay for those programs. A corporation, even given the status of a person by the United States Supreme Court years ago, doesn't use these programs and isn't a person in that sense, so shouldn't pay for them.

DEFICIT REDUCTION

As shown in past chapters, eliminating the income tax and the payroll tax will free up billions of dollars for the consumers to spend in the economy, and that will spur growth which results in increased tax collections that could help ease the Reagan-Bushes debt that accumulated by piling deficit on deficit on deficit over the past three decades. Ending the tax freedom given to corporate freeloaders over the years will greatly reduce the taxes individuals are now paying.

Many liberal, progressive or moderate economists argue that addressing the deficit/debt has to be done with government spending to "prime the pump" to get the economy growing. That was shown to be a valid argument in chapter 11. Just the elimination of the payroll tax, as it applies to the first $25,000 in income, frees up billions of dollars for the consumer class. As stated, states can tap into that to pay for healthcare in HMOs or clinics for their residents and what is not used for that purpose will enable ordinary Americans to help "prime that pump" and government needn't spend as much on "priming."

Whenever the topic of solving the debt problem arises, the millionaires and billionaires the nation always turns to for ideas have the some constant basic ideas. That is to raise payroll taxes on the working middle class and to slash spending in the areas that benefit the working middle class; that is Social Security and Medicare. They also go after the poor with the mantra to slash Medicaid spending. There almost never is a mention to get some assistance from the very people who benefited immensely from the Reagan-Bush raid on the United States Treasury; the millionaires and billionaires who spent three decades loading up on Treasury instruments. Nor is there any mention of requiring the corporations of the nation to contribute any part of the immense fortunes they have sitting in their treasuries that they often use to take over competing businesses, then shut them down, after getting trillions of dollars in tax breaks since World War II.

Social Security, Medicare and Medicaid did not cause the problem; the payroll taxes that fund these programs have been used to cover up the real cause, tax cuts for the wealthy who really didn't need the cuts and didn't use any of the money saved to create new businesses. Tax cuts for corporations, that didn't use any of the saved money to employ American workers, contributed heavily to the problem.

Democratic Capitalism would help solve the problem because it will never again allow giant corporations to exist as freeloaders in the economy that made them massive. Executives of those corporations will also be required to contribute to solving the problems they were heavily involved in creating. Their massive salaries, bonuses and stock-option profits would be tapped for taxation just as the working middle class worker's income is taxed from the first dollar earned to the last dollar pocketed.

It is significant that Congress would enact tax laws that benefited millionaires the most and preyed on the working middle class when about half the members of Congress are considered millionaires. But that must be tempered with the realization that in calculating wealth of members of Congress, primary residences are not factored into their wealth and neither are their salaries of almost $200,000 annually. Then the range of assets owned is so wide that immense wealth can be made to resemble moderate holdings. If factoring in congressional salaries and primary-home ownership it would be clear that there are very few non-millionaires in Congress. And they made the laws that benefit themselves, their friends and the special interests that finance their elections.

When many in Congress leave that institution they go to work as lobbyists at salaries many times greater than their congressional pay and there they reap the major benefits of their tax-cutting legislation.

ILLEGAL IMMIGRATION

Apparently many in the Republican Party believe that the matter of "illegal immigrants" to the United States has gotten out of hand and our southern border needs to be secured with a 700-mile fence to keep aliens out of the country. That the Republican Party has been responsible for the national borders for the eight years from 2001 to 2009 and most of the past three decades may be why the matter has gotten out of hand. While part of the party has its panties in wedgies over the issue the other part of the party brought about the situation in order for business to pay cut-rate labor wages, which helped suppress wages for everyone. Those wages would account for much of the 70 percent of our economy. In building the fence, private property rights—that the GOP claims to adore—are being breached as the structure cuts across property making much of it unusable. And it blocks wildlife migratory patterns further endangering the natural order of the world.

It's all so unnecessary. With employers required to pay a fixed amount in wages and salary and employees entitled to a specific portion of the profit they create, there is absolutely no incentive for any employer to seek out illegals in order to drive down wages with cheap labor. There will be no way to add a dollar to the profit margin by flimflamming employees. Employers will soon learn that their best interest is in hiring labor that will do the best job to increase profit, and when a leader's profit compensation is tied to the number of Americans employed, Americans will be the first hired and the last fired. There should be no restrictions on the number of aliens, legal or illegal, a business hires except that illegals will not count in calculating the CEO's compensation. That will insure that Americans will be hired first and there would be opportunities for immigrants to take jobs Americans "really don't want." Both management and labor should soon learn that the best method of gaining profits is co-operation between the two, not confrontation. And there would never be a need for states to intrude into federal areas of responsibilities as Arizona recently did to enact an anti-immigration bill that smacks of police-state tactics.

Executives who try to use illegals in calculating executive CEO compensation from profits would be "stealing" from employee profit sharing. Those employees would be the best watchdogs to keep executives honest, reducing the amount of government investigations and elimination of workplace raids designed to enforce immigration laws.

One downside of Democratic Capitalism is that it weakens unions by taking from organized labor the power it has to confront management over salary and wages. But, it also takes away from right-wing politicians the devious methods they use to enact policies that show their hatred for the working class of America. And union busting will just be a wasted exercise because nothing can be gained.

Another downside is that without an income tax, donations to charities will decline because there would be no income-tax write-offs, but that can be overcome by providing deductions and credits for donations to charities in the inheritance tax. One possibility is to give a $2 credit for every $1 in charitable donation in a will, then eliminating all government taxes on the remaining thereby making the "tax" on inheritance 33 percent rather than the normal 55 percent.

AGE, GENDER AND RACIAL DISCRIMINATION

The provision that would remove illegal immigration as a negative force on workers' incomes also will make discrimination based on age, gender or race less of a problem. There will be no incentive to hire younger workers at lower pay after firing older workers because they have earned higher pay. The total compensation for the work force must be the same regardless of who is employed. Therefore, ability to earn a profit for the business will be the only consideration on employment matters. If a woman or a racial minority is better capable of providing commercial income, they will be hired and paid as well as any white male.

GAP BETWEEN HAVES AND HAVE-NOTS

Recent reports show that the top one percent of Americans receive more than 23 percent of the national income—up from nine percent at the beginning of the Reagan Revolution—the widest disparity since 1928. And the nation experienced an economic meltdown similar to that following the 1928 condition. That disparity needs to be reversed just as it was by the programs that ended the Great Depression. The answer lies not in seeing the top one percent have less, but seeing that the other 99 percent have more.

Democratic Capitalism will begin to reverse this harmful condition by rewarding with profits those people who create the profits instead of enriching only those who control distribution of profits, mainly to themselves.

OUT SOURCING OF AMERICAN JOBS

Sending US jobs to low-wage foreign nations tends to reward only those at the top while harming the consumer class; it damages the nation in which consumer spending amounts of 70 percent of the economy. Even though consumers may have access to some foreign goods that are cheaper, they aren't better off because the incomes of consumers have been suppressed by the outsourcing of jobs. Millions of jobs of consumers have been eliminated and millions not eliminated pay far less than would be normal because of the foreign competition that creates labor surpluses and job shortages in America results in lower consumer income.

By tying profit compensation of the top leaders to the number of Americans employed, management would hire just enough Americans to raise the executive's compensation without hiring so many that the compensation is diluted. If those hires require bringing some jobs back from overseas, American workers win and CEOs will think long and hard about shipping jobs to foreign lands if it cuts significantly into CEO pay. If adding one employee would increase a CEO's profit compensation, that leader will hire one worker.

The only unresolved issue would be the profits made in foreign operations. As of now, American-based corporations open plants and factories overseas so they can profit from low wages that produce higher profits. That is a strategy with obvious short-term capitalist appeal, but it works against the long-term interests of the American economy by removing Americans from the payrolls.

One solution is to maintain foreign manufacturing as is, but not allow any foreign-derived profit to go to management's profit-sharing income. Foreign workers would be compensated according to the laws of the nation in which they toil. The profit they create would be disposed of according to foreign law, if there are such laws, and the remaining profit would come back to the United States to be distributed to the owners of the corporations, the stockholders. That would also boost income of top management of the corporations, since most would hold numerous shares in the corporation, assuring the money goes into the US economy. It would then be subjected to the profits taxes that support Social Security and healthcare plus costs of war, when applicable. If management thinks it will be beneficial to executive paychecks to bring jobs back to America it will do so, which might cool the "war against workers" that has been one of the cornerstones of Reaganomics.

FOREIGN CO-OPERATION AND PARTNERSHIPS

In the 1992 election campaign that led to the election of Bill Clinton, maverick independent candidate H. Ross Perot complained loud and clear about pending legislation from the departing George H. W. Bush administration called the North America Free Trade Agreement (NAFTA). Perot claimed to hear a "great sucking sound" that would drain real jobs from the nation to be sent to other nations where corporations are permitted to pay near-starvation wages. In a true, long-practiced American tradition, no one in positions of authority listened to him even though he was totally correct. But, Perot doesn't necessarily listen to others either. NAFTA became law in the Clinton administration and that "great sucking sound" has indeed become louder as millions of American jobs have been sent to other nations. But those jobs were from the working lower middle class, so the elites didn't care much. It was their beloved "free trade" in practice.

But real free trade isn't possible when corporations offer near-starvation wages in some nations and remove jobs from nations that require them to provide livable incomes.

Now, many claim to care about that, but they have no solution for the problem. But there is hope.

When Democratic Capitalism is entrenched in the United States, other nations may see its advantages and give it a try. Once their workers' incomes were brought into line with each other, different nations could not prey on each other because of fluctuating currency values, and real free trade could be implemented. Commerce between the two nations would be no different from commerce between North Dakota and South Dakota.

LOW PRODUCTIVITY GROWTH

American business has long suffered from a master-servant relationship in the workplace that relies on fear of losing a job if master dictates aren't successful. Democratic Capitalism offers an escape from such working conditions. When it becomes clear, even to the most-obtuse manager, that cooperation between management and labor is the best road to profitability business leaders might make the effort to know the names of those who work for them, know qualifications, talents and desires and begin using those assets rather than treat employees like mindless drones that can be exploited for a while, then discarded.

And management attempting to increase productivity by driving labor to the point of exhaustion often is not beneficial because it leads to shoddy products and industrial accidents. Labor is best equipped to determine the amount of output it is capable of handling and labor would produce just the right amount of productivity to assure itself proper profits while management would concentrate on the proper number of employees needed for maximum efficiency. A simple rule here is that if labor profits from increased productivity, labor's productivity will increase and so will profits. And we may start to see the end the class warfare the elites have waged against the rest of us that was begun by Reagan and exacerbated by the Bushes.

The stagnation or reduction of wages over the past three decades of conservative rule resulted in a situation that there was less money consumers could put into the economy to spur growth. With greater productivity the labor-consumer middle class will command greater income, which will be spent in the economy creating newer jobs. The cycle should continue to repeat itself until there is an ideal balance between labor and productivity. Increases in productivity will always produce increases in profit and put an end to this drive to lower wages through union busting, immigration for low wages, control of one person over others' lives.

CORPORATE CORRUPTION

If major portion of a person's income came from profit sharing, each and every one of them would keep an alert eye on the shenanigans of the executives to keep them honest. That would reduce the need for government to do so. Shortchanging employees on profits would be considered theft and tax subversion by the employer since an employee receiving less than legally entitled would not be taxed on the stolen money. Corporate tax cuts the right constantly champion did nothing to address the recent mini-depression corporate tax cuts helped produce because most corporations pay little or no taxes to the United States, existing as freeloaders in a society that enriches them.

We should have had enough of the likes of Enron, WorldCom, Adelphia, Tyco, HealthSouth and other corporations where insiders treated the companies as their private piggy banks while stockholders and employees were left with nothing when the cheating was uncovered. An honest business is a solid business and likely to be a profitable business.

It is vital that corporations once again paid taxes on their profits, as the Enron debacles should show.

Enron was able to evade taxes because of friends in high places, so it could list any income as profit, boosting its stock price. The income could come from borrowing, selling stocks or bonds or a contract that was yet to be exercised, but was listed as profit. When the phony "profit" caused the stock price to rise, corporate insiders could exercise their stock options and buy stock at a cheap rate, then cash out.

Say they got options at $10 a share, and the phony profits caused the stock price to rise to $50. High-ranking executives could exercise their options; buying one million shares ($10 million) now worth $50 million then immediately borrow that $50 million from the company, using the stock as collateral. That gave them a $40 million gain on which they paid no taxes. They never had any intention of repaying that loan and no intention of ever paying taxes on their windfall.

When the company's deceit was discovered and the stock price plunged, the company was left with worthless paper and the executives ran off with millions.

A system of taxing profits, as this book proposes, would make corporations more honest about what is profit and what is smoke and mirrors.

CLEANER POLITICS

Absent a constitutional amendment authorizing public financing of all elections and the elimination of special-interest funding, Democratic Capitalism offers the next best thing. Since every cent a business earns comes from the labor of workers, whether owner-employee or hired employee, they should not have their share of what they create withheld from them through low pay so the corporation can send it to corrupt politicians who then shift the tax burden onto those same middle-class workers and off the corporations those workers make profitable, or eliminate their jobs entirely. By eliminating political campaign contributions as a business expense politicians will have to represent the people, not the corporations.

Enron used profits created by its workers to finance corrupt politicians who enacted tax cuts and deregulation that led to Enron's collapse. That money could have gone to the employees in the form of higher pay or shareholders in the form of dividends, but instead was used to harm both groups. Employees lost their jobs and retirements, shareholders lost their investments, and both groups were forced to pay for their own destruction.

The judicial establishment in this nation would go into conniption fits if trials, both criminal and civil, were to be decided on whom or whatever spends the most money on advertising, propaganda, character assassination, who can lie the most convincingly to make nonsense seem superior to reality, or outright "bribes" to politicians, so why should we have our elections decided in this very manner?

The right-wing Roberts Supreme Court has it all wrong.[86] Corporation contributions do not constitute a "free speech" right since a corporation cannot and does not speak as one for all the employees and shareholders of the corporation. It is only "free speech" for the top executive who decides the campaign contribution with money that isn't his or hers and is a way of forcing all others in the corporation into speech they may not agree with. Democratic Capitalism would establish money of a corporation as property of the shareholders and employees. Money corporations now use for politics comes from the firm's general treasury and it is profit that rightfully should have gone to employees who created it or shareholders who own the corporation but was withheld from the rightful owners to be used for matters those owners may not agree with. Democratic Capitalism would protect the rightful owners by stating exactly whom the rightful owners are and their property couldn't be taken by one person or an appointed board of directors to finance the concerns of that one person. That would be theft.

The decision removing restrictions on corporate campaign contributions is only establishing corporations as surrogate government entities regulating speech, which government is constitutionally prohibited from doing. It also opens United States elections to manipulation by foreign or multinational corporations that may not have the best interests of the United States as their concerns. All persons associated with the corporation are allowed to made political contributions with their own money, that is individual free speech. Or the CEO and board of directors could get permission from employees or shareholders to use part of those groups' profit for political contributions but use only money from the "yes" voters for that purpose, and get that approval in the same method already discussed for getting bonuses. "No" voters would get their money in pay or dividends. That also is real political free speech. This requirement should also apply to money spent on lobbying government for special favors. Management should be required to get approval from the stockholders/owners of the firm or its employees if any of their money is to be used for lobbying purposes.

A trial is a government function, created, operated and financed by government. An election is a government function, created, operated and financed by government. In a trial, a government official—the judge—has one

---

86   *Citizens United v Federal Elections Commission*; 130 S.Ct. 876; 2010.

primary function; to regulate the speech of all involved so all constitutional concerns are met. In an election, according to the right-wing judges, no constitutional principles need apply and no government functionary may act as a judge. Government has legitimate power to regulate speech: in addition to the courtroom; it can regulate in the classroom, in commerce (fraud), crime (conspiracy), in the arts (copyright and patents). Government regulates speech in its armed forces and it certainly has power to regulate the speech until death of those of us who served in its intelligence community. But the political right says elections are different.

An Answer to Irresponsible Governance

With Democratic Capitalism calling for the nation's corporations paying for defense, homeland security and related activities plus managing the debt, those concerns may not use government as their private piggy bank. Should corporation X totally escape taxation, executives of corporations Y and Z, who may sit on corporation X's board of directors, could rebel, bringing about self-policing that promises to be effective. Absent public financing of elections, corporate executives might support responsible politicians who would govern for the nation rather than those who only govern for themselves and for special interests. And if corporations want to use government as their private bank accounts, other corporations and businesses pay the tab, not individual taxpayers who will be protected because their taxes would not fund the areas of government on which corporations feast.

But the irresponsibility politicians show supporting their sponsoring corporate clients pales compared to their ideological concerns they wish to impose on the nation.

No sooner than the first session of Congress in 2011, after the Republican successes in the 2010 election, the GOP turned to its favorite subjects about government: cutting taxes for the wealthy and corporations and reducing government spending while abandoned the job-creation mantra its candidates campaigned on. New representatives in the House of Representatives, ushered in with the influence of the so-called Tea Party, called for $100-billion reductions annually in spending while House leadership was willing to settle for approximately $60 billion and the Obama White House was willing to "compromise" with a $30 billion reduction, but settled for a $38-billion compromise. Long-range goal for spending cuts by the GOP were estimated at $6 trillion. In response President Barack Obama unveiled his own plan that called for cutting spending on domestic programs and raising taxes on the richest Americans.

History shows all of these proposals are not solutions.

As already shown in previous chapters, cutting government spending in a recessionary or struggling economy is counterproductive. It has always failed and produces disastrous results. It never saves money on a dollar-for-dollar basis and it damages or ruins careers and families, forces small firms out of business, drives up unemployment, results in reduction in tax revenues while raising government spending for the societal problems it creates.

Herbert Hoover cut government spending in fiscal year 1932 – that began in mid-1931 – and an ordinary depression descended into the Great Depression. The Gross Domestic Product fell from 1931's level of $76.3 billion to $56 billion. Unemployment grew from 15.9 percent of the workforce to 24.9 percent. Franklin Roosevelt cut government spending in 1937 and the successes in recovery from the Great Depression immediately evaporated. Unemployment went from 14.3 percent of the workforce to 19 percent in one year; the GDP fell from $90.8 billion to $85.2 billion. It took two years for GDP to return to 1937 levels; three years before unemployment even approached its 1937 low.

Many on the political left call for a major cut to the Pentagon's defense budget; but that was an important component creating the California Experience – along with a tax revolt. It also won't work.

There is no evidence that Obama's plan would do much good. Reduced government spending could cause negative economic reactions severe enough to wipe out any money raised through tax increases. That would leave high-income taxpayers "poorer" and poorer Americans without helpful programs.

The Republican House, if it had gotten its way with massive spending cuts, would only extend the California Experience to the entire nation; solving nothing and threatening to bring back the Great Recession the nation was weakly escaping. In the 2011 negotiations, freshmen GOP representatives in the House seemed willing to force a shutdown of government rather than compromise on several nonbudgetary issues, two of which – family planning and the procreation process – the United States Constitution does not give Congress authority to concern itself. Critical observers claimed a government shutdown would work havoc of the fragile economy; but what economic damage that might have occurred could pale in comparison to the damage caused should the GOP succeed in slashing spending. This is an area in which responsible government is sorely needed.

A SMALLER INTERNAL REVENUE SERVICE

Democratic Capitalism based solely on a profits tax should result in more than 100 million fewer tax returns sent to the Internal Revenue Service, making it more efficient. The IRS can be divided into the branches overseeing each type of taxation (individual, business, corporation and excises) and will have plenty of employees freed up from processing returns who can turn to examining compliance. As Democratic Capitalism becomes more entrenched, many IRS jobs will become redundant and retirements will gradually produce the smaller IRS the political right claims to want without destroying its duty of tax collection that is needed to keep the nation strong.

Those individuals who still file tax returns with the IRS will find the process much simpler. A professional athlete would get a basic salary, as negotiated between the players' union and the league, and profit sharing. On the tax return, that would be listed along with other income, such as endorsement, book royalties, personal appearances. The Agent's fee would be deducted, as would the $25,000 tax-free income available to everyone. The rest would be taxed as profit. If the team deducts and pays the agent's fee, filing would be even simpler. The whole return could take a half-dozen lines. And because there is no income tax, some athletes may receive much more disposable income than they do now.

MISCELLANEOUS THOUGHTS

There is something amiss in an economy where a professional baseball player thinks $25 million (minus agent's commission) for a few months of playing is insufficient and a football team can lay off dozens of moderately paid employees only to turn around weeks later to shell out $100 million to one player who had been paid several million during several preceding years. Democratic Capitalism would mitigate that situation somewhat.

US businessmen may be the most lame-brained people in our society. They pay themselves millions of dollars for poor performances, which they use to support political parties and candidates (Republicans Reagan and the Bushes now and Warren Harding, Calvin Coolidge and Herbert Hoover in the past) who implement economic policies that harm or destroy the businesses that enriched the businessmen in the first place. Then they turn around and adamantly oppose any government effort to right the economy and rescue their businesses that were established, nurtured and made profitable by someone else while decrying policies under which businesses fare best (Democratic). This, after chasing bigger profit by suppressing wages and salaries which, when done throughout the economy, only destroyed the ability of consumers to purchase their products.

When US voters turn angry at conditions and begin blaming government for all their problems, they are only lying to themselves: they voted for such disasters. In the 1980 presidential primary campaign, would-be GOP hopeful George H. W. Bush rightfully labeled Ronald Reagan's fantasies as "voodoo economics." Voters chose Reagan's fairy tales in both the primary and general election. In the 1984 presidential elections Democratic candidate Walter Mondale rightfully told Americans of the disaster Reaganomics would bring and told them taxes would be needed to prevent that fiasco. He lost in a landslide.

As president, Bush the Daddy preferred to keep the Reaganomics he called "voodoo" in place in hopes of getting re-elected. His personal benefit was more important to him than rescuing the nation from the problem he was among the first to identify, but he lost any way.

Even after 12 years of economic disaster under Reagan and the elder Bush, George W. Bush came back in 2000 and promised the same programs. Enough Americans bought his fairy tale that they threw the election into such a tie that a right-wing Supreme Court tipped the election for more economic shenanigans.[87] Then with four years of steadily escalating deficits the voting public opted for more deficits in an economy that produced no new jobs.

---

87 *Bush et al v Gore et al*; 531 US 98; December 12, 2000. Contrary to public opinion, the United States Supreme Court did not make George W. Bush president with the *Bush v Gore* decision. It only stopped the statewide recount the Florida State Supreme Court had ordered until a statewide uniform system of recounting could be established, contrary to Florida law; then it set a time limit so short it was impossible to meet the requirements. It legislated from the bench. The United States Congress, which counted the ballots and declared the winner under Article II, Section 1 of the United States Constitution, was not party to the lawsuit so it could have refused to consider the Florida ballots until a thorough and fair recount had been completed. It did not; therefore it was the Republican Congress that made Bush president. For those who claim Al Gore kept the controversy alive, Supreme Court cases always list the plaintiff first: the case title shows it was Bush who kept the issue alive.

When the Reagan Revolution of deregulation and tax cutting was beginning its destructive run on America, a third part of the program was to eliminate some federal actions and return matters to the state or local governments. The selling point was that locals were closer to the problems and could handle them better than could the federal government. But many on the political left argued that turning problems over to local control on a "states' rights" argument would be counterproductive because, while taxpayers may get a few dollars saved in federal taxation, their local taxes—especially property taxes—would skyrocket. They were ignored and property taxes in some locales skyrocketed.

The "Now" news program on PBS followed the situation in the western portion of New York's Long Island in early 2010 when the local right-wing Tea Party activists staged a tax revolt over property taxes that had reached five figures on some middle-class properties and began voting out of office reformers and voting in the same type of right-wing tax haters who caused all the problems in the first place. The multimillionaires on the east end of the island didn't get hurt because they received hundreds of thousands of dollars in tax cuts and didn't have the urban problems of those closer to New York City. The political left had argued that all American taxpayers contributing a few dollars to address metropolitan problems would be much more benign than having some local taxpayers contributing thousands of dollars to address the same problems. The Tea Party types now revolting didn't want to hear that. This is another area in which sage advice fell on deaf ears and where Reagan's "voodoo" visions turned out to do the exact opposite of what he promised.

After the 9/11 attacks millions of Americans became admirers of George W. Bush who vowed to "keep us safe" even though he had ignored warnings of impending attacks only weeks before they occurred. He was re-elected on the argument that Republicans are better at national defense than are Democrats.

Voters are apparently unaware that no conservative Republican president, who will constantly flaunt the status as "Commander in Chief," has ever won a war, but the moderate Bush the Daddy did expel Iraq from Kuwait. But he did so against an Iraqi army that had been reduced to ineptitude after an eight-year war against Iran. Progressive Democrats prevailed in World War I, as they did again in World War II by defeating two world-class military powers of Nazi Germany and Imperial Japan and the lesser third power Italy in half the time it took George Bush the Younger to become bogged down in the Mideast. Harry Truman expelled North Korea and China from South Korea; Dwight Eisenhower then settled for the status quo. Lyndon Johnson prosecuted the Vietnam Conflict to a draw; it was lost under Republican Richard Nixon before Republican Gerald Ford cut and run. Bill Clinton successfully ended the Balkans fighting before it could replicate earlier times and spread into the rest of Europe as it did to start World War I. Then Bush the Younger began two wars in the Mideast and could not finish either before leaving office.

When bark comes to bite on national defense, the right can only yap about its prowess while the left puts up a winning fight. Right-wingers such as former Vice President Dick Cheney, who opted out of military service with five student deferments, can only muster up the bluster of Yosemite Sam while displaying the battle mettle of Elmer Fudd. Why the Republican Party has the reputation as superior in national defense is a mystery.

When a would-be rescuer comes onto the scene with promises of "change" trying to preserve the nation, he should get same co-operation from others in the attempt. The GOP assailing of President Barack Obama from the very moment he offered would-be solutions to conditions that existed long before his election is reminiscent of a *Mad Magazine* comic strip from years ago. In a Little League baseball game the home team is down by one run in the bottom of the sixth inning (Little League plays only six). The big fat kid with pimples comes to bat and strikes out. Then a tall, gangly kid with big ears and buckteeth also strikes out. After the scrawny little nerd of a kid with big glasses and tiny hands strikes out to end the game, the first two assail him with shouts of, "You lost the game for us." Even if the last kid strikes out, he didn't lose the American economic game; that lose was done by those who have consistently struck out over the past three decades.

This nation must do better.

BIBLIOGRAPHY

Adams, Guy. "The Brutal Truth About America's Healthcare", *The Independent UK*; August, 2009.

Anderson, Annelise. "It's federal spending, sweetheart!," *USA Today*; February, 1993.

Barlett, Donald L., and James B. Steele. "*America: What Went Wrong?*", Andrews McMeel Publishing; © 1992.

Benedetto, Richard. "Post-election euphoria fades as voters perceive few changes", *USA Today*; June, 1993.

Benedetto, Richard. "Report won't gather dust, says Clinton", *USA Today*; September. 1993.

Berger, Eric. "Enron creditors sue Ken Lay and wife", *Hearst Newspapers*; February, 2003.

Bloom, Allan. "*Closing of the American Mind*", Simon & Schuster; ©1987.

Bozell, Brent. "TV's Most Liberal Programs", *TV Guide*; July, 1993.

Broder, David S. *Washington Post* columnist, in *The Seattle Times*, "Gimmicks won't end our deficit woes"; October, 1992.

Brown, Ellen. "Austerity Fails in Euroland: Time for Some 'Deficit Easing'", Truthout.org; January, 2011.

Buchanan, Patrick. Quoted in "Opinionline: Clinton's plan: 'Sheer audacity'", *USA Today*; February, 1993.

Cauchon, Dennis. "Tax bills in 2009 at lowest level since 1950", *USA Today*; April, 2010.

CFO.Com. "Enron Could Force Kenneth Lay to Repay $94 Million Loan"; November, 2003.

Chambers, Jack. "Reject school socialism," an Opposing View column, *USA Today*; May, 1993.

Chavez, Linda. "Progress, not greed, destroys jobs", *USA Today*; March, 1996.

Chavez, Linda. "Want motive for Unabomber?, *USA Today* Counterpoints; April, 1996.

Cox, Patrick. "New tax rates are wrong" an Opposing View, *USA Today*; February, 1993.

Deets, Horace. "Curb the deficit by targeting *real* causes", *AARP Bulletin*; September, 1992.

DeRosa, Robin. "Clinton hits airways 'hatred'", *USA Today*; April, 1995.

El Nasser, Haya, and Jonathan T. Lovitt. "Growing woes in the Golden State", *USA Today*; March, 1993.

Evans, Daniel J. "Revival: A manifesto for the GOP", *The Seattle Times*; May, 1993

Gertz, Dwsight. "Growth, not downsizing, leads to greatness", *USA Today*; February, 1966.

Goldwater, Barry M. with Jack Casserly. *Goldwater*", Doubleday, © 1988.

Greenwald, Gerald. " 'Downsizing' leaves bad waves behind", *USA Today*; July, 1996.

Guy, Pat. "More Newspapers elect not to choose candidates," *USA Today*; October, 1992.

Hamilton, Alexander. "A View of the Constitution of the Judicial Department in Relation to the Tenure of Good Behavior", *Federalist Papers*; Number 78.

Hartmann, Thom. "*Rebooting the American Dream*". Berrett-Koehler Publishers © 2010.

Hasson, Judi. "Task force on health hit on secrecy", and Hasson, Judi, and Judy Keen. "Ruling doesn't apply to units of task force". *USA Today*; March, 1993.

Henry, Tamara. "ACT scores of minorities rise", *USA Today*; August , 1995.

Henry, Tamara. "Middle-class students most likely to work," *USA Today*; August, 1995.

Hodge, Scott A.. "Taxes not needed to cut deficit? Bunk!", *USA Today*; October, 1992.

Ivins, Molly. "Opionionline: Welfare plan keeps people on the rolls", *USA Today*; June, 1994.

Jones, Del. "Layoffs increase during first three months of 1996", *USA Today*; April, 1996.

Kasich, John. "No end in sight to spending spree", *Seattle Post-Intelligencer*; February, 2004.

King, Larry. The late-night wars and daytime drama", *USA Today*; September, 1993.

Kinsley, Michael. "More GOP Than the GOP", *The Los Angeles Times*; April, 2005.

Krugman, Paul. "Health Care Realities, *The New York Times*; July, 2009.

Kusnetr, David. Quoted in *USA Today's* Opinionline from the *Los Angeles Times*; June, 1996.

Ladenburg, Tom. "Digital History: Unit IX, The Prosperity and the Depression Decades", University of Houston; ©2008.

Limbaugh III, Rush H.. *"The way Things Ought to Be"*, Pocket Books; © 1992.

Mazanec, Jana. "Failed Colorado mine a reform 'poster child'", *USA Today*; June, 1993.

McConnell, Sen. Mitch. "Say no to welfare for politicians", *USA Today*; April, 1993.

McDermott, Terry. "Why inspections of meat fails", *The Seattle Times*; January, 1993.

McKinnon, Douglas. "GOP must reach out to blacks", *USA Today*; July, 1993.

Moore, Geoffrey H.. "The Three Ds of Recession: A Brief History", *econlib.org*.

Moynihan, Daniel Patrick. "The Ominous Rise in Illegitimacy"; Reader's Digest, Octrober, 1994.

Neirkirk, William. "Experts fear budget-cutters will hurt standard of life", *The Chicago Tribune* printed in *The Seattle Times*; May, 1995.

Peterson, Pete. "The Plan", *USA Today*; November, 1993

Phillips, Kevin. "Newt's formula for failure"; *USA Today*, April, 1995.

Pope, Charles. "Just how good a health plan does Congress have?", *The Oregonian*; August, 2009.

Reader's Digest . "Do We Trust Government?", May, 1994.

Republican National Committee ad. "An Important Economic Decision Is About To Be Made And There Is A Clear Choice", advertisement in *USA Today* by the; March, 1993.

Richards, Rhonda. "Disabilities law inspires entrepreneurs", *USA Today*; November, 1992.

Richards, Rhonda. "Prospering airlines hang help-wanted signs," *USA Today*; February, 1996.

Salon Magazine. "White House blames Bush for budget woes"; February, 2010.

Schumer, Charles E., and Orrin G. Hatch. "A Payroll Tax Break for Jobs", *The New York Times*; Jan., 2010

Shanker, Albert. Letter to the editor, *Seattle Post Intelligencer*; September, 1993.

Skar, Holly. "CEO Pay is Sill on Steroids", *Providence Journal*; May, 2005.

Stewart, Sally Ann. " 'No room at the inn,' so inmates will walk", *USA Today*; May, 1993.

Stockman, Farah. "Top Iraq contractor skirts US taxes offshore", *The Boston Globe*; March, 2008.

Tanner, Michael. "Just abolish welfare", USA Today; July, 1994.

The New York Times. "United States: corporate profit outlook", January, 2008.

The Seattle Times. "The drama of Haiti in three acts", reprint from *The Los Angeles Times*; September, 1994.

The Washington Post, reprinted in *The Denver Post.* "Budget analysis: Obama trying to balance his vision with nation's needs": February, 2010.

Think Progress.org. "FLASHBACK: in 1993, GOP Warned That Clinton's Tax Plan Would 'Kill Jobs,' 'Kill The Current Recovery'"; August, 2010.

Tongas, Paul and Warren Rudman. "How to cut deficit to zero," *USA Today*;

September, 1993.

United States Supreme Court. *Bush et al v Gore et al*, 531 US 98; December 12, 2000

United States Supreme Court. *Citizens United v Federal Elections Commission*, 130 S.Ct. 876; 2010.

Urschel, Joe. "Economists are different from you and me", *USA Today*; June, 1994.

Urschel, Joe. "Aristide, No credit to the Catholic priesthood", *USA Today*; September, 1994.

USA Today editorial debate. "Public doesn't hear whole story about taxes, budgets", August, 1996.

USA Today. "Reaction: 'It's a disgrace' to 'It's a smart move'"; September, 1994.

USA Today. "Voices: What do you think is the biggest waste in the federal budget?"; February, 1995.

USA Today. "Republican candidates' proposals"; January, 1996.

USA Today. "Spread pain: Tax and cut", Opinionline; May, 1993

USA Today. "Tax hikes always roll down hill", Opinionline; February, 1993.

Weiner, Jerome and Kosta Tsipis. "Saving found at Pentagon", *The New York Times* printed in *The Seattle Post-Intelligencer*; March, 1993 and "There's room to cut defense budget safely", *USA Today* editorial; February, 1993.

Weiner, Robert, and John Larmet. "Presidential Economics: Myths, Facts", *The Milwaukee Journal Sentinel*; August, 2007.

Weiner, Tim. *Knight-Ridder News Service*, "Quayle council actions now ensnarled in Law; *The Denver Post*; July, 1992.

Wikipedia, the free encyclopedia, using estimates collected by the Bureau of Labor Statistics. "Jobs created during U.S. presidential terms".

Will, George. "The president grabs for power" and "It's only Clinton who needs a crisis", *Washington Post* Writers Group; May, 1993.

Will, George. "Make savings the only deductible": *Seattle Post-Intelligencer*; October, 1992.

Willette, Anne. "IRS audits less as tax gap grows"; May, 1994; and "IRS barely makes dent in $95 billion tax gap", May, 1996, *USA Today*.

Williams, Walter. "Can Bill Clinton Save America?"; *The Seattle Times*, January, 1993.

Wysocki, Bernard. "Some firms cut costs too far, suffer 'corporate anorexia'": *The Wall Street Journal* reprinted in *The Denver Post*; July, 1995.

INDEX

A

Apple Computer, Inc., 50
Afghanistan, 60, 106, 200, 219
Agriculture Department, 13
Aid to Families with Dependent Children, 28
Ailes, Roger, 41
Alabama, 223
Alaska, 40, 124, 126, 187
Alaska Permanent Fund Dividend Program, 124
Alien and Sedition Act, 20
Allen, Paul, 50
Amazon, 70
America: What Went Wrong?, 65
American Broadcasting Company (ABC), 114, 128, 143, 169
American Federation of Teachers, 76
American Management Association, 133-134
Archer, Rep. Bill, 92
Aristide, Jean-Bertrand, 19-20
Arizona, 38, 69, 73, 127, 147, 226

B

Baird, Zoe, 121
Bank of North Dakota, 125
Big Brother Government, 38
Big Government, 12, 38, 148, 199

Block, Los Angeles County Sheriff Sherman, 74
Bloom, Prof. Allan, 27
Blue Cross–Blue Shield, 186, 222
Boehner, John, 92, 95
Boortz, Neil, 53
Boston Globe, the, 100
Boston's Mercer Management Consulting Inc., 133
Bozell, Brent, 39
Breyer, Steven, 121
Brown, Ellen, 124-125
Brown, Murphy, 27
Buchanan, Patrick, 46-47, 108
Bureau of Economic Analysis, 106, 220
Bureau of the Census, 66, 97, 101, 206, 217
Bush, George H. W., 2, 8, 59, 61, 108, 201, 205-206, 208, 218, 228, 236
Bush, George W., 2, 8-12, 14, 20, 24, 34, 40-41, 43, 47, 59-66, 69, 80-82, 84, 86, 88, 90-91, 93-94, 96-98, 101-102, 106-107, 110-111, 116, 120-122, 125, 139-141, 147-149, 165, 169-170, 177, 183-184, 187, 189-190, 194, 198, 200-208, 218-219, 236-238

C

California, 30, 54-55, 58, 68-69, 71-76, 78, 83-84, 88, 91, 111, 131, 143, 147, 150-151, 166, 169-170, 172, 234

243

18026123R00138

Made in the USA
Charleston, SC
12 March 2013